# The Mother I Carry

*A Memoir of Healing*

*From Emotional Abuse*

## Louise M. Wisechild

**SEAL PRESS**

Cover art by Selene Santucci.
Design by Clare Conrad.

Library of Congress Catalog-in-Publication Data

Wisechild, Louise M.
  The mother I carry : a memoir of healing from emotional abuse / by Louise M. Wisechild.
  p.  cm.

   1. Wisechild, Louise M.   2. Incest victims—United States—Biography.
3. Adult child abuse victims—United States—Biography.   4. Mothers and daughters—United States.   5. Psychological child abuse—United States.   I. Title.
HQ72.U53W543   1993
362.7'6—dc20                                                              93-25030
ISBN 1-878067-38-9                                                              CIP

Printed in the United States of America.
First Printing, November 1993
10  9  8  7  6  5  4  3  2  1

# Acknowledgements

I WISH TO thank my friends for the support and inspiration they have given me during the four years I have worked on this book. I am grateful for the excellent women of my dream group, writers' group and voice group and for our work together.

I thank Mary Meyer, Emm Gumley, Arlene Gerlough, Peter Jenson, Ginny NiCarthy, Jane Klassen, Tammy Su Lianu and Marianne Twyman for giving me extraordinary help and love when I most needed it. I am grateful to Jennifer Hopkins for the many ways she has supported this project. Monica Woelful, Nancy Redwine, Robyn Johnson, Sara Deutsch, Pat Pederson and Gail Fairfield gave me thoughtful feedback in the course of various drafts.

I am grateful to Margaret Anderson and Susan Fodor for lending me their cabin and giving me a place to begin. My later residence at Cottages at Hedgebrook gave me the solitude and beauty I needed to shape this book and I thank Nancy Nordoff and the staff for their good care and commitment to women writers.

I thank the people who responded to the letter I sent asking for support, especially Jim Lipinsky, Sandy Swirnoff, Ruth Crow, Helen Tevlin, Mary Gentry, Sally Giovinne-Kerr and Mark and Kathleen. Their response allowed me to devote needed time to this writing.

Holly Morris, my editor, made helpful comments and never once incited Sarah, for which I am grateful. Peggy West did an excellent job typing this manuscript.

Lastly, I am grateful for the wisdom and work of the people I have known as clients and students. As always, their bravery and growth has encouraged me.

# Contents

*To Marianne and Mark*
*And to Mnemosyne, who is Memory, mother of the Muses*

# Introduction

*The Mother I Carry* is the second book I have written about healing from the abuses of my childhood. I began writing these books ten years ago when I was twenty-eight. Together, they are the record of my journey to discover why I felt so fearful and self-hating regardless of the circumstances of my adult life. My questions led me to memories of my childhood. My first book, *The Obsidian Mirror*, recounts my experiences remembering childhood sexual abuse and my work in healing. Although it is not necessary to read that book before reading this one, *The Mother I Carry* continues my journey of self-exploration focusing on my childhood relationship with my mother.

In talking about memory, I am not referring to the memorizing we are taught in school or to distant observations of events outside ourselves. I mean memory as a sensory collage of sound, smell, taste, picture and kinesthetic response to important experiences in our lives. Memory has the power to propel the inner explorer back through time and space to the emotions, thoughts and physical sensations of childhood. The more I looked to memory the more I remembered. I recalled not only how I had experienced my life as a child but also how this had affected me as I grew. Memory made sense of my confusion and showed me why I was in so much pain. At the same time, Memory illuminated my ongoing determination to create, to take the tragedy of this abuse and use it like compost in growing a life better and different from the generations of my family before me.

"Sticks and stones will break my bones but words will never hurt me," I was taught; one more lie among many. In truth words penetrate the unlidded ear and land in the spirit. Words carry hatred and passion and love and fear. Words have the power to shoot down or raise up. Sharp cutting words can whirl for years afterward like the rotating blades of a lawn mower.

The incest made me want to destroy my body. It caused me to fear catastrophe, to stay small and invisible waiting for the events that would take my breath away and leave me speechless. The sexual offenders in my life were all men. In healing I learned to push them away and throw them off.

Emotional abuse is like water dripping every day on a stone, leaving a depression, eroding the personality by an unrelenting accumulation of incidents that humiliate or ridicule or dismiss. Emotional abuse is air and piercing vibration. Emotional abuse can feel physical even though no hand has been raised. The perpetrator may seem fragile and pathetic but still be vicious. Childhood emotional abuse can define us when we are young, debilitate us as we grow older, and spread like a virus as we take its phrases and turn them on others.

For several years I have taught workshops for women who were emotionally abused by their mothers. Together we shared our experiences with our mothers, the ways we still tripped over their long-ago evaluations of us or their neglect and betrayals. One woman, who was also an incest survivor, said, "The incest stopped when I left home, but the emotional abuse is there whenever I talk to my mother on the phone." For all of us, emotional abuse was the pain and powerlessness we felt in the face of our mothers' anger, fear and oppression.

When we begin, the women in my workshops are reluctant to talk about their own experiences or to hold their mothers accountable. Each one of us is aware how much work it is to be a woman, let alone a mother, even more work back when we were children, when women had it harder than they do now and now it's hard enough. We were told our mothers were too weak to stand examination. We were taught to excuse our mothers by saying, "She did the best she could," instead of exploring her legacy and revising it for ourselves and our children. But the most terrible lesson we learned was that taking ourselves seriously and demanding respect was selfish and forbidden. As daughters we learned most of all that other people's opinions and needs mattered more than our own. I was my mother's shadow. I became the child part of herself that she had disowned. She passed to me her hatred of being a girl and a woman. But she did not invent this hatred. She gave me what she had fashioned from the chains of the generations before her and the era into which she came to adulthood. She embraced the conservative Christian beliefs about women and child-rearing that she had been told it was sacrilege to question. She trusted the half-hourly schedules in *The Good Housekeeping* book on parenting, telling her when to pay attention to the child, when to offer food and to always close the door to the baby's room at night. My mother did not question the fact that the author was a man, but then all authorities on child-raising in 1954 were male. At the same time, psychology was tracing the aberrant behavior of men to their "suffocating" and "castrating" mothers. If a woman turned to psychology for help, however, she was diagnosed as "hysterical" or "melancholic" and told it was her femaleness that was the problem, not incest or emotional abuse or the other manifestations of misogyny.

But my mother never would have turned to psychology for help anyway. Nor was she an inquisitive or observant person.

Healing has required that I know my own story better than I know my mother's. Healing insists that I acknowledge my memory as the source of my knowing instead of swallowing the stories someone else tells me about who I am. Healing is like weeding; watching closely for the feelings and messages that restrict, bending down until I am the size of a child, then pulling out the roots and shaking the good dirt back onto my own ground, the ground upon which my life happens. I found I could not talk myself out of my pain and anger. I discovered that core beliefs and feelings are closely connected and that I must get close to my feelings to heal.

Since Freud's ego, id and superego, psychology has conceptualized the mind's ability to talk to itself. Transactional analysis, Gestalt therapy, Jungian dream work and Psychosynthesis have all recognized the multiplicity of the personality. In this work with myself and with other people abused as children, I have found that healing needs to occur at the site of the wound. Healing is a process of cleaning the wound by expressing what lives there. This involves inviting the wounded child selves forward and listening to them.

In writing this book, Memory took me to every age I have been. I honored the child's voice that my mother had discounted or ridiculed. I felt my grief and anger and fear at how I was treated because I was a girl-child. But I also brought my adult knowing to this child, validating her and making new decisions about who I was. I found strengths and gifts in myself that my mother never mentioned. I affirmed my desire for connection and love and attention. I honored the tenderness of my heart, my desire to grow and learn and the fire in me to make songs and stories.

As in writing *The Obsidian Mirror*, working with inner characters allowed me to illustrate the complexity of my inner landscape. The inner voices are the committee of my personality; each of them evolved to hold an aspect of my experience and development. There are children and teenagers, a critic and a healer. As I paid attention to these parts of myself, I changed the way I talked to myself and my responses to the opportunities and challenges of my daily life. I found abilities I feared I had lost in becoming an adult. I rediscovered my childlike spontaneity and eagerness. I learned to call on my natural capacity for new experiences and learning and play. I saw that I needed the passion of my adolescents and even the organizational ability of my critic. I realized that these inner voices, who had developed in response to specific times in my life, continued to grow and learn.

Healing involved hearing the story of each inner voice. But it also involved asking these voices what they needed. From their responses, I created rituals using sound, movement and magic. For memory is experiential; in acting out my healing, and drawing on the power of nature and myth, I created new beliefs and practices. I revised my life. I allowed myself to make up songs and imitate crows, to color with crayons and converse with dragons, practicing until I could manifest a new way of being in my life.

At times the journey into abuse seemed overwhelmingly difficult. Making myself the subject of two books and taking my own side went against everything I learned from my mother.

But now I feel only gratitude that this journey has brought me so fully to myself and given me the opportunity to encourage others in healing and knowing their own truths.

*Louise M. Wisechild*
*March 1993*

# The Mother I Carry

# 1

## *Moving In*

MARIANNE AND I pull on our wool sweaters and don thick caps as the heat generated by hoisting and depositing a car-load of boxes, blankets, lamps and computer apparatus dissipates to the reality of our breath condensing in the unheated and long unused cabin. We investigate the assorted rooms and begin our attack, armed with Easy-Off, Ajax, Spic 'N Span, vacuum attachments and a determined optimism. Crystal Cat prowls the corners and settles for a safe spot on the top of the refrigerator, overseeing the rites Marianne and I first learned from our mothers.

It's the end of January and I'm moving into this island cabin for six weeks of solitude and self-exploration. I have come to remember my childhood relationship with my mother. For six weeks, I have no bodywork clients or work-shops or readings as well as no telephone, no appointment book and no guilt for what I have not yet gotten around to doing. I am protected from obligation by slow moving ferries and the winter bleakness of a neighborhood of summer cab-ins. I sigh hugely and squeeze the mop. Free at last.

This isn't the sort of arrangement my mother would ap-prove of. Even though we haven't been in contact with each other for five years, I can imagine what it would be like if she were here right now. She would shake her head in disapproval at her first sight of this peeling red shack pouring waterfalls of rain from its edges. She would not see the determination with which this cabin squats among the tall grasses, collapsing inward but still standing after years of neglect through Puget Sound winters.

At the door, she would hold her breath as if expecting a disaster and on the exhale would begin talking about the dirt and cold and "look at that lock, anyone could just walk right in."

"I don't know why you have to live like this," she would say.

If I could not hold my tongue, I would mutter that it was a little late for her to worry about my protection.

She would push aside my words with a motion of her hands and tell me I had always been ungrateful.

Then she would say, "Let's not get into this," and give me a can of tuna fish, a baggie of chocolate chip cookies and a Tupperware storage box for my kitchen.

Even after five years, it is easy to hear her voice.

I stop cleaning the mouse droppings from the refrigerator to smoke a cigarette, feeling its burn in my throat.

I have always been good at anticipating my mother's response. All along I knew, deep down, that my mother would get rid of me if she could. But for a long time, I carried a secret hope that this wasn't really true. So even though I told myself that she would disown me some day, I was caught undone when it happened.

Until I was twenty-eight years old, I survived my childhood by not thinking about it too much. But then Memory returned in flashback and dreams, in phantom pelvic pain, anxiety attacks, and suicidal despair as I began to remember the extensive sexual abuse I suffered at the hands of various male relatives and to make sense of my lifelong depression and anxiety. I was twenty-nine years old when I sat in a restaurant and confronted my stepfather with my memories of being sexually abused by him. I wanted him to say that he did it and that he was sorry. I wanted him and my mother to go into therapy. What I got was the sound of my voice telling.

My stepfather went home in a fury screaming libel and how could I say such a thing about him. My mother and I never talked. A week after confronting him I received a one sentence letter saying she did not want to see me or hear any more about this ever. She signed it, "Carol."

I wash the refrigerator racks with hot soapy water and imagine her quickly writing my dismissal, her back teeth tight together the way they always were when the subject was me. I can see her driving it to the post office and shutting me firmly away from her thoughts as the blue box swallows the end of our relationship. My mother was good at firmly shutting up trouble. But she could not stop me from writing down everything I remembered.

I spent many years of devoted effort trying to suppress my mother's voice, but it's still with me. Her voice travels with me in Memory, through time and distance, carrying emotions and responses that I can not easily shed. And sometimes in my own words and thoughts, I unwillingly echo her phrases.

"I'm almost done in the living room," Marianne calls over the sound of Tracy Chapman.

I leave the toilet bowl soaking to admire the rearrangement of sofas and easy chairs. We hug like bears in our sweaters and savor the warmth of our mouths as we kiss. Sunday, she will leave me alone here. I stroke her sweater, seeking the familiar curves in her back, memorizing them with my fingers.

Together we hang a beach mat between the living room and the kitchen to keep the heat in the back of the house. I look wistfully at the Ben Franklin wood stove, the deceptive stately centerpiece of the living room.

"We bought it at the dump for ten dollars, cleaned it up and put it in. Don't bother lighting it. It just fills the house up with smoke. Believe me. Every time we go up there we try it. It never works," I was told by one of the women who own the cabin.

Given my mission, it seems appropriate that there is a large dysfunctional item in the middle of the living room. I put obsidian and rutilated quartz on the stove top and light three long candles in the hope of creating an illusion of warmth.

Marianne and I stop to show off the new shine on the kitchen linoleum and the white we have found under the stains in the sink. I notice that my feet are cold, on more than one account.

I hug Marianne again. "This book seemed like a good idea when I thought of it," I tell her. "But my relationship with my mother was awful! Now that I'm here, I remember that wandering through childhood with Memory the first time was a very vivid experience, sometimes too vivid." Solitude always seems like a good idea until I'm on the brink of it.

The thing about spending time with Memory is that it's like being there all over again. It's a jigsaw puzzle as the memories get beginnings and endings and meet each other in time.

I hardly remembered anything about my past when I began visiting with Memory and now, six years later, many large pieces of my past are in place. Because of that, I am different. I stopped living in a well of despair and helplessness. I stopped telling lies. I began to feel possibilities. That journey with Memory was worth it.

"But to go back and actually invite Memory to show me more about childhood? How do I know that it will get me anywhere?" I ask Marianne earnestly as we put on the tea-kettle and investigate the cupboards to find pastel plates and coffee-stained mugs.

"Maybe this isn't such a good idea. Who knows what happens to people who introspect too much? What if I find too much meaning and explode? You know it might be easier to pretend that I know all there is to know about my childhood and that I have transcended it. If I work on my mother, after all this incest work, people are going to think I'm awfully slow in getting it together. And then there's the fact that I counted the days of adolescence wishing for the magic number of eighteen and leaving home. What am I doing spending my adulthood preoccupied with what I could hardly wait to leave?"

Marianne rolls her eyes at me. "Louise, part of who you are is someone who roots around inside yourself. Believe me, you've been talking about it for months." She recognizes the fear in my eyes and touches my back.

"I'm just not sure I want to spend more time with my mother, even just in my head," I complain. As I say this, Memory reminds me that it's my self I will spend time with. Still, I am beginning to remember that Memory is not casual company.

It's not as if I'm without Memory. Memory comes when I write in my journal and sometimes in therapy. I find Memory in the way I walk and the holding in my muscles. Memory reminds me that the present is a continuation of many moments which came before. But lately, Memory has been investigating my mother.

It began when I noticed that activity makes me anxious. Schedules overwhelm me. I am somehow so involved in what there is to do that I have only sporadic moments of exhilaration at what I have accomplished. My life now involves many public engagements and though parts of me enjoy being heard I worry disproportionately about what people might think of me. All this worry is getting tiresome. And yelling at myself about my insecurity has so far not eradicated it.

I find taking care of my self to be a continual challenge. I spend a large part of my time trying to invent how to do it, wrestling with the matters of daily life. At every turn in this, I sense the presence of my mother. I learned what she taught me so well that I'm often either obeying her or disobeying her, which is not the same as being nice to myself.

I was supposed to have become her, if I had turned out according to plan. I was trained to repeat her life, daughter becoming wife becoming mother. I carry her fears and limitations in weights around my wrists and ankles. My body was molded first by her own body and then by the words she wrapped around her feelings.

I look to Memory, again, to help me extricate myself from what my mother said I was. Memory lets me look at myself through my own eyes. Memory shows me what I carry of my mother and what I've picked up in other places.

"Maybe you could just stay?" I ask Marianne, feeling very young inside and wrinkling my face. "You could take a month and a half off work?"

"I wish!" she laughs. "I'm jealous of you for this time to speculate on yourself." She folds her arms on her gray sweater and examines me warmly through her wire-rimmed glasses.

I never thought I'd fall in love with anyone with copper hair and light freckled skin, because those were my mother's features and I could never imagine being close to my mother. But in Marianne, there is nothing that reminds me of my mother. This has not always been true of lovers in the past.

I reach out to stroke her head, feeling her great flowing cape of curling red hair against my fingers and smiling into her face which looks as often ten or eight or thirty as the forty that she almost is. "I'll miss you."

"Me too. But I'm going to make baskets and necklaces and spend some good weekend time by myself! I love winter! Even without you!" Marianne sticks out her tongue at me right into my mouth and then arms herself with the broom, saluting as she marches from the kitchen into the back bedroom. I trail behind her.

Blackberry vines lean against the window; making thorned archways with shriveled berries dangling in tight black knots. The remaining January leaves have holes in them as if they've been gnawed and then abandoned by small desperate bugs. When I sit low on floor cushions and lean forward onto the board that Marianne and I have set on the Parsons tables, I look up into this thicket. The vines are a nest, protecting me from unwanted eyes and keeping the rain from the window.

This room is the writing studio and bedroom all in one. Unlike the living room and the other bedroom, this one has a working heater and warm walls of stained pine. The ceiling has a cross of brown where the roof once leaked and folds inward a bit, like the bed, whose mattress slopes to a V in the middle of a black metal bed frame. A baseball hat, four decks of cards, a kite, Parcheesi, a red fire hat, a round baby's walker with a lemon plastic tray and dust complete the furnishings. I put the games away in the front bedroom, but keep the kite hanging on the wall. When I walk with Memory, I am myself as a child.

Marianne dusts the walls with the broom, selectively leaving a cobweb in the corner, hung like a hammock of a thousand gray silk threads so that it seems to be solid rather than temporary, with perfect holes for the entrance and exit of the spider. Crystal Cat moves from her perch atop the refrigerator to curl on the new-made bed, a circle of long perpetually shedding fur organized into intricate patterns of black, white and brown.

· · ·

Monday brings the mixed experience of delight with my solitude and unmarred writing time, terror at the prospect of rummaging around in my unknown and a new appreciation for just how cold uninsulated floors can be. The refrigerator sputters and hums, then lapses into silence. Large windows on two sides catch the early afternoon sun as it reddens the browns of bare trees. On the counter are an assortment of small brown bags, labeled in pen. Lobelia, mullein, angelica root, alfalfa: herbal remedies to stop smoking and to heal my lungs. I light a cigarette and look at the bags, puzzled again at how many times I've tried to quit smoking only to return again in a panic, to suck in comfort and the support that I have not figured out how to give myself otherwise.

"When are you going to stop smoking?" I hear a voice inside myself chide even as I inhale. "Everyone else has figured out how to quit. You're thirty-four years old and you just can't do anything!" The only way I can rid myself of this voice when I smoke is not to notice that I am smoking.

I light a second cigarette and blow smoke in the face of this voice, who I call Sarah. I have known for quite a while now that my personality is a collection of inner voices. Sarah is my critic, list maker and general all around detractor. Sarah is the part of myself that apprenticed to my mother. She has a hard face and pokes me on the inside when she talks. "Life is hard," she says. "It's good to suffer." Sarah is responsible for all of my self-critical thoughts.

Sarah is an expert at pointing out that everything can go wrong. For a long time, Sarah was the only adult voice I could hear inside myself. Between her and my mother, I got the idea that adulthood was a merciless state of deprivation and tasks. My inner children used to be terrified of Sarah.

"Sarah!" says another inner voice softly. "We will learn how to be a nonsmoker. But you make us anxious."

It's Carrie. She is a part of myself who is learning to be an adult. She is the self who works with clients and teaches workshops and lectures on healing from sexual abuse. I have had the other voices longer than I have had hers. She is still learning how to take care of me.

"You're just too slow and self-indulgent," Sarah accuses.

I sink onto my floor cushions and lean on the plank table, considering the objects I have gathered to help me focus or to give me something to look at when I can't. When all else fails, Carrie tries to remind me to hold onto something although amidst Sarah's uproar and the response of all the parts of me who are children and adolescents, I sometimes don't get around to Carrie's suggestions. Indeed too often, just reaching for a rock seems risky and unfamiliar. Not like cigarettes which I have reached for since I was sixteen.

Now I take a breath and hold a bloodstone; a stone the color of a deep forest on an overcast day, flecked with red. The properties of bloodstone are balance and grounding. I think of how my mother and I are connected by blood but how little fluidity there was between us.

I hold the photo of Marianne and me smiling together, with rolled up sleeves and the last of summer on our skin on Mount Rainier. I smile at us and try to recapture the morning giggles and solid hugs that are part of our relationship. Breathing into my chest, I try to recapture the full heart I knew last night before she left. But what I find is tightness and a small child voice that says, "I don't know if I can do this."

This is what usually happens next on my journey with Memory. I get scared. My legs ache, my stomach corks itself at my solar plexus. I reach for a novel. My heart beats faster. I surrender and sigh, pick up a pen, close my eyes and notice how hard it is to breathe.

I travel through my body, questioning the tension in my muscles. I am looking for an inner landscape, a metaphor that will tell me something about my relationship with my mother. I find myself at the crooked steps of an abandoned house. It does not look particularly inviting.

"Make yourself at home," Memory invites, referring to this house in my mind.

Behind my eyes, this house looms like something haunted, with tattered edges, falling gutters and a foundation of dubious integrity.

"Does it have to be beige?" I ask Memory. "I hate beige."

I try to imagine a nicer house than the one that sits before my mind's eye, perhaps a nice peach colored Victorian. But this abandoned two-story box with a porch slung on as an afterthought remains. Chipped paint fades beneath a roof that threatens to slip off in asphalt squares. The mangy winter thistle and sharp crabgrass poking up through the hard ground do nothing to brighten its appearance. It looks nothing like any house that I have seen with my outer eyes. But it feels colorless and cold like the insides of the houses I grew up in.

The windows are small and mean on the two-story house as if they refused entrance to fresh air. Back of the windows is darkness as if night were the only occupant of this house. The front windows catch a moment of sun and seem to glare at me like eyes. The next minute the windows seem to sag in their frames, covered with drops of water running in lines down the house as if it were raining, but it's not. Feelings live in this house. They cling to the walls and leak through the windows. It's easy to miss them at first because of all that beige.

I understand that I am to take possession of this house which I have found in my mind. I know this must be important or the house wouldn't remain so stubbornly, but it gives me the willies, even if it is only in my mind.

"What are the willies?" Memory asks. And just then I notice that I am not alone here.

My mother is standing by the door. Between us is a tether, a braided cord of leather, snapped to a ring in the shadow of her belly. A leather tether which crosses my breastbone in front of my heart, circling my breasts and shoulders like a harness. There is no give when I tug.

My mother is the body of my childhood, wearing her hands over her eyes. My mother is the red sound of her voice, repeated and preserved in the inner echo of her words. My mother is a shade of swirling loud air that pulls on the blinds of the inner house, snapping them up toward the ceiling. My mother is how I got here.

I hear my own voice, young and older. "Carol. Carol. Mother. Mother! Mommy, Mommy, Mommy!" A baby crying. I hear myself calling my mother with all the names I have known her by, in tones of distress, pleading, anger and loneliness. Each inner voice names a connection that is blood and body. When I close my eyes I can imagine what these voices look like; I see images of children and adolescents. I see Sarah, angular and sharp, pointing her finger at me. Carrie reminds me to breathe and feel my body even as I imagine coming closer to my mother. Carrie's eyes are lit from behind like shallow river rocks when the sun shines on them.

Each voice is a part of me. Together this cast of inner characters enacts the drama of my life; they are the multiplicity of my self. Sometimes I am playful and curious, but I am also wanting and lost and shy. In my adult life I become ten or fifteen or two years old again in response to my life's experience. Some of the voices are bold and some are frightened. Some are reckless and some are too afraid of what people will think of me. Carrie leads me toward what is healing. Sarah mimics my mother and is always finding new rules to make. The inner voices represent my response to everything that happened to me and all the ways I have ever felt and moved and been frozen. They are the actresses of my Memory and the committee that makes my choices. I am often working to find a harmony between them, so that I can have peace and feel good and excited about my life. But my inner voices also still carry beliefs from my childhood that long ago stopped serving me.

On the porch of the inner house, Carrie says, "I want to go inside and be with every part of our self. I want to witness what we still carry from our mother. Perhaps if I see this, I will know how to take on a different adultness, how to tend better to this self."

I hear a voice that is not mine, but that I have recorded. "Loueeeeze, Loueeeeze." It's my mother's voice, using the long stretch of name she called when I was outside as a child and she wanted me to come in. "Loueeeeze!"

I climb the first step. My mother is waiting for me at the door, white blouse buttoned around her neck and wrists. I can see the outlines of her bra and slip. But even with the vividness of detail, she seems ethereal, as if her body lacked substance. Memory has made her much taller than me. She is pointing a pale finger shiny with clear nail polish. "Don't you ever tell anyone what goes on inside of this house! That's our own private business." I am four and seven and ten.

I fumble with the tether that connects us. I try to shoo her away with my hands. But my mother has never gone far from me. Even when I have wished that my mother would go away forever, she has been here, inside of me; a burning hot air whistling through the cells of my body.

"Honor your mother! How dare you talk back to me!" I am twelve and sixteen.

I am holding my pen like a cigarette. I open my eyes to escape, distracted by the inevitable late afternoon chain saw in the country. Water for mint tea comes to a boil.

I leaf through the actual houses of my childhood. I listen hard, but hear no jokes or laughter or tender shared confidences in these houses. Instead I hear my mother's voice, spinning like a blender, crushing something or pulverizing it. These are my mother's houses and I was always running away from them and being brought back. I am still trying to make myself at home, here, in this body, in my work and relationships and relaxations.

The fleecy gray blanket of cloud has been shedding layers until blue is nearly visible beneath it. The hillside is infused with the flat light of a late winter day. I put on my thickest sweater and go out to walk on the beach. Blue herons stand on one leg in water the color of steel. I watch the sun crown the Olympic Mountains. This is also home.

# 2

## The Nursery

THE FRONT DOOR of the inner house leads to a hallway dotted with dark wooden doors, each one of them closed. The bare bulb on the wallpapered ceiling is lit, but most of the light comes from the open front door behind me.

I turn the first doorknob. Long pale draperies blow by a window. In the corner, crib sides are latched like a cage at the zoo. Two frayed strips of cloth are laced through the wooden bars to hold the baby so that she cannot turn over. On a table next to the crib, atop a pile of diapers, an electric clock has numbers that glow in the dark.

I become naked in this room, uncoordinated in my hands and feet, as I lie on my back in the crib.

My mother is a cloud who lifts me into the sky and feeds me the food of the great spirit. My mother's hair is a halo in the sunlight. I reach up with my arms optimistically when I think she might come.

My mother is a blur who folds diapers and pushes a squat roaring vacuum. Shadows move through the window onto the wall. My mother closes the door between us, leaving me alone with my language of moan and cry. The clock slows to long minutes of partial nursery light which shifts with the dance of draperies. Grating sounds enter through the open window and I tighten against the thick smell of cut grass.

Wanting is a round mouth in my stomach. If I could suck as long as I wanted I would not wake with hunger. If I could find warm stillness in her arms, I would not dread the shadows and the tearing sounds from outside this window.

I stand in this doorway as an adult. I search for words from the time before I had language. I hum a lullaby to myself.

*  *  *

I like to make noise when I'm alone and no one else can hear me. This morning I'm roaring out the hundreds of scared stopped breaths of my life in the city. I am humming, sighing, moaning and growling as if I could shake out my muscles with my voice. Apprehensive muscle fibers relax with the vibration of my exhale. No one can see me or hear how much I sigh, how loud I cry or the audible conversations I hold with myself. Solitude is luxurious in its absolute absence of outside opinion.

Sarah is still with me, of course, awesomely full of inner opinion; of how much I have to figure out while I am away and all of the ways in which I must improve myself now that I have the time for it.

"Ssshh," Carrie says to Sarah. "We're here to listen."

Fear travels on well-worn trails through my nervous system, making me wince and duck. This fear is a part of my inheritance.

The small sawmill town in Western Washington where I was born is best known for a billboard erected by a local turkey farmer in order to disseminate the ideology of the John Birch Society. The general hospital that delivered me would have eschewed birthing rooms as a communist conspiracy. My mother, strapped to a bed in the maternity ward in 1954, had been told that having a baby was the most natural thing in the world and brought fulfillment. But before that she had been told that her vagina was "dirty" and not to touch herself there. As she lay numb on her back, the doctor plunged his fingers into her vagina and hauled me from her in an act that she could neither feel nor see between the gray of anesthesia and the sea of white bedsheets.

Carrying an assortment of related genes, I pushed through this channel in her body, a channel that I too inherited. I have no pictures for the first moments when I traded water for air. I do not remember being placed into my mother's arms or her shadow falling on me from the light. I do feel a longing when I watch my friends tenderly cuddle their infants now. It is not a desire to have a child myself. It is wanting to be held by a mother easy in her body and comfortable with mine.

The sky descends in flimsy white garments as I make coffee and steam milk. Color bleaches from the long grasses. Dampness clings to each link of the metal fence. In Memory, my mother's mouth comes toward me, but it is a far ago time, before I began cringing at the edges on her words. Memory gathers on my tongue: my mother's finger in my mouth; the sweetness of my sucking. Now I suck, drifting on a long curving cloud of smoke.

I was delivered by the same doctor who never questioned my mother when she told him that her bruises were from falling down stairs and running into walls. He cut the cord between us and slapped me. It is the first of many times I am slapped and the only time my noise is greeted with gratitude.

This was before I learned to hunch my shoulders or to pretend to smile when I was tired. I didn't hold my breath then. I giggled and blurted sound in response to wonders and miracles. Every experience passed through me. I took in and responded, reached and was enthralled with the movement of my hand. I was not born with this curtain over my skin, this dullness that covers my senses.

◆*Memory.* In flannel and the slickness of a buried rubber sheet, surrounded by dark wetness, I am small, the night a devouring mouth. I reach up, pressing against the cloth belt that holds me in my dripping loud wanting.

The door clicks and light breaks the darkness. I am carried upward.

To land in a cradle of flesh. Soft singing words enter me through my ears, slowing the turbulent dark river that was swelling in my body. I drink the smell of her skin and the hot air beneath her blouse, circling with my lips. Swallowing, sweet swallowing, and I am whole. I close my eyes to a lighter darkness, floating, tethered to her by my tongue. Her soft enormous hand supports my back, fingers feathered next to the fringe of my damp hair, cupping my head. I cry as she puts me down. She says, "Sssshh."◆

This is as close as my mother and I ever got. But there is no lingering satisfaction in my body, only wanting to hold on. I hold B. Bear but something has come between me and being able to comfort myself.

"I need more time here," I tell Memory. "I'm still hungry. I want to fill up with gentle memories but there aren't enough of them."

I claw the air with wanting. I light another cigarette, seeking the satisfaction and peace that I have learned enters only through the mouth. Instead, the smoke makes my tongue thick and dry.

"Stroke me, stroke me," my skin demands.

I stare at my fingers and the lifeline etched into my palm. Beyond my fingers is only the stained ceiling. I am trying to conjure up a mother's smiling face, a meeting with her eye to eye. I am trying to imagine that she is just holding me, not feeding or bathing or diapering.

When Memory speaks again, I am caught behaving like my mother; sticking food and non-food in my mouth, tossing myself stuffed animals, engaging in a flurry of activity instead of staying with what I'm feeling in my body. Memory brings fear. I'm afraid of what I cannot have but need, like love and safety. Memory requires me to sit with my fear over and over again, reminding me that I must feel my fear before I can receive comfort.

With my breath, I allow the full crazy feeling of lostness to permeate me until I no longer feel the edge of the bed. Memories float between the arches of blackberry vine. My head shrinks into my neck and my tiny fingers wave like the cilia of feeding barnacles. My lips have gotten stiff, like old worn rubber. I begin moving them, twisting my mouth until my jaw works open and large frightened sounds come forward from back of my shoulders.

I want to ease into my mother's arms, but I can't conjure up more safety from her. Instead I feel wary, like the picture of me at three months, propped up on chenille pillows, surveying the world with a solemn stare, beginning the lines that are now etched indelibly into the rectangle between my eyebrows. Inside, I am already wanting food and touch and kindness. The seeds of my later hatred of clocks, calendars and schedules are already planted. My mother has too bright eyes that come too close and squeeze too tight. Eyes that turn cloudy and far away. I lean toward the smiles of strangers in the supermarket, especially the ones that reflect me back in their eyes. I cry indignantly when the Episcopal preacher puts water on my forehead. What will be done with me next and why is it so hard to get what I'm asking from my mother in my language of heart and stomach?

I return to this language, holding my emotions like a sacred rattle that I shake for my survival. My crying hunger, screeching frustration, howling aloneness, inhaling surprise, giggling excitement, screaming danger, danger. I will grow up and be given words for these emotions that are much less than the sounds I first knew them by. Memory takes me back to the emotions I was supposed to have forgotten.

◆*Memory.* I am folding my body inward, ducking my head into my shoulders. The air in my parents' house vibrates. The sound is hitting skin slapping falling sound sound of mother screaming sound sound my father booming, beating. I want to cover my ears, but my hands bat the air instead. I want to be under the bed but I can't even turn over. My skin is breaking out in rashes, oozing irritation. I pierce the vibration with a song of hunger and fear, a stream of vital energy that fills the sky over my crib, but this time there is no magic only an exhaustion and a grit in my eyes.◆

Memory releases me to the sound of crows and a barking dog. I peer out from behind the living room blinds to make sure that no one has heard my wild crying and sent an aid car. I open the door to the large cold front bedroom and look in the closets to make sure no one has snuck in. I tell myself, "I am safe. I'm safe." But I feel like a baby.

A beige long-haired cat raises her feet high through the long grasses, glances quickly at Crystal who is perched atop the patio picnic table, and disappears into a hole that leads to a maze of pipes and dirt under the cabin.

.  .  .

My mother once told me that she'd met my father on the rebound, after the soldier she'd been engaged to died in the Korean War. The soldier was named Bill and I thought he probably looked like Prince Charming, though my mother never said anything specific about him or what she liked about him. My mother did not consult Memory or reminisce. I have assembled the skeleton of her life from the sentences that slipped through her lips in rare unguarded moments.

My first twenty-one months were spent with my mother and father in a small house just behind the railroad tracks. My father and his mother administered a Standard Oil distributorship. After the divorce, my mother stopped talking about my father, except to say when I asked that I didn't have one, that he didn't pay child support, and that his people weren't like ours; they drank, they bought fancy clothes and they did funny things with the company books. My brother Jim was born just before we left my father and his house. In my scrapbook, Jim is lying alone on our mother's lap like a beached animal while she smiles determinedly at the camera, her fingers curled into her palms on the outside of her thighs. She never learned to hold either of us.

As the house vibrated with the passage of trains, my mother began to think of herself as a parent, turning her back forever on having been a child. My mother's mother passed on ancient unquestioned child-rearing from the Bible and the Midwest where children were a way of creating a work force. How to diaper and burp, the temperature of bottles on the wrist, strapping the baby in the crib so that she cannot turn over, mashing home-canned vegetables into slush. Warning my mother never to spoil the baby by picking her up too much or coming every time she cried. A spoiled child was the worst possible outcome. A child with moods or wants or a voice was at all cost to be avoided.

◆*Memory.* I'm six years old, sitting on a chair in my mother's back bedroom at my grandparents' house, where we moved after the divorce. Aunt Bev and Uncle Todd are visiting. Bev's baby is crying from the front of the house where she was put down for a nap.

I am chaining my wiggles to the iron frame of the folding chair. Waiting for the words "good girl Loueezy" which I earn if I sit very still. The baby's cries turn to screaming which ricochets through the dining room and the kitchen, down the narrow corridor of coat hooks to the back bedroom. I imagine her face turning red as the sound rises to the ceiling like the organ music at church, swollen and demanding.

The grownups talk about growing corn and the new minister. My aunt looks shyly at my mother and grandmother, as if she's going to apologize to them for something, and begins to rise from her chair.

"Let her cry," my grandmother says. "It's good for her to cry it out. If you pick her up every time she cries, you'll spoil her." My mother nods and my aunt resettles.

The sound is choking now and I'm holding my breath and turning red. Streams of wetted baby sound change to gasps and hiccups. My grandmother pours more hot water over spoonfuls of instant coffee. The warm sun patch that touched the leg of my chair shrinks away on the carpet. The air is thick with coffee fumes and a new silence marked by the clink of spoons against cups.◆

It was accepted in my family that my mother's mother liked babies and as soon as you could do anything for yourself, she was gone. I would add that my grandmother was long gone by the time I knew her, becoming an old vacantly smiling woman by the time she was fifty. In truth, she did not live in her house, but outside in her garden where she plowed dirt, planted vegetables that lost color as they boiled for dinners and rows of dahlias that were never brought inside the house. My grandmother loved concrete and poured several sidewalks. She was also competent with a hammer and mouthful of nails and endless rolls of wallpaper. She never mentioned her childhood, though I knew that both she and my grandfather had grown up on farms, milking cows and "not laying about." My mother was the only daughter of my grandmother's five children. To my mother fell the housework my grandmother abandoned and the tasks of serving my grandfather.

My mother was always obsessive about housework. But even though she tended the house, my mother, like her mother before her, could not pierce the darkness of oppression and abuse that lurked in their houses.

My father's mother is a shadow to me, sharing the dark features of my father evident in the small wedding pictures which are all that my mother did not destroy after the divorce. I will forever see her and my father in a row of corsages, lined up in the social hall in the basement of the Presbyterian church, looking more polite than happy. My mother was also to learn from the shadow of her husband's mother. After my mother's divorce, her mother-in-law stormed her wedding presents, burning Revereware, ripping bed sheets, shattering crystal, in revenge for my mother leaving her son. Just as my mother would go on rampages through my teenage room, dumping dresser drawers in a pile on my bed.

I will never know if my mother also once pledged that she would never be like her mother. She did not begin sentences with "When I was your age." Instead she said, "Just wait until you're a mother. You'll see how hard it is."

I notice the thorns on the blackberry vines as I think about my female relations. The more I think about my mother and about her mother the more uneasy I feel. Interwoven in their lives is the tyranny of their marriages, the arrogance and cruelty of their men, the narrow trench allotted to women of their time. In my known relatives there is no matriarch, no woman who escaped the conventions of her time, no woman who talked back to a man, no woman who put her foot down or who had the last word. I am the direct descendant of a family of wimpy women, a fact that often fills me with despair and uncertainty about what it is I think I'm doing and what right I have to do it.

"You better not talk like this," Sarah threatens. "Those women did give birth, you know, and that's no small task. Something you haven't done, by the way."

I have the distinct sensation of treading irreverently on holy ground. A ground held irreproachable by right-wing conservatives and feminists alike. Although women are mistreated, mothers are considered sacred. For the conservatives, motherhood is the purpose of women, their highest calling. Mothers are up there with the flag and apple pie.

Celestial Seasonings prints dripping sentimental tributes to mothers on the sides of tea packages. Mother's Day cards abound with impossible virtues that women are supposed to possess because they gave birth. As a feminist, I find that mothers are heroines or powerless victims, but in either case, they are not to be held accountable or examined. Then, as we come together in groups of women, we trip over the criticism, competition and fear of judgement that more than one of us learned from our mothers.

I know I'm alone in this cabin but I feel surrounded by taboo and a disapproving gathering of mothers. A few have dark circles under their eyes from not sleeping enough; from rising to feed and walk new babies. Among them are stitches and scars and stories of labor that turned out every way other than what they'd expected.

"Everyone wants to blame mom for what they didn't get."

"Every time there's a serial murderer, it's always made out to be the mother's fault."

"Overworked and underpaid. Overworked and underpaid," they chant.

"It's damn hard work, to be lovingly present as well as to keep the house reasonably tidy so that no one trips and breaks a leg on the Legos left in the hall."

The pen starts to slip away from my fingers. I think about my friends with children, of the stories only now being written of raising children, of agony, confusion and poverty and occasionally of reward. I am older than my mother was when she had me. And I have grown into womanhood, taking on housekeeping, career and errands.

I attempt to respond, trying diligently to be fair. "I admit that it's hard to be a mother. For all of written history it has been hard to be women and to be mothers. But mothers are not all the same and I am not sure that pregnancy is enough of a qualification for the job."

I spent a weekend with friends, in honor and support of

our friend Betsey's coming birthing and transition to motherhood. We sang to her and fed her healthy food. We watched her dance and wrote her poems and chants in support of her upcoming labor. We gave her more support and love than my mother's family ever gave my mother.

I wish my mother had had friends instead of her family. I wish she had been rebellious instead of scared turning mean. I wish she had learned to protect herself from men instead of casting me to them. I wish she had been praised so that she knew how to give praise. I wish she had liked herself and her body. But none of this happened. At every crossroad my mother closed her eyes and told herself how hard it was to be a mother and pleaded with God to make it all okay. She never learned to solve problems or to ask the questions of herself which might have led to a different outcome.

Sometimes I see a woman like my mother in the aisles of Safeway, yanking and slapping and screaming at a two-year-old, threatening to leave her among the canned soup, walking away from a stranded small person crying in the aisle. I hear mothers' voices in campgrounds saying, "You're bad, bad. Don't you move from that spot!" I see myself in solemn young faces that explode with crying and anger because there is no other way to express the enormity of the forces coming toward them.

"She's tired, she didn't really mean it," the chorus claims. "She's not really abusive."

"But why do mothers have to change sides, abandoning the wisdom they might get from remembering their own childhood?" I ask. "Why do we spend so much energy defending mothers and so little considering the effects of their behavior upon us as children?"

. . .

I stare out the window into nothing. I am fighting Memory by spacing out. In my life, I've spent many hours in this state of dead time. Sarah yells at me to "do something!"

I tie my tennis shoes with determination and stomp out of the house in frustration. I check my pockets three times to make certain I have my keys, returning once to make sure there are no appliances on, besieged by the fear that catastrophe will befall this cabin and it will be my fault.

It's still waiting to rain. I squat on the sand, trying to feel the ground, to put some circulation into my legs. The beach is deserted so I let out explosions of sound from a rolled spot in my belly, letting out more air than I take in. I put my forehead against an ancient chunk of granite salty from spending half its life submerged. I want to drain the tension from my body out into this rock, but my muscles refuse to release me.

Two tall blond dogs materialize, running straight toward me, barking sharply, unattended, circling closer. Fear condenses, forming a yellow sweat that radiates out from my skin. I'm afraid they'll smell my fear and leap on me with their teeth. The dogs are barking like deep male yelling. Memory breaks through in the moment of fear rising. I am yelling "Go home, go home!" fearfully.

◆*Memory*. My mother and father are screaming beyond the door. The air in my room is shock waves on my skin making me howl with the intensity of the sound against my body. The door opens too fast and my mother's footsteps shake the crib as she gets closer. I am wet and raw. My mother's breath is hot on my belly, "SSSHH!"

Her hands come toward me but they pick up the pillow. My loud open mouth is stopped open full of pillow and my nose is pressed flat and closed. I clutch and then cease so that I am perfectly still. I float away from my lungs that can't get air, leaving my body behind, a bit of me floating in air on a string, away from my suddenly still body under the pillow and away from her.◆

I exhale slowly, shaken by this triggered Memory and the intensity of buried time coming forward. I jerk my attention back from inner to outer. The more ferocious of the dogs prances nearer to me, snarling and then wagging his tail. Do I yell at them or try for truce? I offer my hand and the other one comes cautiously toward me on wet sandy legs, head down, tail wagging. He cowers as I bring my hand up to pet his head and I wonder if he has been hit too. He stands by my side as if in approval and the other stays at a distance until they run into the icy January sea.

I turn toward the boulder again, weak in my body from the implosion of fear and dogs and Memory. In Memory, my mother removes the pillow from my face; I am floating above us and can see our shapes. She picks up my body and holds me against her shoulder saying "Ssshh, it's all right, it's all right." I find a way back from shock, back into my skin, but I cannot relax in her arms, nor do I have any energy for active resistance. I am unmoving on the beach until Carrie reminds me to unfold bit by bit, to inhale and do small wiggling movements.

When I was an adolescent, I turned against this infant self who had struggled so valiantly to continue breathing. "Who cares?" I chanted. "I wish I was dead." Even now, though I no longer entertain suicidal fantasies, I find that I must remember to breathe, that what at first came naturally has become clogged and erratic.

When I was in college, my mother told me that she was suicidal before and after my birth. We were walking from a restaurant to my apartment. It was one of the few times I have seen her eyes turn inward and the smile fade to a feeling that lurked beneath it. She had never told anyone else this.

Two years later, when I had just begun therapy, my mother sent me a letter in her looping penmanship, which began like all of her letters, with the mundane details. "Today we went out to eat at the new Mexican restaurant. I have often wished you were dead. Visited Steven in the hospital." One sentence, inserted into the middle of the letter, disconnected from any event before or after. I rushed to therapy with the letter, disconcerted yet validated. But I never confronted my mother with it or demanded an explanation. It was only what I already knew.

Currents of wind skid the clouds across the sea, forming elephants and tin men, then eroding them into blackbirds and vultures. The sky dances the shifts of Memory, the swirling patterns of what was and how it became the climate. In the clouds I see the violent shadows of my beginning, the hands turning from cradles to weapons. The moments of regret will shorten; my mother will stop saying she's sorry and begin to assume that I deserved it. The residue of uncertainty will become a dull guilt for which she will hold me responsible. She will tell me in many less direct ways that I am wrong for being alive.

.  .  .

The door to the kitchen is closed and the vines seem to press against the window. The bedroom floor is strewn with index cards and yellow legal pads where I have been writing glimpses of Memory: the high chair, the playpen, the tender hands and smiling faces of strangers, the temperature of my parents' house and how rapidly it could swing to an extreme. When I cry, I begin with loud yelling and drop to a level of repeating moans. I wrap myself in blankets and sit next to the space heater. Crystal Cat sleeps through all of it in a furry mound on the bed. I go to pet her and end up lying down on my back and staring past the ceiling.

"Quit acting like a baby! Grow up, act your age," Sarah says crossly, just like my mother did. "Louise is a baby, Louise is a baby," Sarah chants, discounting these moments spent in meeting my self, mocking my need for comfort.

"Remember what you have learned about safety," Memory instructs.

I return to the nursery in the inner house. I take out the crib and put a cradle in its place. I pretend to be the baby that

I was. I imagine lying on my back in the cradle, looking up into my grown-up face. I am looking into Carrie's face, into the face of my self who is the teacher, the healer and the student. I am looking into the face that Marianne sees when she feels small and I am comforting her. With young open eyes, I am trying to see the part of me my clients see, the healer who is loving and compassionate. I am looking for eyes that greet me with gentleness and delight. I imagine all the hands that have been kind to me, resting on my skin, covering me with touch.

Memory reminds me of Kate, my first therapist. I was twenty-four and terrified of letting anyone know what was really going on in my feelings and thoughts. I leaned against her office doorjamb and told her about slashing my wrists when I was thirteen and how my mother had said she'd kill me if I ever tried that again. My words were a flat monotone. Kate said that my mother hadn't given me the care that I needed. Then she said that I was lovable. It took me a long time to believe that was true. But eventually her listening and the way she took my side seeped through the walls I'd built to keep everyone far away. For the first time in years I felt alive in my heart and my chest and enthusiastic about the idea of love. Over time, I realized that love was more than a warmth sought in others, but was a life force that lived within me and longed to expand and encompass.

"Love requires safety," Memory instructs. "Safety so that all of you is included and accounted for, so that you need not hold anything back. Love does not live in shadows."

When I was twenty-eight years old I discovered "floating" in isolation tanks. Naked and shut in my own private room in a coffin-sized box totally without light or sound, I floated on water buoyant with five hundred pounds of Epsom salts. Though I had had many massages, being a massage therapist myself, floating was my first experience of total physical trust. I would send my breath into all of my muscles and tell myself, "I am held by salt and water. Nothing bad is going to happen to me here. I do not have to hold myself up or prepare for a disaster. I am held safe by water." Then I would sigh a lot, with sound.

I have camped beside rivers and imagined them flowing through me, removing the vestiges of holding; the water loosening muscles held tight in postural memory. I have sung and written loose tensions and cellular Memory, finding freedom in giving voice to my experiences. It is as if I have been resuscitating myself.

I have been journeying from isolation tanks to connection. I have loved friends and confessed my alienation and struggles. With Marianne I've found a safety and communication which allows the free flow of love and skin, of baby and adult. In these fifteen months of our relationship I have often felt naked and new.

"It's remarkable," I tell Memory. "I remember when I felt that no one really liked me, when I felt alone even when I was there with them. Now I know I have friends and I don't feel lonely when I'm with them."

But right now there's an emptiness, a familiar disconnection. "When I'm away from Marianne I can't feel her," I tell Memory.

Instead, I have a sharp and ancient longing to have had what I didn't have. I want a mother who picks me up and feels happy looking at me. I want a mother who's doing it because she wants to, not because she was supposed to. I want a mother who likes me and who is glad I was born.

"Your mother did the best she could," I was told by the women of my childhood. "Your mother really loves you, mothers do."

But I never felt it. I cannot find it when I search in my cells. I know it is possible to cut off feeling; that makes it impossible to love because love is also a feeling. When I wanted to know the joy of loving, Kate said, "The choice is to feel or not feel." Feeling does not let us pick and choose among the range of emotion. My mother erupted, but she did not feel.

I am propelled out the door to seek solace in walking. I sit against a log on the sand and let the ground meet my body. I remember a bookmark my friend Cara gave me, of Kuan Yin, the goddess of love and compassion, standing on the world and reaching her hand toward a baby. I call for her. Kuan Yin waves from the trees on the bluff. She sings in the continual wash of the tide. There are ways of learning what my mother never taught me. The trees and stones and spirits hold the mysteries. Goddesses and heroines, friends and lovers, gifts and challenges are all teachers. "Passion and compassion," I whisper, "enough time. Joy and safety and confidence in my breath."

"Teach me the ways of nurture," I ask of Kuan Yin as I close my eyes and hold a rock I've picked from the beach. "I want to know what it feels like to be wanted. I want to hold myself well and wholly. I want to breathe and not be afraid."

I walk farther down the beach, empty in my mind, but full of the feeling of my feet on damp sand.

"It will happen, gradually, the way it always does," says Memory. "You are spilling the pain of the unloving. And just after you think you are empty, your most immediate memories will be of loving and they will keep you good company in your heart."

# 3

# *Tayla and the Room of Errors*

THE INNER house has narrow halls of dimly lit dark wood. I carry a flashlight and a notebook.

Next to the nursery is a room built for a giant. In this room, I am like a bug that crawls around its old carpet. Forbidden artifacts are strewn enticingly on a tall table. I curl my arm around a wooden leg, bringing myself upright and reaching. Stretching to touch the glossy red of a magazine cover, to put my finger in the magic ring left from water in a glass, to bring the pair of earrings in brass and stone close to my face and into my mouth so that I can join with their shininess. I am two and three and four and five.

My mother's voice fills the room with sentences that circle in the curve of my hearing. "Don't touch that!" "Don't climb on that!" "I thought I told you never to do that again!" "Take that out of your mouth!"

I pretend I have antenna like a beetle to warn me about the "thats." I have antenna on both the front and back of my head. I keep forgetting to pay attention to them.

My mother is radar turning always in my direction, intercepting the path of my hands. The first word I learn is "No," but I am not allowed to say it. Only grownups get to say "No." My mother swoops down, catching my arms which wander constantly and which I am supposed to keep folded in my lap. My mother steers and pulls my shoulder while yelling at my feet for moving too fast or not fast enough.

I want to touch and taste and run and laugh. I want to hide behind the dark brown and green curtains but they don't reach to the ground and my legs show. Something bad always happens afterward.

My mother holds a magnet and I cling to it like the dots of metal filings that make mustaches and eyebrows on the clown beneath the plastic on my toy. I go to her from instinct; I think "I want" and turn in her direction—but what I want is never what I find with her.

"Mommy, mommy."

"Ssshh, be quiet. You just want attention, now behave yourself."

I stand in this doorway as an adult. I pull out my notebook and flashlight. I am no longer two or three or four or five. I've come back to pick up my wanting. I enter the room and stoop to pick my desires up off the floor. I straighten and shout, "Mine! Mine! I want! I need! Look at me. Look at me!"

.   .   .

When I was fifteen, my mother took me to a restaurant where we sat by the window and looked out upon a waterfall and down upon cloth napkins and elegant glasses and china plates. Below the window was a trail with a grate so walkers could watch the salmon fight their way upstream and leap over the concrete barriers. My mother brought me there to tell me about her divorce from my father who I hadn't seen or heard from since I was two. Before, she'd always said that I didn't have a father.

My mother looked at me conspiratorially. I felt taller, as if my mother had finally seen that I was growing up, old enough to share secrets.

"Mom and Dad always said it was a mistake to marry him," my mother said, picking at the chips from her roll.

"You don't know how hard it was to be a woman alone with two children."

I shifted uncomfortably in my chair. She'd told me how hard it had been as long as I could remember and it always ended up being my fault. I didn't ask to be born, I thought, not for the first time. But if I said that, she would say she had taken me out to a nice restaurant and this was the thanks she got. Before she started on hardship, I almost felt sorry for her. I put more sour cream on my potato and began eating the skin.

"Your father hit me. I never told anyone. I didn't want anyone to know I'd picked the wrong man. When Mom was visiting, just a couple of weeks after Jim was born, Dick hit me during dinner. You started yelling 'Daddy hit Mommy. Daddy hit Mommy,' from the high chair. Mom stood up and said I could come home any time, but that she was leaving now."

"He never hit you kids though," she said, scraping at her potato, looking down at her plate.

How would you know, I wondered.

"He never paid child support like he was supposed to. I was so ashamed of being divorced. No one was divorced then, not like now. I went to an attorney who patted my arm and said, 'Carol, you're just lucky to be out of there.' And the superintendent of schools was so nice to me. He said, 'Keep your chin up, Carol.'"

I ordered orange sherbet for dessert. I didn't know about battered women. I did know that my mother was a hypocrite. What about when she slapped my cheek or hit me with the yardstick? What about that paddle with holes in it that the father of one of her students made for her, which sounded like thunder coming to wipe out my child self? That was "spanking," that was supposed to be different. Sometimes I wanted to hit her myself. But she was too big.

I have been lying awake in the cabin bed, wandering through Memory, aware of how few secrets my mother told me. I can hear the blue tarp on the neighbor's woodpile flapping with the wind, accompanying the roar of loose fiberglass on the carport.

I can feel Memory in my stomach and my right shoulder. Memory says, "Remember when you fled your father's house with your mother?"

"I remember no such thing," I tell Memory. But I've never really thought about it before.

I can feel Memory coming closer, brought by the storm wind that is sheeting across the roof and whistling into the gutters. I sink farther into the ditch that runs through the mattress. "I'm sleeping," I say to Memory. "Go away!" I roll over and pretend that I can go back to sleep.

"But I'm always here," Memory responds. "And you're easier to get in touch with first thing in the morning."

Normally I get up and smoke a cigarette before all else, but I crumpled them into a garbage can by the beach yesterday in an act of bravado. The cigarettes don't ever really keep Memory away but they do help subdue the rising anxiety of Memory coming forward.

"You wanted to know," Memory says.

"Fool that I was," I tell Memory sarcastically. But really I am afraid of being two and three and four years old again. My shoulders feel as if they're suspended on metal scaffolding in anticipation.

"To know you is to love you," Memory says. Memory takes me to the back door of my grandparent's house.

◆*Memory.* We squeeze through, pushing aside the screen door. I'm afraid I'll fall without Mommy's hand. Sometimes my knees wobble. Grandpa and Grandma are standing in front of us. Mommy's holding Jim who's wrapped in blankets like a moth. The three of us close together, Mommy's hand on my two-year-old shoulder, wetting my dress at the back.

"Mom?" "Dad?" Mommy says and I get confused,

caught up in the swirling unspoken that made Mommy hurry and me handing her diapers and Jim crying all the way in the car till I wanted to pinch his nose.

"Daddy, Daddy, where's Daddy?" My body is jiggling up and down with the urgency of my question. I want Daddy to carry me high on his shoulders.

"Daddy's not here right now," Mommy says, "We're going to stay here with Grandma and Grandpa."

I hear undertones. "But Daddy. . . . " I scream.

"Now Louise, you hush. You've got to be a big girl now," Grandpa frowns, a leaning gray tower. His voice knocks against me like wind. Mommy pulls me by the shoulder farther into this house that I am reluctant to enter. She is smaller when she passes through the doorway. Inside the brown room, I am not sure she is even as big as me.◆

"Breathe," Memory says.

I don't want to go inside their house. It's brown and cold and mean. I sit up and attempt breathing into my abdomen. Inhaling and counting slowly to five, exhaling and counting again to ten, I try to accept and observe the squeezing of my chest and the way my shoulders are burning.

I didn't see a photograph of my father until I was twenty-four. My mother tore most of them into bits during her separation, as if she could pretend that none of it had happened, save for the presence of Jim and me.

When it came to "the kids," my mother stood with my grandparents as if she had never been a child herself. There were no stories about her own childhood in this house. I didn't know which room had been hers and which rooms had belonged to my four uncles. I didn't know what games she played or if she had had a favorite blanket or doll. I only knew that the Baggs were a hard-working, church-going family, a pillar of small-town respectability headed by my grandfather, the family patriarch.

Through the back door we passed my grandmother's wringer washer where she threaded sheets and underwear. From there a tilting ramp floored the hall between the kitchen and the rest of the house and my mother's back bedroom where Jim and I were supposed to confine our playing. My grandparents entered her room without ever knocking and sat every evening while I played on the floor and my mother corrected papers.

Most of my grandparents' house was never used; the vast table in the dining room lay bare except for rare gatherings of aunts and uncles. The cavernous, cold brown living room housed us only on Sunday evenings for Walt Disney and Lawrence Welk. Up the stairs and through a maze of dark flowered wallpaper was a room Jim and I shared and two other bedrooms.

My maternal grandparents were the extent of my known roots. After they eloped, my grandfather had brought his bride away from Iowa to the Pacific Northwest, to the house I lived in between the ages of two and ten. We always called it "Grandpa and Grandma's house," never our own. It never occurred to me that my grandfather and grandmother had once had parents. This lack of a distant past allowed my grandfather to pretend that he was a king, presiding over us with no predecessors, in league with the Almighty. He was the only one allowed to want. And whatever he wanted, it was our duty to give him, without asking questions. Questions were bad.

◆*Memory.* I am trying to keep track of my mother, following her from kitchen to bedroom, hearing the hemline of her skirt swing against her nylons. I feel my arm thick with wanting to grab a fist of the fabric, but she's always more than an arm length away and I am too old for that now. Too old for hugging or hiding, a big girl. I am four. I can make four on my fingers. My mother flies through door frames with laundry to put into drawers and closets.

"Mommy, is thunder really God bowling?"

"Mommy, why do you have to fold clothes?"

"Mommy, why's the sky blue?"

"Mommy, can I help?"

"Mommy, why do people die?"

"Mommy, why do we have to live in this house?"

"Be quiet Louise! You ask too many questions. Why can't you just be quiet. I'm busy. Go play outside."

I have been talking to her back. "But why do I have to go outside?"

"Because I said so. Now shoo."

She's always saying, "Go outside." I feel a sharp cut in my chest, because I know she doesn't care about my questions. I breathe in hard and try to be still, to stop more sound from coming out of me or my mother will yell or slap or drag me outside by my arm.◆

The doorway to the room that begins childhood is thick with the sound of my voice, rising up, and my mother's, coming down.

"Mommy won't love you if you act like that. No one likes a little girl who whines or screams or cries or throws tantrums."

Being Mommy's good girl meant not making my sounds, giggling only when Mommy wanted to giggle, sitting still instead of discovering the ground of my body. A good girl wanted only what Mommy wanted.

A crow paces the fence rail and calls to another in the apple tree. Crow pivots and announces herself to the neighborhood, squawking pointedly at Crystal Cat. There is no question about the crow's self-esteem or her right to be here on this fence post, making noise. The crow does not know that being on her best behavior would require her not to be a crow at all.

Crystal Cat dashes inside, racing in a circle around the bedroom, springing on and off the bed and dashing into the kitchen to jump on and off the table in her storm dance.

I don't notice the wind as I walk to the store fixated with the idea of buying cigarettes. What I really want is to relax my shoulders and unwind that coil of old bad times in my solar plexus. Instead I buy cigarettes and try not to tell myself that I'm a failure. I can't seem to stick with simple breathing. Burning my throat is a habit. It keeps my voice at a controlled volume. It keeps my mouth preoccupied.

◆*Memory.* My mother is holding me on the swing in Grandpa and Grandma's yard and rocking us back and forth with her foot. She hardly ever holds me like this, with my head on the softness of her chest. I want to be so close to her. I say, "Milk?" remembering a far-off time of warmth.

I am off the swing and set upright on the ground in a buzz and my mother pushes against the swing backward so that there's a cold canyon between us. "Don't ever say anything like that again!" she says.

"I just wanted a glass of milk," I say quickly, trying to fight off the shame that is coming from my feet all the way up to my head.

She walks away and says that if I want a glass of milk I'll have to come in the house and get one.◆

But other times my mother pulled me away from my dolls and sandbox. "You're all Mommy's got," she'd say, squeezing me. Her needs felt like oil pouring out from her hands and chest. I forgot what I had been playing because I had to make Mommy feel better. But then it was hard to breathe. And I began to see that I was going to have to choose, her or me.

I scramble eggs and steam milk for coffee, puffing away and wondering if cigarettes are the imaginary friends of my adulthood. Going without them evokes a longing I invariably succumb to eventually, a desire to hold on, to take in. I want something and I haven't figured out how to give it to myself.

.    .    .

The bedroom is toasty and full of the sound of rain dancing on the roof. I have crayons and I'm sitting on a magic carpet. I am playing with Tayla, the part of myself who is two, three, four and five. I call forth this child in me until my hands feel small and curious and I can feel an interest in my eyes. I'm letting myself do whatever Tayla wants with no rules.

My mouth fills with new words and syllables that become songs as I sway back and forth. "Bah, bo, bobah, ba—nana, ba—nana, bus, bus, buzz-bee, buzz-bee," I sing as I make lines and circles and scribble hard in yellow, red-orange, sienna and blue. I taste words and pick colors, happy with the sound of my voice and the stories I invent on the spot to go with my pictures. "Raahr, RAAHR!" I say as if I am a lion. I draw a jungle on my paper.

Just as I'm getting into it, Sarah says, "Stop!"

I sit still and wait, motionless. In my mind, I hear my mother's voice like arrows with tips that sting. "Can't you play without making noise? What are those crayons doing all over the floor? Don't make me take you to Grandpa for a spanking!"

I stop. I stop playing. I stop making noise. I'm always telling myself to stop.

"Children should speak when spoken to," Grandpa said when I wanted to show off my talking at dinner. "Keep your voice down," my mother would say, raising her own.

I was good when I repeated the words my mother wanted me to say but bad when I learned words on my own or strung them together into sentences. Speaking up for myself still makes my heart pound.

Now I kneel over paper, close to my crayons, toasting my

thigh on the grinning orange teeth of the space heater. Tayla and I are tired of being quiet.

I begin naming all the items in this back room in my four-year-old stretchy voice. "Candle, bear, dictionary, chair. Paper, kite, windowsill, light." Plucking words from the room with my mouth, smacking my lips around them, rocking with my rhythm, tossing sound around the room like colored balls. Recalling the joy I felt when I discovered the kingdom of names.

The same word knocks at my teeth, repeating itself in a string in my mind. The forbidden word. I want to pound my crayon into the floor. "NoNoNoNoNoNoNoNoNo," I say while wondering if I will ever stop now that I have started. I make staccato dots with the tip of the red crayon.

◆*Memory.* I am sitting above a spreading swamp of string beans. I level a mashed potato hill, drawing with the tip of my fork on the Melmac plate, making a new road.

"Quit playing with your food, Loueezy," Grandpa's voice falls from the sky.

My fork clatters to the floor.

"Now look what you've done!" my mother says. "Eat your beans!" Since we moved here, Grandpa yells first and my mother follows him, like thunder and rain.

"Me no like beans," I say. "I'm not going to eat them."

My mother cuts a corner off the margarine and puts it on top of the beans like a hat. "This will make them taste better," she says, stabbing them on her fork and bringing them toward my mouth.

"No!" I toss my head from right to left faster and faster.

"Don't you say 'no' to me, little girl," my mother says between her teeth, grabbing my shoulder and shaking. "Do you want to go to bed right now?"

What I want is not to eat beans.

"You're just going to sit here until these beans are all gone!" My mother and grandmother take the other plates to the sink.

Sitting and sitting and sitting and sitting. I stab the beans viciously with my fork. "Me kill you!" I tell them.

"What are you saying over there? Don't you know there are little girls with no food who would be thankful for what you have?"

"You be good for your mother," Grandma says.

I stack the beans like a woodpile on my fork, watching the seeds hang out cut ends. My mother and grandmother swell above me. I hold my nose and shove the beans in my mouth.

"Now that wasn't so bad was it?" my mother asks. I learn a new way of anger in ignoring her. The half-chewed beans are a large angry pill at the back of my throat.◆

My mother and I fought for control of my plate, my body, my mind and my room. If I said "no," my mother said I was "willful." If I said, "I want," she said I was "selfish and spoiled."

"What do you want?" I ask Tayla inside of myself. She picks a string bean green crayon and I scribble as fast as I can from edge to edge of my paper, melting the crayon into a pile of wax, pouring out agitation and roaring like a lion.

"Fuck shit damn I want a cigarette," Fuckit says. I reach immediately for a cigarette but can't find any matches. My higher instinct prevents me from lighting it with the candle on the altar.

Fuckit is fourteen and fifteen and twenty-two. She holds the anger I began collecting when I was Tayla. When I was Tayla, it was too dangerous to be angry out loud. I had to get taller before I could do that.

Fuckit is an inner teenager developed in all the times I thought, "This isn't fair," "I hate you," "I am important anyway," "I'll show you, I'll be famous one day." "I will have the last word." "So what if I'm bad, so what?"

"I can smoke if I want to," Fuckit growls. "And she can't stop me."

By the time I became a teenager and Fuckit became a more solid entity, I had learned to make my anger self-destructive. I had long forgotten how I had fallen to the floor, kicking, pounding, and howling with the fury that came into every inch of Tayla's body.

◆*Memory.* "No I'm not," I hiccup and sob as my five-year-old body spins far away from thinking into flailing circles.

"You are going to have an enema," my mother yells into the whirlpool of sound, slapping at me with her hands. "Knock this off. It won't hurt. What's wrong with you!"

But I knew enemas meant lying on my stomach on a towel on the bathroom floor. There wouldn't be any place to put my head while my bottom and stomach were being blown up with water. "Hold it in, hold it in," Grandma would say and I couldn't tell her I was afraid I would burst and be dead.

"No, no I'm not!" I chant in screeching refusal, falling to the floor and pounding with fists and feet, rolling from side to side, insisting with every muscle and the loudest reaches of my voice.◆

My grandfather said everything that happened was God's will. He called it predestination, a word with too many consonants. My mother took me to him for spankings. He carried me into the bathroom off my mother's room where he lifted up my skirt and pulled down my underwear and put me across his lap while he sat on the toilet. The fall of his hand took my breath. My mother said I had to learn. Spare the rod, spoil the child.

Punishment was called discipline. It involved hitting and yelling and the soapy washcloths my mother cleaned my mouth with if I said the wrong words. Every year I held myself tighter until moving my adult body seemed like too much work. Discipline became depression.

Inside of me, Tayla is twirling in circles, faster and with amazing speed.

"Maybe we could go back to having tantrums," Carrie suggests to Fuckit. "I think it felt better to throw ourselves on the floor than to smoke or swear at drivers on the freeway."

"Too hard," Fuckit says. "It's easier to smoke. Quieter too."

"I thought you were supposed to be a rebel," Memory says.

"Just fuck off. Don't tell me how I'm supposed to be." Fuckit throws her used match on a coffee table in the inner house.

"Pay attention to me," Tayla says.

I start crying, bellowing tears which sound like chords on a harmonica. It's been a long time since I tried to be quiet when I cry. I blow my nose like a foghorn and toss more Kleenexes to the floor among the unboxed crayons. I try to draw my feelings as Tayla. My mother is an enormous scarlet pointing finger. Tayla is an unformed green blob with black dots in the middle.

"Don't, don't, don't," my mother said.

"I can't, I can't, I can't," I said.

"It's so hard to take care of you," she said.

"Too hard to take care of me," I repeated, weaving my muscles into a net to hold myself in place.

I draw a midnight blue line vertically between my mother and me, pressing hard and going up and down until I have created a barrier between us in this room of error, a soundproof wall between her words and my belief. I tape every picture I've drawn onto the pine walls and sign Louise-Tayla big on every one of them. I stand and yell, "No," until I feel it shake out my solar plexus and vibrate my fingertips.

My grandparents' house was bordered by a cemetery and

a gravestone company. When I was in college, the house was torn down and replaced by a crematorium centered in a parking lot. The poplar hedge which looked like an ominous fortress when I was a child was cut down to make more ground for caskets. Boards were pried apart and flowered wallpaper from fifty years of my grandmother's application turned to dust in the ruins. Did the ghosts fly out from between the boards? Was there an explosion when the last walls fell that released the stew that was always brewing?

I imagine that I am tearing down the house with my hands and feet. I pull and pound and bite. I can hear the sounds of walls crashing and the long screeching groans of nails built to hold forever, pulling out and splintering wood.

. . .

The gulls are bleating into the cold fog that has replaced the wind. I couldn't bring myself to leave the house yesterday, although Sarah ranted about exercise and fresh rather than smoke-laden air. Sometimes taking a walk is too hard and the best I can manage is saying "No," over and over again and hanging up pictures.

I am glad I made it out the door today, because walking reminds me that I can move, I can go where I want, I can throw rocks and shout and mess up the beach with my footprints.

"Tell me I'm good," Tayla says inside of me. "Tell me I'm special."

"Don't go getting a swelled head," my mother would have said. "You're supposed to be good. You shouldn't need any rewards for it." There was no such thing as self-esteem.

"I don't want to be too good," Fuckit objects. "Good has to be earned through doing what I don't want to do. Good means pleasing someone else and displeasing myself. Forget it, Tayla."

"You'll never be good enough," Sarah says, sounding like Eeyore from *Winnie-the-Pooh*.

"Tayla gets to have whatever she wants," Carrie says.

"That's the point—finding what we want. I think that when she says she wants to know she's good, she means that we have a light shining in us and when it's acknowledged we feel full of ourselves and Tayla feels like she can do anything."

Tayla nods her head enthusiastically as Carrie gives language to just the feeling I had when I was small. A feeling of being special and important, of rising up and wanting to be noticed. A tender hopeful feeling that got squished and kicked about.

When I'm in the city I take voice lessons from April. Tayla likes to come out and play and make up songs as April listens and laughs. I sing and crawl around on the floor. Sometimes April says, "I love you Louise," and Tayla likes that because it makes me feel warm and light. I imagine that April is with us, playing on the beach. I imagine that I am Carrie, holding Tayla's hand. "You are wonderful, you are valuable, you are smart," I sing to Tayla. I sing back as Tayla, "I am wonderful, I am valuable, I am smart," in a chanting five-year-old voice. We begin to skip and it feels like I can keep going across the sand forever, skipping and singing to myself.

I invoke the spirit of the crow, loud and raucous and self-centered. I run and caw and pretend to fly and gossip from the branches of the fir. I yell, "Habondia, Habondia!" invoking the goddess of abundance. I thank her for the endless changing treasures on the beach and the room for wild running and the drumming waves and the miniature specks of water caressing my face. I reach my arms all the way out from my sides, feeling the distance. I hold my hands in front of my body and then pull toward my chest, reaching out, bringing back to me, hands opening and closing in the fog, my flesh seeming to glow against the white.

I suck in the salty air, making an O with my lips and tasting my mouth with my tongue. The sea exhales in long draws over the rocks. "Sing with me," Habondia says and I sing, "Mother I feel you under my feet. Mother I feel your heart beat," clapping and stomping. And I know that the Mother I'm singing to loves noise.

Standing on the beach, being five and singing, Memory reminds me that I am irrepressible.

# 4

## Tinsel's Dreams and Nightmares

I HAVE FOUND narrow steps leading to an attic in the inner house. Here there are windows with no curtains, only yellow blinds rolled up to the sky. My mother comes up here, but she's not here all the time. When she's not here I try on faces and act out stories and stretch myself out into all different shapes and sizes. I am six, seven, eight and nine.

I am a mouse, nosing Tinkertoys, scampering through the leaves patterned by sunlight on the carpet. I'm so little and fast that no one can catch me. I am a shopkeeper with tins of green beans and boxes of macaroni, counting pennies into tall copper towers. "Pay attention now," I tell Barbie and Chatty Cathy, tapping my one-foot ruler on the table. I print my name on the blackboard with white chalk.

A monster grabs at me from the corner. I am building a fortress of blocks between us, scratching a moat in my sandbox. I pretend I am Heidi, who plays with goats and sleeps safe in a loft with straw. The monster has big poking, squeezing hands.

When my mother comes, she closes the window and says, "Pick up your toys."

I tell her I am building a fort to keep the monster away.

"There are no such things as monsters," she says, pulling down the blinds and tugging at the bottom of my dress to pull the wrinkles out. She has a brush in her hand. "Now hold still," she says, dragging the brush through my hair, "We don't want to be late for church."

I pick up the Tinkertoys that I have shaped as a bridge. "Look, Mommy, look." I imagine that I am as tall as her so that she'll see. I like to put things together to make something else.

"Put that down. You can play later. Now hurry up."

I stand in this room as an adult. I make an exotic world from the Tinkertoys. I hold the dolls tenderly against my chest and stroke their hair. I make lucky charms from the pennies. "I can play if I want to," I say out loud, "I can play if I want."

. . .

My mother wasn't the only one to interrupt my play, but at least I had a word for what she did—she yelled at me. I learned, as I grew older and tried to tell other adults about my mother, that they did not think being yelled at was serious. It was chalked up to the exasperation of motherhood. I could not describe the emotions that flavored her words, the taste of her hatred and guilt and fear; the limitless places that words could go, the way they echoed and made me flinch. Even then, I knew my relationship with my mother was about feeling, words and the sound of her voice.

I didn't have names for what Grandpa did when he took me away from play. When it was over I tried not to think about it, because the memory made me feel bad and made my mind feel too small. I forgot the specifics of what happened for twenty-four years, until I remembered my history of incest. But I never forgot how everything around me felt wrong.

◆*Memory.* I am playing patty-cake in the bathtub, giggling as water jumps up from my six-year-old palms. I like to hold my blue squeaking fish under water and watch bubbles come out from under it and when I let it go it bounces to the top.

Mommy and Grandma are watching TV and Grandpa's supposed to help me take a bath. "Time to get out now, Loueezy," he says. I jump up because Mommy says I'm supposed to do everything that Grandpa tells me.

He scrubs my skin dry with the terry cloth towel and tells me to raise my arms for the T-shirt on my top.

"Grandpa has a story," he murmurs, pulling me against him and holding his arm across my chest. "Once there was a cave of secret treasure." Grandpa's hands are moving lower now, toward my most private place. "And a brave explorer went in and found that treasure and took it out." I twist. He holds tighter. I shiver, naked, without skin.

No, Grandpa, don't, are the first words that come to my mind and they pull my body forward but he is there too, on all sides. And inside my mind, more familiar than my own words are my mother's words, strong from repetition. "Don't say 'no' to Grandpa. Never say 'no' to Grandpa. We're lucky we can live here. Without your grandparents we would never have a place to live."

"Now put your jammies on," Grandpa says in his voice that sounds cold and gritty. "And go kiss your mommy goodnight."◆

While my mother was a sharp hot danger, my grandfather was a thick smelly grabbing rubbing which began when I was five and continued until I turned ten. I didn't know the names of what he did or even the names for the private places he touched me or for the penis he put in my mouth. I know now that what seemed endless to me took him only minutes. In some photographs, he appears in sleek suits and hats, sneering in a way he imagines to be authoritative. But in others, he is in suspenders, cotton shirts and baggy belted pants, his head shifted sideways with narrow eyes and an arm around me. I am leaning away.

Once I heard my mother and grandmother in the kitchen, talking about men.

"You just have to humor them," Grandma said. "They're like little boys. They can't help themselves. You have to make them feel they're smart and important."

My grandmother and mother shooed me outside with instructions to "help Grandpa," which often meant being led to a dark corner of an outbuilding or into his car in the garage, where he opened his pants and raised my dress. He said I was a good girl and then a bad girl for making him act like this.

Memory opens out, like a fan. "Mommy, don't make me go help Grandpa." "Mommy, I don't like Grandpa." "Mommy, I don't feel good."

I threw tantrums because I did not want to help him. Or sometimes I'd be just sitting still on the couch and an irritation would seem to force its way up my throat and into my five-year-old arms. Then I would tease Jim or pick up magazines and drop them to the floor or start whining. When being slapped on the face and being told to "stop that" only made me cry harder, my grandmother had me sit in a washtub of cold water in front of the heater in my mother's room. I quieted, inhaling in a succession of little stabs. I ran my seven-year-old hands across rose thorns and had one continuous sore throat for which I was prescribed doses of penicillin. My vision deteriorated until I could only see what was right before my eyes.

I tried to pretend not to know what might happen next even though my skin prickled and my stomach ached with warning. I invented magic formulas to keep me safe. If I could learn the alphabet, if I made my bed right, if I always smiled, if I didn't speak unless spoken to, then he wouldn't come. But it was too much to hold inside and then I would scream or throw a ball onto the roof or cut myself on rose thorns.

At first I thought that my mother would notice how my eyes were too wide with dazed shock, how I floated above my body, how what Grandpa did raised storms of electricity that didn't stop when he stopped touching me.

Instead she and my grandmother said I was too sensitive, foolish, emotional, wild, childish. I was behaving in the noisy bothersome way children were known for. I was having a six- and seven- and eight- and nine-year-old phase. The solution was more discipline so that I would learn to behave properly.

Still, for a long time I wished they would help me. I wanted my mother to become a ferocious bear, who would leap from her chair in front of the television, bringing a claw to my grandfather's chest. "You hurt her, didn't you," she would snarl, showing teeth. "How dare you," she would growl, flexing her claw nails, knowing from his eyes and the way he hemmed and hawed that he had done this. She would slash his cheek for what he had done. Sparing my cheek from her slapping, she would hold me in her giant warmth, telling me this would never happen again.

But I can't imagine her—with her pale freckled body and dazed eyes—doing anything to protect me. I can only hear her saying, "Don't tell stories. Grandpa loves you. Now smile like a good girl so that people will like you." I am not even sure my mother knew that protecting me was part of her job.

"Help me, help me," I say as I sit in the director's chair in the kitchen. The rain is dripping from the gutters into sprawling puddles. All of the crows are somewhere dry and hidden.

I wait for the inner child who is saying, "Help," the part of myself I call Tinsel. She is older and shyer than Tayla. Tinsel represents the years of my grandfather's abuse and the fear of my little girl body. As Tinsel, I began to believe I really was bad. I was yelled at every day; and told I was "old enough to know better." When I was six, seven, eight and nine, the world became more complicated and I was expected to know much more, often without any instruction. I was aware of trying to be good, of trying to figure out what was expected, of having large feelings and questions that I was supposed to keep to myself. There was no room for mistakes.

. . .

Tinsel is the part of me struck with stage fright before I lecture or teach. Tinsel is sensitive to nuances and connotations and whether I am good enough. Tinsel is my vulnerability and the ways I feel fragile.

The day ahead is eternal, too full of the feeling of spinning and wanting. Picking the scab off an old wanting for a mother, a protectress, a witch with advanced powers who could hold me safe in her spell.

I was seven when I had a serial dream—a story spanning a week of nights, opening each night where it had left off the night before. I was searching each room of my grandparents' house, looking under beds, in the corners of the bathroom, in dresser drawers. I knew that my mother was poisoning me and I was trying to find the poison. On the seventh night, I went outside, near the berry house where my grandfather often abused me. The poison was leaning against the swing set, looking like pink lint, the color of girls, strung to a square wooden frame. I picked up the poison and took it to the front of the berry house, where my mother stood in her pleated skirt and pointed glasses. "You're trying to kill me," I said, accusing her in a strong voice that shocked me with its certainty when I woke.

"That's not poison," my mother said and laughed.

It was the same kind of laugh I heard when she and my grandparents were watching Art Linkletter on TV. He would be kneeling beside a little girl, asking her what her favorite game was. She would tell him with many words, getting up from her seat to act it out, earnestly trying to teach it to him. Then Art Linkletter would face the camera and say, "Kids say the darnedest things, don't they?"

"What is wrong with you?" my mother said when she caught me sulking. I decided that something was wrong with me. Sarah began to take form in my personality, a part of me just to memorize my mother's answers and rules and to remind the children in me of how to be. I began to be my own victim. Like Chicken Little I worried the sky was falling. My skin was too tight. They said I was clumsy, but it seemed impossible to manage these arms and legs and the harder I tried the more I tripped and knocked and ran into things.

Now I want to stop trying harder to do better. I want to know what good enough feels like. I want Tinsel to feel safe enough to straighten out and to learn by doing, asking for help when I need it. I don't want to feel so alone and mystified. I want Sarah to quit telling me what's wrong with me.

"Why should anyone want to help you?" Sarah says. "Get over it!"

I get up and open the refrigerator and begin eating chunks of cheese, staring at the yogurt and salsa.

My mother would say, "Quit dwelling on the past. God helps those who help themselves." But I can't think of one instance of help I can attribute to the God my mother conversed with.

. . .

I draw closer to Crystal Cat, brought into morning by her exuberant affection, as she leans purring into my ear, enthusiastically licking my chin with her textured tongue. One of the great liberties of growing older is the freedom to sleep with anyone I want.

I pretend I am a cat and lick the top of Crystal's head in return but she knows that I have the wrong tongue and moves away. My mother would be appalled at Crystal's presence under the covers, to say nothing of my licking Crystal's head. "Where do you get those crazy ideas? Dirt! Germs! Do you want to get fleas?" she would say. Then she would pick up Crystal and throw her outside.

Fuckit would tell her that cats, like kids, don't like to be displaced. And add that studies have proven the human mouth to be a far greater source of infection than a cat's tongue.

Tayla and Tinsel wish I had been raised by cats. Then I'd know how to scratch in self-defense, to insist on affection, to be curious about movement in the grass, to stretch thoroughly, to take naps when I need them and to sit with graceful self-assurance.

I stretch on the bed, making little sounds in my throat. It is never too late to learn from felines.

"Get up, get up, get up," Tayla, Clingbaby and Tinsel are saying with good cheer, pulling on my hands. When the inner children are in accord, they are a chorus of Younger-Ones. "Play, play, play," they say.

Today I am going to make a Valentine's present for Marianne. I have promised the playful elements of myself that this day we will make something just for the joy of it.

"This means you just bug off," Fuckit tells Memory. "Enough is enough." I make shooing gestures with my arms.

"But you like to give presents and to make things," Memory says. "This is quite well-documented." Memory shows me a picture of myself offering bits of my chewed-on cookie to Jim. And a long line of poetry books I wrote and Xeroxed and gave as presents to my friends.

"But we're talking about having fun," Fuckit tells Memory. "And so far, I have had less than a good time with you. So just blow off and do not remind us of those Popsicle disasters we were forced to make in grade school or that series of geometric string pictures we made in high school that the nails all fell out of when they were hung on the wall."

"I am never opposed to playing," Memory says. "You're

on this journey to get your sense of play back."

"We are?" Tinsel asks.

Steam condenses on the bathroom mirror while imagination whispers possibilities into the shower. "Freedom!" YoungerOnes say inside me.

Still damp, and for once oblivious to the cold, I study the jumble of treasure on top of the wood stove with child eyes, taking time to notice color and shape and the relationships among the stones, bones and shells. I have an idea of stringing them together into a mobile that will remind Marianne of me and of the qualities of our relationship. Driftwood and deer bones, crab shells, rocks, and feathers, solid and light, like this relationship now, full of discarded shells and a mutual love of sea-washed bones and magical feathers.

I have no idea how it will actually come together; only that whatever I set out to make always ends up looking different when it's done. After I've made it, whether it's a story or a craft, I often spend a long time looking at it, wondering that it made its way out through my arms and sits as itself, meaningful to me but separate.

My fingers feel impossibly large and indelicate as the thread slips from my grasp. Thread is a medium of ferocious integrity when I try to untangle it and alarming fragility when I tie a rock to it. Still I persist, because my wanting takes me past giving up.

Because my mother was an elementary school teacher, I was blessed with an endless supply of colored construction paper, faded on one side from where the sun bleached it on her bulletin boards, but richly colored on the side where it had been tacked against the wall. With blunt tipped scissors and a bottle of Elmer's glue I made stories by layering paper. This was not considered as significant as multiplication tables or learning to make my bed and wash the dishes. As I grew older I retreated to my room and made books with my poems written beneath pictures I cut from magazines. Creativity has always come from being full, full of playfulness and ideas or full of despair.

But I still feel myself waiting for my mother's voice to tell me that this absorption and wholeness called play is less important than the serious suffering business of work.

Halfway through my knot tying I realize that the mobile must have a frog on it for Marianne is big on frogs. Indeed, on more than one occasion we have set off across a pasture at night, armed with a weak-beamed flashlight, searching for the big-eyed baritones we could hear from the road. But frogs are small and hard to find; often we'd get our shoes muddy without seeing a single one. Nor is tying a real frog onto a mobile a desirable exercise. Happily, Print Shop, my computer graphics program, has a most satisfactory frog. I print it out big and color it with crayons and green glitter. I draw a red and yellow heart around the frog so that the frog can be supported by love as she leaps into the sky. Hanging the frog on the mobile once more alters the balance, but I am almost done.

"All right! All right!" the YoungerOnes cheer as the mobile hangs from a wall hook. I look at it and look at it and look at it. Ever productive, Sarah starts talking about making an entire line of mobiles to sell at fairs. Memory coughs, reminding me that perhaps appreciating what I have already done is enough.

I move slowly now, the lethargy of spent imagination a warm pull in my muscles.

．　．　．

The clouds hang low in the sky, gathering weight. The ferry is a rumbling box turtle dipping between waves. On board, I'm with more humanity than I have seen for three weeks. Leaving the cabin is a relief; I was beginning to feel claustrophobic, surrounded by so much Memory and a little discouraged by the accumulating pieces of paper, dense with handwriting, showing neither plot nor salvation. For all Sarah tells me to "do it on the computer," I need to form each word by hand. Then Sarah says, "You're just pretending to write a book," talking to me in second person, the way she usually does.

But the truth is that I'm mining, following the underground veins into my childhood. I feel my way through days without alarm clocks. Days peopled with Memory and walks and rituals of healing, punctuated by coffee and eggs and enormous pots of chicken soup. A couple of times I have touched my cheeks and only then realized that I was crying, so freely did I begin to let myself cry. Although it's good to come out for a while, I am sensitive to the laughter in the green vinyl booth across from me and the sidelong glances of the man walking down the broad linoleum aisle. It is definitely time to dust off my social skills.

My first stop in the city is therapy. I go there to learn new skills and to remember to breathe as the old ways of coping fail me.

I was sixteen years old when I first heard about "therapy." I knew then that I would be in therapy someday, though nine more years passed before I got around to it. I began when I realized I had to stop pretending and tell something to someone before the swirling inner heaviness devoured me.

In real life, I was shy about talking and self-conscious about the rites of social convention. My mother had always told me to smile at other people, to be nice to them and to make a good impression. Forbidden topics of conversation were legion. I wasn't to talk about myself or to brag. I wasn't to ask personal questions or to raise my voice. I couldn't talk about what went on in our house. I must never be disrespectful in talking to a grownup. I must never interrupt an adult conversation. I loved to talk, longed to talk and was scared to death of it.

"We can take care of our problems ourselves," my mother said. "Those counselors just want to blame the parents for everything." Mostly my mother didn't like to believe we had problems, or if there was a problem, it was in my attitude. She didn't need help, she said, she needed me to behave.

For myself, I have found it is infinitely wiser to buy help than to pretend not to need it. And over the years, I have found that I enjoy therapy, that I like my therapist, Jean, and I like having a place where it's all right to talk for and about myself.

I have been many ages in this room of towering bookcases and large windows showing oak trees and shingles. I have read the calligraphied sign on her desk, "To create one must decide," and pondered the difficulty of creating a long-term decision. From her desk in the corner, Jean often pulls out an article from *The New York Times* that she has Xeroxed for me, usually an interview with a writer about her work. I accept the gifts with interest, touched that Jean thinks of me and does this. For years my mother sent me articles from *Reader's Digest* entitled, "I am Joe's Lung" and "A Doctor Talks about Emphysema," but never sent information on quitting smoking. Jean does not use threats.

Here I bring out my inner world and give it air, seated in my familiar corner of the couch next to the Kleenex, across from Jean's winged chair of black corduroy. Here I also meet fears of revealing myself to another person. "No one will like you if you act like that," my mother frequently warned. Repetition carved deep into confidence, so that I am never sure that I'm wanted.

At sixty-two, Jean is two years older than my mother. But where my mother was judgement, Jean is a witness, whose words are often more salty than sweet. I have been every part of myself here. Jean listens, entering my world and broadening it. When I first began seeing Jean, I was overwhelmed and immobilized by Memory. Seven years later, I have written one book about finding Memory and begun another, been in and out and in and out and in relationship, struggled continuously with finances, scheduling, lack of courage, clients and always this ongoing quest of mine into childhood and belief. In this room I rant and rave, sob, consider, say mean jealous things about people I'm mad at, walk with Memory, laugh and once in a while long to hide under the desk. After all these years, Jean has seen almost all of it.

I sigh, stick out my tongue and say "Bleah! I'm discouraged. How many years have I been working with Memory? And I'm still haunted by basic issues which rise up and glare at me, like feeling loved and being faithful to myself." Jean raises a brown eyebrow. I pause and look at her meaningfully. Sometimes I argue that I don't know anything, that I'm as lost and miserable as I always was, that I am chasing my own tail. At about that point Jean recites a list of how when she first knew me I couldn't do my laundry, found taking a walk an idea totally out of my capacity, drank Scotch excessively and considered killing myself every waking moment. She reminds me of how far my steps have carried me, adding that whatever is ahead of me is another series of steps.

"I guess it's that I still want to fix it," I tell her. "Carrie devises rituals and I have exquisite moments invoking crows and goddesses. But it's hard to hold onto. Some days I can hardly move with the Memory of feeling trapped and powerless. It seems like I ought to be over the grief of feeling unloved, but I wake up with it. Tinsel says, 'Nobody loves me, nobody loves me.' I must have told myself that ten thousand times when I was growing up. I don't even miss Marianne—because I don't feel connected with her when I'm away."

I reach for the small funny-looking blond duck that appeared two years ago, becoming the first and only stuffed animal in Jean's office. I work the shaggy blond fur away from the duck's eyes. "When I was little I thought that if I could only be good enough my mother would love me.

"Will I ever fill up and not want a mother?"

Jean fingers a large brown seed strung between turquoise stones on her necklace. "I think we get bits of mothering as we go along. You're learning to take them in." Jean says, "But wanting one person as a mother fades."

"I wish you'd adopt me in the meantime," pops out of my mouth, preceded by no conscious thought. Uh-oh. This is what comes from spending so much time talking only to my cat—I have lost the barrier I keep over certain words that live in my jaw. This old familiar child's wish that my teachers would take me home and care for me was part of my intensity. It made them wary of me. But Jean knows about my neediness and sits in silence, neither rushing forward nor backing away.

"Worth a try," I mutter. Jean keeps waiting, working with patience instead of potions. I look up at her from my shame and understand that the next move is still mine.

I lay my crayon pictures on the carpet between us and Jean retrieves her glasses. The inner house cries from its windows, in thistle, sienna and wild strawberry. The tether between my mother and me is a black X on my chest. They are a child's drawings.

"Isn't there something else I'm supposed to be doing?" I ask, pleading for a formula that will make it all better. "Say the magic words, help me."

"I think that the children in you want to be known and that's what you're doing. It isn't a matter of fixing them, but of knowing the parts of yourself and coming to trust what is you. I can't tell you how this knowing might change you, but you know how listening to yourself and telling your story has changed you already." Jean smiles, reminding me again of my progress.

I tell her about my days at the cabin and how each crayon color stood for a feeling. As I talk to Jean, I see all the ways I was treated as a child; then I see myself as a thirty-four-year-old woman in jeans treating myself with the same impatience. Of course I wanted another mother. It was a wanting that kept me reaching out to women, allowing me to learn from women not my mother.

In my adult self I know there will never be a mother like the one I needed; it is not possible to begin again. I can only keep making new memories and revising the decisions I made on the basis of my childhood experiences.

Inside, Memory says I am never without assistance as I explore this inner house, that freedom is releasing the feelings that were trapped within the walls of my body and making something of them.

Still, there's nothing like a good hug and knowing I'm held in affection, which is how I feel when I leave Jean's office. It's an amazing feeling to be liked no matter what I say, no matter how I rant and rave or want. It's good to leave feeling tall and not frightened at the taboos I have broken in speaking. I have not always left therapy feeling this good.

.  .  .

I arrive at Marianne's door with a bag of laundry and the mobile. "Happy Valentine's Day!" I say heartily, freed from introspection to the joy of this life, this time. Her mouth tastes warm and new and we hug in light spirit, anticipating celebration and the giving of gifts.

We part—she to do last minute wrapping and me to do emergency surgery on the mobile. "Play, play, play," YoungerOnes say contentedly. "It's a holiday!"

All good holidays remind me of Easter, because the year I was eight, I found an Easter basket beneath the dining room table in the jungle of chair legs and table beams, an exotic cellophane flower blooming in the desert. When I noticed Jim's present hidden behind the green rocking chair I met my mother's eye and she gently shook her head, saying, "No, let Jim find it," with her eyes. This was the only easy secret my mother and I ever shared. I learned then that the YoungerOnes love presents and holidays so now I celebrate them grandly.

Marianne returns and we sit cross-legged on her brass bed, sharing our triumphs and frustrations over a meal of cold cracked crab, champagne, winter salad from her garden, lemon curd in puff pastry and a small box of chocolates. Tinsel says, "You love me don't you?" knowing, now that I'm here, that the answer is yes. Here in this warm room of handmade baskets and wheels of naturally dyed wool, in the touches of Marianne's lips and hands, I know perfectly well that I am loved.

We began early in the relationship to introduce our inner children to each other. Tayla calls Lucy who is the same age as herself and Tayla roars while Lucy makes frog sounds. Then Tinsel comes out along with Marianne's eight-year-old self who is named Little Bo Bo. Tinsel talks about Memory and the inner house and feeling lonesome. Little Bo Bo talks about making dream pillows and stuffing them with mugwort and complains about the meanness of Marianne's inner critic, Judge McNeil. "We know just what you mean, Sarah gets anxious when we're having a good time too," Tinsel agrees.

We lick our fingers and go on to talk about the food we had growing up and how exciting it was to discover foods beyond meat, potatoes and casseroles. Marianne tells about her first experiences with lasagne and spaghetti among the Italian friends of her parents.

"This dinner makes me think of Suzanne," I tell Marianne after sucking the last remnants from a crab leg. "She and her husband lived next door to us when I was six and seven. She was from France. She had a round table with an enormous tablecloth that dipped toward the ground. She ate pastries and drank coffee from a flowered cup, sitting in her apricot dressing gown, smoking and looking like a movie star. I would have lived in a corner of her house if I could have, listening to her warm foreign voice and wanting to go near her when she beckoned. She liked children and good food and scenery and suffered greatly being married to a man in the U.S. Army. My mother always ended up standing between her and me when we went to visit, but I would lean over to watch her and tell myself that when I grew up I would be like her and that one day I would go to France and smoke cigarettes and drink coffee. All of which I've done."

Marianne and I decide to go to France together someday. We kiss between bites of crab and I fill her in on life lived backward, the antics of cats and how I forget that I can return here. My heart is accustomed to turning itself off, a child-heart that can not hold love at a distance yet. She talks about work and women's health care and roommates and books and gardens. Finally, amidst the hollow crab shells and artichoke leaves, we exchange gifts.

She exclaims with satisfying enthusiasm about the mobile and hangs it immediately from her ceiling where it revolves above us on the bed and is a true sparkling sensation as the glittered frog catches light. She has beaded a necklace for me, a round tube of tiny green, brown and black beads. Marianne says that it was like making a snake, the way it writhed and wiggled as she fashioned it. We both love snakes, especially when we are feeling like ten-year-olds.

It took many years of learning how to speak for myself and learning all that I did not want before I found what I have, this gift of relationship with talk as fulfilling as sex. We have no "You made me" or "It's all your fault." We have tears and laughter. We avoid compromise in favor of having all of what we each want. It is easy to tell her my desires. It is easy to listen. I want great happiness and fullness for both of us. And because we both want this, and have both thought about who we are, we have crab and candlelight, talk that is easy and deep, inner children playmates and love in our making.

# 5

## *The Book of Customs*

I AM WAITING, waiting for the Book of Customs; the book where growing up is written down. The book with a complete list of all the rules my mother and my teacher tell me. I am six or seven or eight or nine and I want a way to hold the truth still so that I will know for certain how to be good and so that bad things will stop happening.

I am in a room near the center of the inner house, where a living room should have been, but instead it is an old schoolroom like the one my mother used to teach in. I can almost smell the gymnasium down the hall and smoke from the teachers' lounge. The volumes of the World Book Encyclopedia tilt backward on the bookcase that came with them; gold letters on green and white binding. Volumes like those my mother bought from a salesman after enticements with coupons from the booth at the fair. Thick books in this room of desks and blackboards. I am reading my way through the encyclopedia because my cousin Jas is reading it and I have to prove I'm as smart as him. We are the same age, wearing glasses and confusion, acquiring similar reputations for being different and smart.

I hold to one reference from Volume G; a drawing of Lady Godiva riding nude through town on a horse to protest her husband's taxes. I am waiting for them to mention her at school but I hear only about Columbus, Magellan and Washington crossing the Delaware, wearing a white wig in the prow of a boat.

I hold textbooks passed through the small fingers of students, with threads dangling from the bindings. A book says World War II and inside is a girl my age. My stomach aches when I see her. I take her inside of me, wrapping her within the slow dawning horror of mushroom clouds, dead animals lining beaches and the fall-out drill. *The Weekly Reader*, a magazine for children, shows pictures of the world's fair and sheep shearing.

I answer questions on mimeographed handouts. It is all a game, these fill-in-the-blanks, and I go along with it because I like it when the teacher says, "Good, Louise, that's very good." I like the warmth and quiet of the classroom. I listen to the phonics record; suddenly I can read and spell through sounding out words and memorizing rules. I know the days of the month and fractions and i before e except after c.

My mother is the trouble I get into. My mother invites my teachers over to dinner and bribes them to turn against me, to stand firm on my mother's side. I chant phrases to protect myself, "Don't trust her. Be quiet."

I am like tinsel, shiny and slight. I bring my heart here, to a schoolroom. Someday I'll find the Book of Customs and I'll have it all figured out.

I am an adult in this room now. I add the poetry of Adrienne Rich, Judy Grahn and Marge Piercy to the shelves. I take down the American flag and hang a banner that says "Viva la Learning." I put up a bulletin board with pictures of Maya Angelou, Audre Lorde, Barbara Jordan and Geraldine Ferraro. I draw pictures on the blackboard with colored chalk. I say, "I don't care what you think of me," out loud.

·  ·  ·

Kindergarten was small chairs in circles, marching around the room to music, graham crackers and milk, and lots of people about the same size as me. The first thing I learned in kindergarten was that eccentricity was strongly discouraged. Trying to nap between the wall and the piano or wearing bobby pins cleverly crossed on my head occasioned conferences between my teacher and my mother.

One night over dinner, my mother said my teacher said that I refused to learn to tie the laces on the cardboard shoe that we'd colored. I hated shoes and I hated the way my foot got squeezed when they were laced up. My mother began to use words like slow, retarded and stubborn. I knew then that my future hung on those laces. I saw the other kids tie their shoes and get gold stars and smiles from the teacher. I set to work on my cardboard shoe with fierce determination and finally got my star. To this day, my laces work themselves out of my running shoes and flop on the sidewalk. People, even complete strangers, continue to tell me that my shoes are untied.

◆*Memory.* In first grade, we read stories about Spot, Jane and Fluff as we sit in small groups around our teacher. I can read better to myself than I read out loud, but I'm still one of the best readers, I think.

One day my teacher signals for me to come with her to the second grade classroom where she picks out books for me to read because I have finished all the ones in our room. All through recess that day, I skip around the playground with my own specialness. All day, I open the cover of my desk to make sure that my new second grade books are there. I press them against my chest on the school bus, deaf to the big boys in the back seat.

I am tall when I get home. I forget to shrink when I open the door. I forget that I'm not going to tell my mother about anything special anymore. "Look, look! My teacher said I was the best reader in my class!"

"It's not nice to brag about yourself," my mother says. "If your teacher knew how you were carrying on, she never would have given you those books. Don't go thinking that you're smarter than everyone else."◆

I never got used to the transition between school, where learning required opening up, and home, where survival demanded shutting down.

Although she was a teacher herself, my mother was wary of too much education. At home, reading was like everything else—once I learned to do it, I was expected not to do too much of it. A person who read too many books was distrusted and accused of having "highfalutin'" ideas. Practical hard-working people did not ask questions and did not read many books, especially secular ones. At the same time, I was supposed to be a good student because my mother was a teacher.

Memory is a thumb pushing into my solar plexus, pinching the bundle of nerves at the base of my breastbone, between my chest and stomach. I have always wanted to rise up out of my family. Instead I split in two, torn between school and my stifling home. The rules at school were more predictable and there were fewer secrets. Home required the total taming of my mouth, the swallowing of the truth that lived on my tongue along with the bitters of Grandpa's penis and the solution my mother painted on my nails to make me quit chewing them. School required talking. A good student was supposed to raise her hand, to volunteer. I discovered a special part of my brain that was only loosely connected to my body. I could memorize poems and practice penmanship and figure out math problems and raise my hand with the answers. When I did all this, I didn't have to think about home or try to understand it. The confusion that swept away the ground and made me cry and stomp at home could be kept away by blackboards and gold stars.

The right answer guaranteed the teacher's attention. I know the answer, I would think, waving my hand with wild excitement. When the teacher called my name I'd wish I was a cat and could sit in her lap. When she called my name, I felt real, like the Velveteen Rabbit. "Who will volunteer to clean the blackboard, to run this note to the principal's office, to watch the room for a minute while I'm gone," the teacher asked. "I will, I will," my hand said. I would do anything for her attention.

I watched the teacher closely. What if she found a new rule? What if I couldn't really count on my brain? "Is this right, teacher?" I would ask, checking my paper at her desk too often. But what if this brain let me down the way my legs did when I couldn't run or the way my eyes cried when I squeezed them tight. I checked my test answers out of the corner of my eye against Sally's paper. "Keep your eyes on your own paper," the teacher said. But what if I didn't really know anything? I was always making mistakes at home.

◆*Memory.* I am sitting in the dirt against the house. I crawled between the rosebush and the flowers so that I could hide. Four boys yelled "fatso fatso" at me on the playground after lunch and all day I just wanted to cry.

"What do you think you're doing sitting in the dirt?" Mommy asks. "You come out of there right now!"

I like how soft the dirt is. When I sit in the dirt I can feel my bottom and I don't feel like I'll fly away any minute. I can't go toward her. A great tiredness is pulling at my limbs.

She walks closer until her shadow makes me cold.

"The boys called me names," I say, looking at the ground.

"You're just too sensitive," Mommy says. "Just pretend you can't hear them. They can't hurt you."

I want to bury myself in the dirt. She reaches for my arm and starts pulling. Why can't she just understand?

I would rather feel lonely and sad than hear her tell me it doesn't matter. I sag against the house and start crying, too full of my feelings to pay attention to Mommy.

My crying makes her angry and she pulls harder. "You stop that crying or I'll give you something to cry about. Grow up and act your age," she says and gives me one more pull. I am seven and I have no idea what that is supposed to look like.

I scramble up with tears falling in wide tracks across my cheeks. If only I had the right words, maybe she would listen. But all the words I know are for objects outside of me; I have no words for this turbulence inside that is a tornado. I am waiting to be lifted like Dorothy in *The Wizard of Oz*, tapping my heels together. I cannot stop crying.

My mother's voice is a swarm of stinging bees: "You just stop this nonsense."

I can't stop crying because I can't believe she's still yelling at me. My crying says, Why is she being mean to me? Why can't she just hold me and be gentle?

She is never going to do that. I have to stop wanting. My tears slow to ragged swallows as I repeat these truths in my mind. The hurt has left my nose and throat and eyes so that when I open them the yard is shimmering. In my clarity I think, someday I'm going to leave here.◆

. . .

The island road is a serpent turned on its side. On my bike, I glide down and push myself up, scaling hills that looked like mountains when I was at the bottom of them, surprised when I get to the top without dismounting. I am pedaling a rust-ridden ten-speed along unfamiliar roads— the trees a corridor of dark giants, the sky a low gray roof. When I ride a bike, I am always eight. Like much else that feels truly liberating, I did less of it the older I got.

I was skeptical at the sight of my own first bike, July 26th, 1962. How could I remain upright so far from the ground on two narrow wheels, I wondered, when my world was always tipping from side to side like a ship about to capsize. I was saved from training wheels by our neighbor, Mr. Makone.

He held the bike while I mounted and suddenly was no longer there as I continued on my own. Here was a miracle. I was filled with the feeling of possibility, glimpsing a life free of limitations and stillness. I flew in endless circles around the driveway that looped the garage, around and around the walnut tree, squishing the green nuts with my tires. Out to the edge where the driveway met the street and back down again, tracing the shape of a giant tennis racquet in the asphalt.

The neighbor kids rode their bicycles on the street. "You'll get hit by a car if you go out there," my mother warned. I was confined to the driveway, within sight, for my safety. "They're just delinquents," my mother said. "Their parents don't even know where they are." I was not to leave our yard or talk to them. But I watched them from the edge of our driveway as they shared secrets and penny candy, drooped over their handlebars.

My mother and I always had different opinions about safety and danger. She worried about me falling from my bike or getting hit by a car or being subject to bad influences. I worried about getting yelled at or Grandpa touching me or not knowing till too late what constituted bad.

My mother said she worried because she loved me, but her worry was angry words so full of fearful dislike that they had a force as tangible as the way her hand pulled on my shoulder. Having a body was dangerous, I decided. So was moving around.

"Don't stare. Don't wiggle. Quit slouching. Pick up your feet. Hold your stomach in. Stand up straight. You are so clumsy!" I took the sentences into my body and grew unsure with them, losing grace to self-consciousness. For years I have feared that people were staring at me in weighty evaluation of my posture. I worried about keeping my knees together and not spilling on my dress.

When I was eight I wanted to ride away from all of this danger on my bike. I wanted to ride far away from my worries. They chased each other round in my head and for all that I worried, the danger did not recede.

Twenty-six years later, I have yet to escape my worries. I dismount the bike and call to a donkey behind a fence. The donkey chews and stares back at me, then flicks an ear. Sarah is worried that it will rain and makes me get going again, afraid that something bad will happen to me if I get wet.

I return to my cabin, pulling up on the spot of gravel, walking my bike through grass to the back. I push against the door with my body to enter, met by the chill dark breath of the cabin. I walk cautiously through the shadows, peering beneath the bunk beds in the front bedroom to make sure no one is hiding, waiting to jump out. I still think of danger as hidden, when for years it was directly in front of my face. Even God was dangerous, and according to my mother, he was everywhere.

◆*Memory.* Grandpa sits at the gray kitchen table, stirring a cup of coffee with a spoon. Jim and I are supposed to sit quietly. Mommy still wears her teaching clothes; a high-neck white blouse and pleated skirt that she spot-cleans with the corner of her napkin. Grandma has tight lips above her housedress and one button coming loose. The air is gravy and string beans. At 7:00, Jim and I will probably have to go to bed even though I'm not sleepy.

"The planets will be lining up tonight, just like Dr. Kramer wrote about." Grandpa has a red book between his hands. I think about the pictures of Saturn and Mars on the second grade bulletin board.

"God said that he would never use a flood again to destroy the earth, but Revelations tells us it will be by fire and earthquake. Tonight the planets are in the pattern that Revelations spoke of, the one that brings the end." Grandpa clears his throat. He sounds like the ministers we listen to on the radio.

"I colored a picture of the ark in Sunday school," I volunteer.

"Ssshh, this is grown-up talk," Mommy says. "Time for bed soon."

"These are the times we're in," my grandmother adds. "The final days, when the chosen will be called to heaven and the earth destroyed."

My mother nods and picks at her fingers. "Has it happened before, the way these planets are?" Her voice is small, like mine.

"Not like this," Grandpa says in a low tone that makes me shiver. "God gives and God takes away."

"Mommy," I say, trying to turn her attention away from this. I have questions. My heart is beating from my stomach.

"What is it, Louise, now hush." She pulls me up from the table by my arm and tells Grandma she'll be back for Jim.

The trip to my bedroom is more than a hundred footsteps. In my head, I see Sunday school pictures in vivid color: the Tower of Babel broken into pebbles; Sodom and Gomorrah eaten by flames; Abraham holding a knife over the child Isaac's bound body. "Mommy, is the world going to end?" I ask into the air ahead as we climb the stairs, me first. It's not fair, I think.

"Hush now, you just get ready for bed." She kisses me on the top of my head as I stand in my flannel pajamas. "Now I lay me down to sleep, pray the Lord my soul to keep." Her voice is loud and dutiful, leading the prayer which makes me afraid to go to sleep at night. "If I die before I wake, pray the Lord my soul to take."

"Mommy!?"

"Now you just go to sleep now. That's a good girl." She gives me a hug, squeezing tight. I wrap my arms around her as if I could keep her with me but I am easy to unwrap.

I stretch my arms flat out at either side of me, holding tight to the curled corners of the mattress. If I hold on tight, I won't be thrown into the crack that will split the earth in two.◆

The end of the world has always counted among my worries. But now, it's the men in charge of the world who frighten me.

Jim and I rode our bikes through the cemetery next door —through grids of vacant level roads set in large squares around the gravesites. I was fascinated by the rectangular holes covered by forest green canopies, the sound of the sprinklers hitting the canvas. "The worms go in, the worms go out, the worms play pinochle on your snout," I sang as I rode my bike. My mother said I had to respect the dead and never walk across their graves. I couldn't understand why, if heaven was in the sky, bodies were buried so far from it and so close to worms. It was another grown-up mystery.

"I hate you, I wish you were dead," I yelled at my mother when I was mad at her.

"God will kill you for saying that," she replied. "He can hear every word you say."

I used to worry that he would send lightning or split the world open and activate all the mountains so that they became volcanoes. I saw my baptismal certificate once and was certain that the year I was going to die was written on it in cursive following the words: "In the year of our lord." Fifteen years later, when I saw it again, I realized the year referred to was the longhand spelling of the year of my birth. Now I worry about breast cancer, lung cancer, automobile accidents, snipers, nuclear war, pesticides and overpopulation.

But it's the quality of life that concerns me most. It's wanting the worry to end so that I can feel the bicycle wind on my cheeks. I would like to stop holding so tight to my mattress. I am no longer sure that safety comes from holding on or pleading with the almighty. I want to run down the puddled January pavement to the pay phone, call Marianne, and ask her to tell me that I'm not dying. She is a doctor.

Instead I get out all the bones I've picked from the beach. A delicate facial bone from a small duck with one oval eye shelter still intact. Long clean leg bones from deer and cattle. Translucent bones from unknown fish. Bones are to the body like walls to a house. These are bones rocked in the tides and aged by the moon, holding the mystery of what survives after all other identity passes on.

I look at the bones and admire the curving at the end where the joints connect with each other, the fine construction of balanced weights and rounded edges. Their structural beauty continues beyond decay. I think of the fine lines of my own body, held by the solidness of bone, bones beyond my mother's inspection.

I was teethed on dying instead of life, so that now I must begin to count my survival. Rising from the deaths of self-expression in which I was as silent as a pale body in a coffin. Being alive means taking on a boldness which still comes hard through my fears and my learned passivity. Being alive means being noisy and asking questions. Being alive is traveling down unknown roads instead of repeating the only route I learned, leaning on the integrity of my bones and allowing Tinsel to be enchanted.

◆*Memory.* A thin stream of smoke is wafting from the berry house and my seven-year-old brother Jim shoots out the door as my grandmother comes running yelling and my mother screams. "What was Jim doing in there?!" my mother demands as she shakes my shoulders. He'd been playing with matches, of course, I'd seen him and I knew we weren't supposed to, but we weren't supposed to do most things.

In the meantime, Jim has run away. My mother does not go looking for him. Instead she calls Kenny, a neigh-

bor boy she won't let us play with. He's on his bike. "Go
find Jim," she tells him, "and tell him that if he doesn't
come home right now, I'll call the police and they'll come
take him away for being bad." ◆

My mother would always use anyone she could find. The
world was populated with people who never told her, "Do it
yourself," or "Don't you care how scared he is already?"
   "Ha!" Fuckit says. "We're never going to get away. I hate
this. I hate going back and listening to her again. I think we
should just tear down the damn inner house and live in a
tent."
   "We'll get in trouble for writing this book," Tinsel says. I
leave the back bedroom and the writing table. I try to close
my eyes and imagine Carrie hugging Tinsel in the inner
house. But I don't feel this nurturing healer self. I am not in
the mood for softness or meditation. "Enough already!"
Fuckit says. "I just want to tear apart walls." I clench both
fists and stomp through the house, then grab the car keys
and pull on my coat, in adolescent rebellion against Memory
and childhood.
   Limbs and fragments of greenery fly over the road as the
wind pushes against the side of the car. I push on and off and
on the radio, looking for loud raunchy music and pissed off
when I get only static or the news. Ted Bundy is being exe-
cuted today. The newscaster says that parents have brought
their children for picnics outside the maximum security
prison and that people are wearing T-shirts that say, "Roast
Teddy Deady." In his last interview, Ted Bundy says that
pornography caused him to rape and murder, and that he
hoped no one would blame his parents because they were
wonderful.
   "Right Ted," Fuckit says out loud, punching off the radio
again.
   I drive and roar, squeezing dissatisfied air through my

lungs. I feel like Gulliver, bound by a thousand clinging strings. "I'll never have peace!" Fuckit screams. "I can't get away from my mother."

This is a familiar feeling. For years it seemed like my mother was everywhere, with her own personal network of spies and informers. She loved to tell people how much trouble I was. My mother knew no boundaries. She had no loyalty to me, only a deep desire to find fault with every move I made. Or perhaps she was haunted by the premonition that I would tell the secrets, the ones she fought so hard to keep. I am telling them.

But the big problem is that I keep reacting as if my mother were still with me.

◆*Memory.* "Bad girl, bad," my mother is pulling on my arm because I have knelt to get closer to a resting butterfly on my way to the school bus. Inside my head, I repeat her words to myself, memorizing how to be mommy.

"Bad girl!" I tell my Betsy Wetsy doll when she cries for me to pick her up. "You just lie still and be a good girl." I pull her diapers up tight and pin them with a safety pin. "You're just so much work, always wetting your pants." I tuck her in and yell at Jim not to get dirty as he plays with his dump truck.◆

"You're just selfish," Sarah says to Tinsel now. "All you care about is yourself." Sarah is how I turned myself against myself.

Tinsel reminds me of how it felt like people were always turning on me. I used to have stomachaches on the nights of PTA meetings, because I always got in trouble afterward. I never quite understood that I shouldn't talk about my teachers because it made my mother jealous. When she knew I liked a particular teacher, she tried to befriend her and convince her that I was bad.

In reality, I was better behaved than the runabouts and far

too cowed and shy to be the class clown. It's only now that I realize that I don't know exactly what my teachers told her. Despite my A's and my accomplishments in reading, my mother said that my teacher said I stayed in the bathroom too long or wiggled in my seat or talked to my best friend in class. I lay in my bed and held my stomach going over every recollection of my schooldays trying to figure out what was going to get me in trouble. My mother would start out saying what a good person my teacher was, how they had a good talk and how she's going to give me some cupcakes to take to the teacher. Then she'd say that I had to learn to keep my hands to myself and obey the teacher. She'd say when would I learn to be quiet. Then I would have to take cupcakes and put them on my teacher's desk and hear my teacher say what a good mother I had and that I should be nice to her. Then I'd get back to my desk and Johnny would call me a teacher's pet. To this day, all worry goes to my stomach.

I eat malted milk balls and smoke Marlboros after eight days of cigarette abstinence. "She was like a poisonous gas, she was like God, she was like *1984*," Fuckit says.

Carrie points to the cigarette and says, "Poisonous gas?"

"Oh blow off!" Fuckit says.

"I would be glad if we could figure out how to care for this self," Carrie says wearily. I feel the familiar sense of being an adult and not knowing enough. "Between Tinsel's fear and Fuckit's anger and Sarah telling us no one's going to like us if we say these things, I'd be glad to find a different way to be," Carrie says.

But first I have to know what an alternative looks like. If I do not become my mother, who do I become?

◆*Memory.* My mother and I have been driving away from town, on a road between trees and under low-hung clouds. We pull into the gravel circle of Ann's driveway. She is leaning on a hoe, smoking a cigarette as the wind pulls at her yellow-gray hair and billows the large men's shirt, teasing it from the sturdy waist of her gray trousers. She nods as we approach and for a moment it seems that she is planted there, between dancing brown cornstalks and raspberry vines.

She walks with us, leaving footprints of grid marks from her logging boots, stomping her feet firmly against the doormat on dirty linoleum. Ann is a friend of one of my mother's friends and we have come to visit, my mother and I, bearing cupcakes. Ann is the shape of a tree with a mighty trunk and I would like to wrap myself around her legs, certain that they would hold me up.

She is not "good" with children and does not try to talk with me, but gives me a glass of water and nods to a corner of her large couch where I sit quite still with my short legs in front of me and look up from under my bangs trying not to stare at her.

I have noticed that most grown-up talking is about people I don't know or what the minister said at church. Ann's husband is in a frayed armchair, holding an ice pack to his armpit because he has boils. He showed one to us, it was oozing.

Ann has a wart on her chin and eyebrows which sweep up in long hair from her eyes. I have never seen a woman who looks like her, whose voice is so loud, with laughter and smoke that comes from the back of her throat. My mother is squirming a little over the ways Ann is acting that are wrong. She tightens her chin and makes cheerful, careful comments to which Ann delivers a loud roaring sentence and slaps her hand on her thigh.

When we leave, I stare at the gray twill of Ann's legs and the solid buttocks that squeeze against the top of her pants. I look at the slippery nylons on my mother's pale legs. I remember Ann planted in her garden, watching the crow flying into the wind. When I grow up, I want to wear play clothes and get dirty like Ann does. I want to grow long exuberant eyebrows and have the loudest laugh in the room.◆

•   •   •

I slam the car door as the first big drops of rain thud on the narrow road outside the cabin. "I just want to drink wine!" Fuckit says.

"I want to walk in the rain," Tinsel says. I put on my slicker and leave the wine in the refrigerator. As soon as I hit the beach I play dragon. I bellow and breathe fire out my nose. I stomp loudly through the edge of the tide. I throw rocks one after the other and say, "I'm tired of being scared. I'm tired of being good! I'm tired of being shy!" I make more noise than Tinsel has ever made.

Then I act out Sarah. I squeeze my face up like an old dried out potato and point my finger and complain. "Your poor mother did the best she could," Sarah rants. "And these trips backward aren't helping one bit. Get on with it. The past is the past. You're never going to get Tinsel to feel good about herself or Fuckit to quit smoking!"

"If the past was the past you wouldn't be saying these same old things," Carrie retorts. I pick up a moonsnail shell and put it in my pocket.

"I want a mom," Tinsel says. "I don't want to do this all alone."

"I want to be a good mom to you," Carrie tells Tinsel. "Sometimes I think I'm better at caring for clients or teaching good workshops than in paying attention to you. But I like you, younger self. Thank you for your sensitivity and honesty. Thank you for your sense of justice and your compassion. Thank you for your unstoppable voice which tells deep truths even though you're afraid. Thank you for teaching us to ride a bicycle and to read. Thank you for wanting love so strongly that we kept looking for it." I feel tall as I walk through the rain and talk to myself.

I imagine bringing into the inner house my childhood teachers, and Jean and Kate and Marianne and every friend who has held me and listened. I paste the walls with stories of their patience, kindness and wisdom. I learn from their tenderness and instruction and hope for my future. I study their customs.

I take down my hood and open my mouth to the downpour. I am washing my mother off my skin. My jeans are soaked beneath the edges of my coat. I yell, "I'm soaking wet and I like it." I run flapping my arms down the beach. "I can fly. I can fly," Tinsel says. A seagull hovers above me, riding the current. I am awed by our synchronicity. "It's magic," Tinsel says and Carrie nods in agreement.

Back in the cabin, I fill a casserole bowl with fine sand and place it on the kitchen counter. I run my hands through the softness, lifting a palm full and watching the sand make rivers and waterfalls through my fingers. Outside, the rain has stopped. I have filled the kitchen with candles and their light is doubled in the dark bare windows. The space heater adds orange to the night and the quiet.

I let myself be eight again but this time I have crystals and a magical red lump of palm resin named "dragon blood" that I bought for fifty cents at an herb shop. I am freed from the sermons that threaten the end of the world, free from the Bible and sin and from ever having to go to church again. Because I am an adult, I am free to be as magical and enchanted as I please.

Tinsel holds my magic. She believes in fairies and tree spirits and healing stones. She believes because she feels the existence of the unseen with her sensitivity. She is drawn to what is shiny and tender and genuine. She does not need faith, because she has knowing.

I sit in my chair by the kitchen table, wearing long underwear beneath my faithful blue sweats, and a sweater of thick Australian wool I knit when I was seventeen. I cry about how hard and unceasing the time as Tinsel felt when I lived with my mother and grandparents.

I begin humming and playing with the sand in the casserole dish. Tinsel arranges the stones in a circle, giving each one a meaning. The chunk of milky calcite that has always looked like a mountain is turned upside down so that peaks become wingtips. A round of hematite, metal and heavy in my hand, gives grounding and the support of my feet. Green calcite is for joy. I trace a path of sand with the tips of my fingers, a spiral, a maze. The design is from a Memory much longer ago than childhood. In the center, bloodstone, shiny and tumbled, represents this journey through childhood and to self-nurturance.

Tinsel opens my paper bags of herbs. For luck and good fortune, I sprinkle vervain along the path of the spiral and plant a golden star anise at the beginning of the path. Next to it I put the root called Helping Hand, because it is in the shape of fingers and palms. Tinsel's sand play is about help, both seen and sensed.

I have made a play, a movable sculpture. I move my writing and put the dish of sand on the writing table. "That was fun," Tinsel says. "It made me feel hopeful and like I could wave a wand and make myself happen."

"Ah yes, this will make a fine Memory," Memory says.

"It will be one of my customs," Tinsel says, as I drink cocoa and watch the candlelight illuminate my gems.

# 6

## *Lulu*

I AM OUTSIDE the inner house, in the yard of dried grass. In the corner, three pine trees grow close together, with long swooping branches that touch the ground. Beneath the arching branches is a protected patch of dirt, packed like a floor. Treasures of rock, shell, feather and marbles are in the ledges and pockets of the protruding roots.

Inside the shelter of tree limbs I am in my own world. I am the tallest one in it; no adult would be willing to crawl in because they would get dirty and they hate that.

In here, I eat jawbreakers and Butterfingers, watermelon sours and Sweet Tarts. I have adventures by turning the pages of books and making up stories about forts and treehouses. I rearrange my treasures and sharpen all my colored pencils. I make up songs and sing them to myself. I am ten.

My mother doesn't like my having this place that she can't enter. She wants to chop the limbs off the tree and trim back the branches. My mother says it's not nice to make up stories. My mother says there is work I'm supposed to be doing in the house.

I make a sword from a branch and carve Z's into the air like Zorro.

My mother says girls shouldn't play with sticks.

I am an adult in this yard. I put up a hammock between

the trees. Next to me on the ground is a pile of notebooks and novels. I swing back and forth pressing the ground with one dangling foot. I close my eyes behind my mirrored sunglasses and wait for the stories to come to me.

.  .  .

*My name is Lulu and I am ten*
*And I have things to say,*
*It's time you paid attention*
*to what I'm all about,*
*I've been here a decade,*
*I've figured some things out.*

*My name is Lulu, I like to play*
*Can hardly wait till morning to have a day,*
*Smashball is my favorite,*
*I like to skip about*
*I like writing, I really like to shout!*

*My name is Lulu and I am ten*
*And I have things to say,*
*Don't yell at me when I play,*
*It's what I need to do,*
*Don't tell me what's wrong with me,*
*Just keep your mind on you.*

*My name is Lulu and I am ten,*
*And I have things to say.*
*It's time you paid attention*
*to what I'm all about,*
*I've been here a decade and*
*What I have to say, Counts!*

"Sarah is having a cow," Lulu declares at the end of her favorite song. I've been standing and singing since I got up this morning. I wrote "Lulu's Song" in my voice class a couple of months ago.

"Tomfoolery! Laziness! Self-indulgence! Procrastination!

Daydreaming! Wasting time! Get to work!" Sarah is on the roof of the inner house, yelling down with a bullhorn.

"Sarah, what are you doing up there?" Carrie asks, alarmed.

"I am making sure we get this book written," Sarah says, "I am saving us from uselessness. I am holding us to our commitments. I am God."

"Oh God, Sarah," Fuckit sneers from an upstairs window, craning her neck through and looking up.

"This is my chapter," Lulu announces, "and I can sing if I want to. Can't I, Carrie?"

It's not easy to get permission for singing. My favorite play was standing in the front yard strumming my tennis racket, and pretending to perform for an audience of passing cars. I was caught doing it on more than one occasion and told to stay in the back yard, where no one could see me. I had seen a man play the guitar and sing all kinds of sad and funny songs. But singing in the back yard involved making noise and noise, especially kids' noise, got on the adults' nerves.

Singing was the saving grace of Vacation Bible School though. I learned "Michael, Row the Boat Ashore", "All Things Bright and Beautiful", "The Lord of the Dance" and "Kumbaya"; songs that became long-time friends. The teacher played the piano as we sang along, and sometimes a teenager came and sang to us with a guitar.

I wished we could sing all day long, not just for an hour, but the rest of the time we colored and learned Bible stories. Bible stories made me wiggle. All the girls in them got to do was have babies or anoint Jesus with oil or cook food for him. Not like the disciples who got to travel and camp out and have adventures and watch miracles. The more I thought about these stories, the more questions and objections I had. Sometimes, I said my thoughts out loud accidentally while the teacher was telling us stories and we were coloring the pictures that went along with them. Then the teacher said,

"We're listening now, Louise," and I felt stupid because I talked.

So I tried to figure out the questions by myself. I wasn't sure I liked God. He did terrible things to people and if that was his will, then he must not be very nice, I reasoned. If he could do anything, why did he make Jesus be killed when Jesus could have kept on doing miracles and entertaining everyone? I would never want to be Job, I thought, boils are gross! If Job loved God so much, why was God so mean to him? We colored pictures of Moses coming down the mountain with an enormous block of granite in each arm; he looked ferocious because he could see the people admiring the golden calf. I would rather see a calf made of gold than be told thou shalt not do things. I hope God can't really read thoughts, I thought, because if he did those things to people who loved him, what would he do to me? I resolved to be extra good and sit still to make up for my thoughts.

I liked Bible School because my mother and Grandpa weren't there and because we got Kool-Aid and cookies every day. Although the subject matter wasn't very cheerful, there were treats and songs and running around in the parking lot.

"But Girl Scout camp was the best!" Lulu says and I sing "Donna, Donna," for old times' sake.

"You've played long enough now," Sarah says. "Write something down! Right now!"

I want a cigarette but I've thrown them away again. It's been five days without them. I always feel a little tense when Sarah wants something. I start moaning, standing and raising my arms above my head and letting them fall. I sing,

> *Daughter of Light,*
> *Fairy of Spring,*
> *Come take me with you.*
> *Mother of Hope,*
> *Dragon of Fire,*

*Carry me with you.*
*I am tired of dark,*
*I am weary of pain.*
*I can't hold any more.*
*Come take my hand.*

◆*Memory*. I am, at ten, the youngest girl at camp. I sleep in a big yellow canvas tent over a wooden platform. I have three other tentmates and I can hardly talk to them because I feel so shy but I like how the tent smells. Next to my bed, I even have my very own wooden box for my cup and toothbrush and my Girl Scout book that tells me how to make fires and how to cook on them and how to bandage wounds.

We eat at long tables on two open covered porches next to fir trees with long draping branches. After dinner, three girls do the dishes at each table with huge basins of water while everyone else sits at their tables and sings. Turtle, who's a counselor, wears a cowboy hat and green Girl Scout socks held up by garters with little yellow flags. She plays the guitar and teaches us songs by singing a line and having us sing it back to her. We learn a lot of songs because we sing after each meal and around the campfire, too. Camp lasts a whole two weeks and this is the very best part.

And there are only girls and girl counselors. Almost all the counselors are great even if I'm too shy to talk to them much. But I think about them a lot and I am going to grow up to be like them.◆

I begin to sing camp songs, playing the chords I have known for nineteen years, "Joggin' Along," "High Up, High on a Mountain," "Where Have All the Flowers Gone?" I sing to an audience of trees through the windows. I know they hear because their branches move as I sing for them.

The television weatherman slips his pointer theatrically across the fast moving white clouds cascading in an arc across the Pacific Northwest. The radio announcers echo him, quoting the proclamation of the National Weather Service, "Zero temperatures predicted with snowfall. No end in sight."

It's hard to take them seriously as I walk to the neighborhood store in my sweatshirt and sweatpants to buy my daily quota of red licorice. Snow in the Pacific Northwest, while not unknown, is uncommon and temperatures below zero are rare. When I was ten, my mother, Jim and I listened attentively to the radio when snow was forecast. If more than an inch of snow fell, school would be canceled or at least begin late. I spent those mornings glued to the window, watching and praying to the sky for fast-falling mountains of snowflakes.

On the trip home from the store I'm blowing into my hands to warm them. In the cabin, the implications of cold begin to register: I am in a summer cabin built far enough above the ground to make the crawl space a fun house for the neighborhood cats. The floor of plywood and linoleum is seeping cold air that's coming in fast, littering the sky with satchels of sagging clouds. Maybe I should jump ship and move in with Marianne.

"Babo ho ba," Clingbaby says, enticing me with the thought of hugging Marianne in her warm and friendly communal household.

"So you're just going to turn your back on this writing and play in Seattle, aren't you?" Sarah chides, making me feel guilty for the thought of leaving. I have less than two weeks left here.

I put on both sets of long underwear and my wool sweater. I notice the single-paned windows and think about the way the pipes crawl, exposed, under the house.

"What will we eat?" Tinsel asks, thinking of the meager

offerings of the corner store. "It's going to be cold, isn't it?" she worries.

"I don't like having to wear so many clothes to be warm," Tayla complains. "They make me feel like a mummy!"

"It would be pretty," Carrie says, "with the grasses and vines outlined in snow. It might be like that time we were at the ocean and the protruding rocks collected snow only on the sides where the wind blew it, like frosting." Carrie imagines meditating as the snow falls; sinking into stillness.

"Yech! Double yech!!" Lulu shouts. "What are you talking about? It's going to snow and you're content just to sit and watch it?! No way, no way!" Lulu says, stomping her feet and waving her arms about. "We go to Marianne's right now and spend time playing in the snow. Snow is a gift from the weather goddess. If we don't go play in it, then I will go on strike and make us thoroughly miserable!"

Sarah grumbles, and Crystal Cat growls from the cat box on the front seat, but it feels good to drive away from the cabin which looks bleaker by the minute, under the darkening sky. I imagine a giant insulating housecoat around the cabin and protective warmth under the pipes.

Inside me, Lulu is chanting incantations to the weather goddess. "Snow, snow, please snow, please, please snow" until I start singing a long completely made-up song about the inner voices, with an occasional chorus of "Let it snow, let it snow, let it snow."

I had a lot of therapy before Lulu got strong enough to re-emerge. Tinsel was so sad, frightened, and full of incest, Clingbaby was so hungry for comfort, and Tayla had so completely lost the habit of making sound that Lulu was squished. She emerged in bits and pieces in play with lovers and in songs that broke through the fear, inertia and prohibitions. But in the past several years, Lulu has become more distinct.

The snow begins within an hour of my arrival at

Marianne's where I am met with the smell of long-simmered bean soup and chunks of hot buttered garlic bread. We put on our hiking boots and long coats and walk through the flakes that fall like feathers under the streetlights. The snow turns her hand on the neighborhood like a magician, bringing light to the winter dark evening, turning houses into castles.

◆*Memory.* "We're going to move!" my mother announces, smiling at me with a sidelong look, both of her hands on the steering wheel of her car.

I straighten in my seat, brought to my full height by the holiday music in her voice. I am ten.

"We're going to move next door, to the house that Mom and Dad rent out." She is smiling as if she means it.

"Grandma and Grandpa too?" I ask anxiously.

"No, just the three of us. We're going to be a family, just you, Jim and me. Things will be better now. It will be like starting over. You'll have to help out though."

"I can do lots of things," I say.◆

"Do you ever wish for one act that could just change everything?" I ask Marianne.

"Like the lottery?" she says.

"Yeah. Or like the way I think my life will change completely when I move to a new place."

"Sometimes I think I'll just wake up knowing what my life work is," Marianne continues. "No more process, just knowing!" Marianne went to medical school, practiced family medicine, did research, left it all to try to make a living as a gardener, and is currently working as a part-time clinician in women's health care. "One morning, all the confusion will be gone and I'll just know what I want to do. Of course if I'd known all along maybe I never would have taken this time to learn beading and gardening and basketry and sewing."

"I want to play every day, that's what I want," Lulu announces.

At first it was exciting to help my mother more. I could iron! I could vacuum! I could turn on the oven! I could help Mommy grade her papers, even though she taught sixth grade and I was only in the fifth. Some of the boys' papers had smudges of dirt on them. I could spell better than lots of the kids in her class too.

But the best part was that I got home on the bus a whole hour before she and Jim did and I could do anything I wanted then. Although I was supposed to be doing my homework, she wasn't there telling me to do it.

An hour wasn't enough though, for all I wanted to do. "You're going to have to do things you don't want to do in this life, young lady," my mother said when I said, "I don't want to." "You never think about anyone except yourself," she continued. "Stop whining and be glad for what you've got."

I began to notice that I spent a lot more time doing what I didn't want to do than doing what I wanted. My mother had a lot of plans for my time and I was informed of her decisions, without consultation.

◆*Memory.* It's Saturday morning and I have a stack of new library books, Sue Barton, the Hardy Boys and the Lennon Sisters adventures. I can hardly decide which one to start first.

The kitchen blender shakes me loose from the hospital I have just entered with Sue Barton. "Louise, have you made your bed? I'm making some cupcakes to take to Joe who's in the hospital with his hip, then Emma next door and poor Sally who can't get out much. We're going to leave in an hour."

"Do I have to go?" I ask, making it clear that sitting in a room of grownups is not my idea of a good time.

"Don't you think about anyone except yourself? Don't you think there are other things I'd rather be doing today?"

The question, "Then why are you doing this?" forms so clearly in my mind that I can see it as a typewritten sentence, as if I were living in a book.

"I have an eggbeater for you. Now why don't you wash up these dishes while I get ready. And don't get anything on your blouse or you'll have to change."◆

"Marianne," Lulu says.

"What, Lulu?" she responds, recognizing Lulu's voice.

"Why do we have to do so much of what we don't want to do? And how come hardly anybody gets paid to write and sing when lots of people get paid to sell insurance or to be in the army?"

"I just call it the patriarchy," Marianne says. "And then the Puritans made it all worse with their dedication to suffering. Even if they got to heaven, they wouldn't know how to enjoy it."

◆*Memory.* I've been on my knees wiping the dust from the top of the molding with a rag and Spic 'N Span. The kitchen floor has left marks on my knees. Now I'm supposed to dust. Some Saturday.

"And after that you can do some ironing," my mother continues.

"I don't want to!" I say in frustration. "I have my own things I want to do." I want to be in my room by myself with my pencils and books.

"You'll do what I tell you," my mother says, raising her voice.

"You just want me to be your slave," I say. "Jim doesn't have to do this. He gets to practice baseball and mow the lawn. I'd rather mow the lawn. You're always telling me what to do!" I can't stop my mouth talking.

Sentence finds sentence, not whining but declaring.

"How dare you talk back to me, young lady." My mother has moved closer now; the shadow of her hand crosses my cheek, then the sharp sound and sting. "I don't want to hear any more about this."

I touch my cheek and stare at her. I think, I never want to be like you. I don't want to grow up spending Saturdays yelling at children or washing molding. I don't want to spend my time doing what I'm supposed to do instead of what I want to do. I'm never going to be like you.

"You only want me to be like you!" I accuse her. "You don't care who I am." I don't care if you hit me again, I think, but look at me first, I am getting taller. All the thoughts I have collected for ten years are finding their way past my jaw.

"How dare you!" my mother's voice fills the room. "After all I've given you, after moving us to this nice house and working all day, I come home to a daughter who can't even help her poor mother around the house. I'll tell your teacher about how you never do anything around here."

I go up to my room and sit on my bed. I decide that I am going to grow up and do something important. I don't know what it is, but I feel it on my tongue. And I won't let my mother see it or take it away.◆

"I'm tired of this Memory stuff," Lulu says to Marianne. "I don't want to think about it anymore! And I'm not going to!" I scoop up a handful of snow and fling it at Marianne. "I just want to play and throw snowballs."

Whereupon Marianne becomes Beth, who is ten years old herself and also Lulu's best friend. We throw many snowballs at each other and then fall to the ground holding hands, making ourselves angels.

.   .   .

My sled is a yellow plastic shell with a seat and two steering handles which look like the ears of a dog. I asked for it for Christmas after the last great snow which was three years ago: a great snow being any snow deeper than six inches and lasting longer than two days. My friend, Paul, who always gives me just what I ask for, braved the holiday lines at Toys R Us to get the one that matched my specifications. It has lived in closets and basements for two and a half years and this is its inaugural voyage.

Lulu and Marianne-Beth sprang from bed this morning, which is not always the case. We cooked a play-day breakfast of scrambled eggs and oatmeal pancakes, donned our mittens and hats and oohed appreciatively at the white world at our doorstep.

Beth pulls with gusto, dragging the sled and me over the sidewalk, as the cold sun picks out glitter in the snow and an occasional car moves in a lumbering metallic rhythm. Her hair trails from beneath her wool cap in a billowing path over her long tweed overcoat while her well-used hiking boots crunch on ice. Looking up at her from the ground, I see she looks exactly ten and I feel full because I have a best friend and an adventure.

I bump over sidewalk snow and laugh a clean gleeful laugh knowing that nothing can pull me down from my yellow plastic throne.

"Beth, Beth!" I call between laughs.

"This is wonderful," Beth says. "Hold on!" she yells and begins running across the street so that her momentum propels me and the sled up and over the curb. A man with a newspaper folded under his arm passes and pretends not to look at us.

"Grownups!" Lulu harrumphs. "It just kills them to see someone having fun, they can't bear it. They just walk around grumpy and worried and scared to smile at each other."

"The best part of having grown-up bodies is that we can pass for adults when we need to," Beth says.

"And we don't have parents telling us what to do!" Lulu adds emphatically.

Pulling Marianne on the sled is like having a pretend dog at the end of a rope. "Come on yellow dog!" Lulu shouts and runs at the curb, easily pulling the sled and Marianne-Beth up and onto the sidewalk.

We are the tallest people with a sled at the park. A couple of adults are on skis, the rest are standing with their arms folded, watching their offspring whoop and holler on hills.

We find our own private undisturbed slope. Marianne-Beth says "go" and pushes my back to get me started. I sail through a sea of leaping snow, laughing so hard that I can not even begin to understand the steering mechanism, too weak from laughter to get up after tipping over near the low wide boughs of spruce.

Beth masters the steering first, gripping and pulling the black handles while whooping and screaming. "I'm happy. I'm happy," she announces as she reaches the top of the hill and prepares to descend again.

I feel a release when she says that, a subtle relaxation in the nerves near my belly. If my mother was happy, then it was safe for me to be happy. If my mother was mad or depressed or tired, then I had to be nice to her, do everything she said and certainly not look happy myself. But watching Marianne glide expertly down the hill in her Beth-self, I see that she can make her own self happy and that I can be as I am.

Just as I'm getting pain in the tips of my fingers and my chin is going numb from such an intimate association with the elements, a man and a woman crest the hill. He wants to know how much the sled cost. I offer him the rope while Marianne says, "You can take a ride in it." We are both gleefully anticipating sharing the discovery of such wonderful entertainment with a possible kindred spirit.

"You go," he tells the woman with him who looks at the ground shyly.

"You're the one who's been talking about it," she says to him. "You go."

"No, you go."

"No, you go."

Finally Marianne says, "Well if you're not going, I will," and slides away in a spray of snow and giggles. I remember when I used to play the same game with my boyfriends. My mother taught me that to want something myself was rude and selfish. She thought it was better to tell other people what they should have than to have a preference herself and ask for it. But I have found it is more direct to ask for what I want. And I don't have to guess what Marianne might want, because she's good at saying what she does and doesn't want.

We decide to catch a bus before our faces freeze and fall off. We enter the city bus clutching the sides of yellow-dog sled and grinning with the self-satisfaction of an afternoon well spent. The bus is full of intrepid commuters who went to work although most of the city was closed down. They avert their eyes, as the snow dribbles off the treads on our hiking boots onto the impervious transit floor.

Lulu leans over to Beth and says, "Let's go trick or treating on Halloween."

. . .

Now that I have only eight days left at the cabin, Nora at the grocery has connected me with a man reputed to be a master of wood stoves. Harry arrives, a thin handsome eighty-year-old man with a full head of thick white hair. He chops cedar with a hatchet from the box of wood he brought, then warms his hands round the coffee I have given him. We sit in the cavernous wintery dark living room, feeding morsels of wood to the fire and ignoring the smoky column working its way from ceiling to floor. He cups his ear as I

speak as if he could catch my words in the palm of his hand.
He tells me his history of fires, and talks of the strong scent
of burning driftwood which clung to his jacket for months
after he returned from hitchhiking down the West Coast
when he was nineteen.

As he speaks, I can imagine the cuffs of his sleeves rolled
up, the ease of finding temporary work on the jobs young
men were hired to do. I see young men gathering in groups
and fearless on the sand dunes, drinking coffee and sipping
from silver flasks. Then I imagine Harry sleeping on a blanket and pillowing his head with a jacket, the sea in his ear.

I remember pictures of teenage boys being hippies, hitchhiking with backpacks, and the way my legs ached wanting
adventure and escape.

♦*Memory.* "So what do you want to be when you grow
up?" Uncle Ed asks, visiting our home on a business trip.

"I want to be a teacher," I say.

"Just like your mother," he says and smiles.

Really I want to be president and talk on TV, and answer questions like those men in the debates we watch. I
want to write books of course, but I said I wanted to be a
writer once and everyone laughed so that's a secret. I also
want to see lots of other countries, especially Africa because of the zebras and elephants there. I want to be a
singer, too, although I don't know how people become
one. Someday I will learn to play the guitar.♦

When I got older, I secretly hitchhiked to Seattle a couple
of times. It was an hour away from Bryce, but I was too
scared to keep doing it. The air was saturated with stories of
bad girls picked up by truck drivers and businessmen and
raped or maybe even killed. "What did they expect, out
there just asking for trouble," my mother said.

Harry leaves me staring mournfully at the fire which
sighs heavy thick breaths at the effort of trying to heat the
living room. "It's not fair!" I shout. "What boys get to do!

What girls can't do." Boys get to feel their oats, girls are held captive in elastic harnesses of bras and garter belts, sanitary napkins and girdles. Boys get to grow up and have money and run countries; girls get to be their secretaries and become mothers. "It's not fair!" I shout again.

I open the front door for air and smoke a cigarette on the porch, underneath the dripping overhang. It's one of several smokes I bummed from Harry.

"Hell, he can still breathe," Fuckit fumes.

Free-roving dogs bark from the center of the street. Their fur spiky from rain and mud, they jump at each other and play with their noses. It pisses me off to see them doing whatever they damn well please. "Raff, raff, raff," I bark at them, feeling like a disgruntled housebound bulldog.

◆*Memory.* Every Wednesday I get to wear my Girl Scout uniform to school with its shiny gold pins and my sash full of embroidered badges. Sometimes I rub my hands over my badges and remember all the things I learned to earn them. I could learn anything, I think. Sometimes my mind is like lightning and I know the answer at the moment the teacher finishes asking the question. My hand almost always goes up before anyone else's.

We get to write stories and I always get A's on them, except the teacher says that my penmanship is getting lazy. It's just that the words come out faster than I can write them if I try to be neat.

I sold five hundred boxes of Girl Scout cookies and got a prize. Mommy sold a lot of them in the teacher's room, too. I feel kind of funny about the ones she sold because she wants me to be grateful that she did it. It's not like I asked her.

I feel funny about the spelling bee, too. I liked the way we lined up in class and were given a word. We said the word out loud, then we spelled it, and then we said the word again. I outspelled everyone in the class and represented our room in the school fifth grade spelling bee. Mommy was a friend of the vice principal and knew that the spelling words would come from the back of the *World Book Dictionary*. She quizzed me on those words and said I couldn't tell anyone that I knew which words would be asked. I won and my class gave me a party but I didn't feel as good as when I won the first one all by myself. It felt like the time when I was little and Mommy took away the picture I was coloring and started coloring it herself and then sent it to a contest under my name.◆

I was good at memorizing and reciting back what I learned word for word. But I was twenty-four and had dropped out of graduate school to be a waitress at a pizza restaurant before I realized that I was really smart. After we closed I'd go around the corner to The Home Plate and talk with Bill, the bartender. He taught me to drink "White-Label-water-high" because it lasted a long time, and debated me endlessly about politics. He was a Republican, I was a feminist, and when it was closing time, he'd always tell the others at the bar, "She is a smart one, this gal. What a mind! But she'll get conservative when she gets older."

"No chance," I would say, clear that conservatism was forever behind me.

But I always left feeling exhilarated by the discussion and by the way I could argue from facts I had heard or read and not thought of again until our discussion. He's right, I thought, this is my intelligence. It's not that I can memorize facts that some teacher wants to hear. It's that I can find meaning in the pieces.

My mother believed in memorization. She had many sets of flash cards with multiplication tables and questions about history. To her, this was learning. For as long as I knew her, she mouthed the beliefs and opinions she had memorized in my grandparents' house and never expanded on them.

I imagine Lulu in the inner house. She writes stories and

poems in pencil on a wide-lined tablet. She makes up tunes and learns history by pretending she was there when it all happened. Lulu is good at pretending.

"It doesn't matter that she didn't even look at my picture, but nodded her head automatically and, 'That's nice,'" Lulu says, bouncing a foursquare ball. "It didn't hurt that she was too busy to hear my story and said she'd listen later but never did. I don't care that every time I sang around her she told me she needed quiet then." Lulu sticks her chin out. "I don't have feelings anymore," she says, "I've made them all go away."

"Then what's that aching in our stomach?" Carrie asks.

"I just wanted to be important," Lulu says. "I thought that if I didn't let them see my feelings then they would listen to me and be happy because I could write poems and make up stories. I was so excited after I wrote them that I couldn't keep them to myself, but she was the only one there, except for Jim, and he wanted her attention too. She just thought the most important thing was to clean the house and make a good impression.

I am crying now, long and loud. My stomach has stopped aching, but my chest is filled with a big grief. It's the first time I've cried as Lulu. I am crying as if I were ten, with long deep broken sounds that come up with hard breaths.

I put a log on the fire and open the door to let out more smoke. I am a girl camping out in the winter, all by myself. I am a woman who writes books and lets her house get messy. I know this and I keep crying in big gusts all evening. In the morning when I wake up, I begin crying again—because I spent too many years memorizing flash cards while wishing that someone would listen to my stories instead.

. . .

"Count your blessings," my mother would say when I protested her decisions. "There are a lot of people in the world who don't have what you have."

Today, when I think about my mother, I think that living well truly is the best revenge. And for this living, and the many ways it is different from my upbringing, I give thanks.

On this last evening of solitude, I thank the cabin and the land around the cabin for keeping me safe, for harboring my emotions and my inner children and for being faithful. I burn candles in all of the rooms and light a token fire in the wood stove. In the back room, on the writing table, hand-written papers are stacked beneath crystals and bloodstone.

"Notes!" Sarah says accusingly. "Where are the chapters? Nothing is typed! You have spent six weeks scribbling! How are you ever going to finish this book?"

I stand above the teetering mountain of yellow legal paper and Post-it notes, looking at the plank and the pillow I have sat on for these nearly six weeks, surrounded by crayon drawings on every wall.

"This work requires research," Memory says.

"So what did we get from all this work and all these feelings?" Fuckit asks. "Sarah is right, this book is going to take forever."

"What do you mean, what did you get?" Lulu asks indignantly. "You got to spend time with us! Just because it wasn't easy, doesn't mean it wasn't valuable!"

"Yeah!" Tinsel shouts and then Tayla roars like a lion.

"Bo boo boo ba bo!" Clingbaby says, making sound in the general excitement.

I light cedar and sage to cleanse the cabin and to invite friendly protective spirits to stay with it. I imagine the inner house room by room and notice that there are still closed doors that I have not yet opened.

"All in time," says Memory.

# 7

## *A Woman's Work Is Never Done*

THE INNER HOUSE resounds with ticking as seconds, minutes and hours march across the faces of the clocks. The clock my mother feeds me by, the tiny painted Swiss clock with a bird on it that says "cuckoo" by the hour, the alarms that wake me up, the school bells that divide my attention, the clock I measure into client hours and workshop days, the red digital numbers I race to make time for writing and songs. On the hall wall in the inner house, a round clock with bold black numbers sweeps away time with steady continuous hands.

"Are you ready yet? We can't be late. Don't waste time. Hurry up. Go faster." My mother is always counting the minutes as if there were never enough of them.

Old school calendars mark the right angle of this hallway of dark wood and forest green wallpaper. Dated papers show the years of endless preparation for the tests, the next grades, the future, college and work. All the years of getting ready for the next event.

"Time to grow up," my mother says. "You're old enough to know better. You're not a little girl any more."

There are no toys on the floor; no blocks or balls or crayons or dolls. Childhood ends at the bend of the hall.

I am always looking at the clock. How many more minutes do I have to finish? How many more minutes before I must start? How long until it's over? Once a minute has passed it is forever gone; on to the next one with no consideration for what has been.

"Time to eat. Time to go to school. Time to get a bra. Time to go to bed. Time to work," my mother says, peering anxiously at her wrist.

In this hall of ticking and chiming, there is no room for thought, hickery dickery dock. No time for play or feelings or rest. The clocks are a metronome for "Onward Christian Soldiers," which is playing throughout the house. Good soldiers go forward and don't let anything stop them, even if it kills them.

I am just past ten years old. I am pressed against the wall, opposite a large grandfather clock. I want to get away from it, but I'm hypnotized by the pendulum and cannot move or close my eyes.

New hair and sweat and breasts form to the rhythm of an unseen inner timepiece. If I don't think about them, they will go away.

My mother says, "What's wrong with you?! No one's going to like you if you act like that. Be neat, be on time, be obedient. There's a lot of things to do around here. Just take your mind off whatever it is that's bothering you. Do something for someone else for a change."

But I am always doing something for someone else. My mother holds my minutes and assigns them tasks. There are more tasks than minutes so there is no time for rest and play and laughing.

For many years, I have been trapped in this corner. This corner is what it meant to grow up. I stand eye to eye now with the grandfather clock. I practice tai chi in the corridor, coordinating movement to breath. I bring toys and shells and musical instruments into these passages. I wear earplugs so I can hear my heart beat. I practice moving in accord with my own rhythms. "I am going to tame you!" I tell the grandfather clock.

. . .

"Can't you see what time it is?" Sarah yells. "Get moving!"

"Just a minute," Lulu says. "This doesn't sound like any fun." She drags her feet in the inner house, pushing her body ahead with great effort and slowness.

"Time for a cigarette," Fuckit decides.

My mother's mail was piled on one manageable corner of her desk. She did not give to causes or subscribe to journals or get on feminist mailing lists. She didn't get letters from people she'd never met thanking her for writing a book or wanting a referral to a therapist in Arkansas or telling intimate stories of childhood. She did not write ideas for books, essays, poems, workshops, songs or plays on scraps of paper, nor did she have a trunk filled with journals, requiring four people to carry it. My mother wrote form letters and Xeroxed them for holidays.

As a writer, it is natural that I am surrounded by paper, but sometimes all this paper makes me tired just looking at it. It floats from spreading pile to spreading pile from table to floor to mattress depending on the ever-shifting, unending arrivals of new deadlines. Or dreadlines, as they become, laden with the fear of not doing well enough and of someone thinking I'm a flake.

I don't know how to make my life big enough to hold all of this paper. Sometimes I fear these papers run my life. I resort to subliminal tapes. I look with interest at books that tell me I can learn in my sleep or better yet, manage with only four to five hours of it. If only I could do more than one thing at the same time, if only I had a clone, or six arms or a secretary or better yet an entire staff. How much can one person get done? Is it possible for a Type A personality to develop Type B traits without sacrificing ambition? I am thirty-four years old and still struggling to be a grownup.

How do I balance meaningful relationships, being present with my clients, preparing, advertising and giving workshops and lectures, writing books and songs, figuring quarterly tax payments and keeping up with my inner life?

"Work, work, work," Lulu complains from the bottom of a familiar depression. "Responsibility. Commitment. Obligation. It's the end of us kids, that's for sure."

◆*Memory*. "You are going to sit at this table until you get those thank you notes done," my mother says. "Just hurry up, so I can go to the post office."

I think of the Avon pink powdered bath mitt my godmother gave me. Girl stuff! It made my nose itch even before I unwrapped it. "Thank you for the nice bath mitt," I write. Each word takes forever; I have to work hard to make them come out because my shoulders don't want to write them down. I keep stopping and looking out the window.

My mother gathers up the cards, addresses the envelopes and puts stamps on them. "Now you can go in and clean up your room before you set the table. There's a lot of work to do around here."◆

Each task was followed by another in unending sequence, with no time for taking a walk or gazing out windows or meditating. No one in my house whistled or sang while they worked. No one seemed to take genuine satisfaction in what they did.

Now I find myself thinking I must go as quickly as I can from task to task. Sarah recites lists of errands and deadlines, beginning first thing in the morning. All of this rushing and reciting makes me tense and uncomfortable. I lose my tolerance when life interrupts my outlines; I get anxious and stop breathing when I am in a hurry and I have to wait in line or stop for fifteen minutes in traffic or add an unexpected chore to my list.

YoungerOnes say it's all too hard; it's just too much work. I rebel against hurry by crossing my arms and engaging in procrastination. This incites Sarah to tell me that very bad things will happen unless I get moving, which makes me more anxious. Finally I grit my teeth and set into the task. I know this is not the most efficient use of energy but it sure is familiar.

In my family, work was the opposite of play. Play was frivolous and unnecessary. Play was selfish because it came from my own desires. Play was suspect because it was fun. My Protestant forefathers believed they had to work to get into heaven, sort of like working off the rent in advance. Heaven is expensive though, so it was important to work hard, being as solemn and sober as possible. The more suffering involved, the better. God did not create people to have a good time.

"Idle hands do the devil's work," I learned. The solution was to be perpetually busy so that I would not be accused of "daydreaming." Chores and embroidery and ironing sheets were good for me, not like reading library books or staring at the pebbles in the sidewalk and making up stories about them. Now I seem to convert all of life's activity into the category of work, which takes the fun out of it but justifies my attention.

Work meant doing the same task over and over again. Picking and snapping beans, shelling peas, peeling carrots and potatoes. My grandmother roped Jim and me to the plow and we played "horsey," pulling my grandmother and the plow through the furrows of dirt. Neither Jim nor I ever got to steer, nor did we plant seeds. The garden was work, a continuation of the Midwestern farms where my grandparents had grown up. I was not awed by its seasonal transformation. I preferred wild grasses and bugs. Children were for working. And work was not about wonder.

"So are you a good help to your mother?" the ladies at

church bent over to ask.

Grandpa did not abuse me after we moved next door, but "helping out" my mother was still doing what I didn't want to do. After I turned ten I had what my mother called "responsibilities." I ironed, dusted, washed floors, moldings and woodwork, set and cleared the table, and washed or dried the dishes. I scrubbed under the burner covers with SOS pads and coated the appliances with Spic 'N Span. My responsibilities came in boring and worrisome multitudes which chewed up evenings and Saturdays.

Jim did not have the same responsibilities and I began to realize that this was woman's work and I was supposed to learn to do it so that I could be a wife. I learned to spend as long as possible doing my homework since reading school books and writing qualified as a legitimate use of time. I wasn't supposed to want to play anymore. It was time I learned to work and that meant doing what I was told promptly and without a fuss. But inside my head I thought about what I read in the history books about indentured servants and slaves.

I am still rebelling against what I was taught about women's work. And I am still suspended on the outside of mysteries my mother failed to teach me. I was given chores which required no thinking, but never taught to cook. My job was to put cookie dough on cookie sheets or to ladle cupcake batter into paper cups, or to take a casserole from the freezer and turn on the oven. My mother liked to cook; children were supposed to do the jobs that adults didn't want to do themselves. Being old enough to work did not mean more rights, it only meant more work. Nor did it mean more reward; Jim and I weren't supposed to notice that my mother ate steak and fed us hamburger.

I was not yet eleven when my mother decided it was time that I "learned the value of a dollar." "Money doesn't grow on trees," she said.

"Okay, okay," I scream at her now as I balance my checkbook and run my hands through my hair. "But where exactly does it come from?"

◆*Memory.* I'm waiting for the bus to pick up strawberry pickers, wearing my sweater and coat and T-shirt. It's still mostly dark in the gas station parking lot, and all of the houses are still. I'm wearing the same clothes I wore yesterday and the day before. My pants have flattened strawberry prints on them from the knees down. At ten, I am the youngest kid here, except for Jennifer Merkif and her mother is the row boss. The smaller kids have to work behind a bigger kid, scavenging for the tiny berries that the big kid didn't bother to pick.

A row boss comes and checks my row and if she finds one strawberry, like she did yesterday, I have to start all over again in the same row. The most I have picked is one and a half flats. In the afternoon it is hot and dusty and my mother has been packing strawberry Jello in my lunch which melts into sweet goo. I don't know why she sends strawberry.

When I fill a flat I have to stretch my legs across wide bushy rows while carrying a heavy wooden crate. The row boss yells if she sees me squish any berries when I step across the rows. The older boys yell at me too and laugh. The checker is a long way away and sometimes she says that my boxes aren't full enough and then I have to go all the way back to my row and pick another box full before she'll punch my ticket. Friday I turn in my ticket which is all wadded up and crumpled after being pinned to my coat. I get paid fifty cents a flat. I'm supposed to give some of it to the church in my offering envelopes. I hate that.◆

My mother acted like an agent, setting up outside work for me. Unlike an agent, however, she did not try to get me a good deal. She told her customers that I would babysit and clean house for much less than the going child labor rate.

Once she even ordered napkins imprinted with Christmas slogans that Jim and I were supposed to sell door-to-door. We grossed about five cents a package. Most people didn't need Christmas napkins, unlike Girl Scout cookies that could be eaten, frozen or mashed with a rolling pin into pie crusts.

"It's not nice to talk about money," my mother said even as she was saying, daily, "We don't have enough money for that. We just don't have enough money. It's not like there's a man in the family working."

I was supposed to work hard, to be conscientious and polite, but this effort was not supposed to lead to money. Instead, it was supposed to make people like my mother, because she had such a reliable daughter. I believed that if I worked really hard, then people would like me too.

My family was suspicious of money. It was ungodly to have too much of it, but God was punishing you for your sins if you didn't have enough. Money was saved against a rainy day, not invested or enjoyed. My grandmother and grandfather grew vegetables and sold them to neighbors, at rates far below store prices, because it wasn't nice to ask for money. My mother opposed the teachers' union when they finally struck for higher wages. Despite the fact that schoolteachers were far behind most other professions in salary, and ignoring the reality of our own poverty, my mother thought teachers were just being mean to the school administration. My mother did not challenge authority.

Instead she regularly took cupcakes and cookies to the minister, the dentist, the school principal and the family doctor, going to their homes with paper plates of Betty Crocker goods even though she did not know them outside of their offices. When I think about my mother and authority, I imagine her in the Middle Ages, trying to escape the Inquisition by damning the witches and taking pots of porridge to the local priest.

For a number of years, I followed in my family's footsteps, diligently working for minimum wage. I worked as a file clerk, a waitress, an office temp, a research assistant, a work-study consumer protection advocate and a graveyard shift clerk at 7-Eleven. I've been paid to pick up golf balls at a driving range, to clean Motel 6 rooms and to make plant cuttings at a wholesale plant nursery in a greenhouse of women who were all paid less than the men who carried cans and drove trucks. I graduated summa cum laude from the University of Washington but knew nothing about finding a job that paid well or throwing myself into the currents of the middle class. My mother assumed that working was something to fall back on until a girl married and something to save her if she were disgraced by a divorce. Work was what I *had* to do, not what I wanted to do.

By the time I had to think about supporting myself fulltime, the days of playing school and imaginary store, of being excited when I learned a new skill, were far behind. It would only take a month or two on a job before I had to force myself to go to work in the morning, muttering about how I didn't want to go and watching the clocks eat time on the wall. I believed that my real life began after work.

I attended massage school in 1979. For $350 I learned a skill that would eventually propel me into the ranks of the self-employed. I made advertising leaflets using press-on letters and stick figure people miraculously cured by massage. I acquired business cards and learned to read tax codes. I learned by error as well—what questions to ask prospective clients, how to say the words "my fee is" without looking down. I even set the driers in my apartment on fire from the oil in my massage sheets. But no matter how much I have figured out, new mysteries of making a living are perpetually presenting themselves.

Self-employment requires a level of organization my mother never achieved. She was unable to determine priorities. Every task was cause for stress and worry. She was continually overwhelmed by the activity in her life and unable to stop it.

"Don't think too much of yourself," my mother said. "You think you're so smart but you don't know anything. You'll see how hard it is."

But she was, at least, under contract, given insurance, paid vacations and guaranteed an income. She did not have to sell herself over and over again. She did not hoard time for writing or singing or crayons.

"You're a failure," Sarah says, comparing me to the "real women" in power suits in the grocery store.

I am never sure when I have worked hard enough. The older I get, the more the words "financial stability" send a chill to my aging bones. During the inevitable slumps in self-employment I read all the Help Wanted ads in *The Seattle Times*. I inevitably find I am qualified for exactly the same work now as I was before I spent ten years writing and editing books and teaching workshops and doing body-mind integration work. I get depressed for a while and then launch a series of classes.

"Do your best," my mother always said. "Think about what other people want. Don't be selfish."

Every Saturday from the time I was ten, my mother was up by 8:00 a.m. and in the kitchen, preparing cupcakes for her housecalls on her day off. She did not approach visiting for the joy of spending time with someone else, but as a mission dependent on her tireless labor. Women were supposed to take care of people and not have any needs themselves.

I have gone in and out of political activism, in and out of letter writing, meetings and demonstrations. I have ended up an activist again, giving readings, lectures and workshops on healing from abuse. My work is always wider than the money that I make doing it. If I am happy with my writing and my life has achieved a rare balance or I've just had a vacation with Marianne, then I am full and I give total attention to my work. Hours of preparation pass easily. But then Sarah tells me I should do more faster, and I begin working just to get it done so I can do something else. I start feeling used up, unable to stop and replenish, as if I were a soldier on a long march.

Two months ago, I was in the cabin making pictures with crayons and playing in the sand. I listened to the wind and studied the movement of the trees. Now, I hardly even notice the weather. I don't talk to the YoungerOnes either. Lulu complains to Marianne. But the only way I know how to work is by winding myself up and not stopping until everything is done, which it never is.

. . .

"I am unable to listen to my answering machine without smoking a cigarette," I announce.

Jean raises an eyebrow and swivels slightly in her chair. She writes books, she speaks at conferences, she sees clients, she gets mail and phone calls from women in distress and she seems to have a life as well. What is the answer to this puzzle of doing? Why does doing seem like so much work?

"I feel too responsible!" I cry. "I have converted doing what I want into work and now I don't like it. I feel like Sarah's standing over me with a whip saying 'More, more, you're not getting anything done.'

"I want to make a contribution to my time," I tell Jean, feeling self-conscious, aware of psychological theories about delusions of grandeur. "I want to give what I can but I have an aversion to work. Oh, I do it, but the fact that it's work ruins it. I can't enjoy it. I feel inadequate. I compare myself to, um, other activists. When people thank me for what I've done, I'm too busy to bask in the gratitude even for a minute. I spend more time responding to other people than I spend responding to myself."

Once I was visiting a friend and we went to hear a Tibetan lama speak. We went early, in order to receive Buddhist names. This involved writing our name on a piece of paper which the lama then briefly meditated on. My name translated from Sanskrit meant 'Activity of All Good.' My friend got 'Queen of Great Bliss.' She gets to spend months just sitting still and breathing.

"I want to be Superwoman," I say, "I want to embrace this work. I just don't know if I'm cut out for it.

"On top of all that, I'm always worried about what people think of me. Am I measuring up? Am I polite enough? I get so worried that I say 'yes' to what I don't want to do and then get pissed off that they asked."

I feel stupid crying about this. But I'm afraid that my own visions will be torn away and I will be swept down an enormous river of everyone else's demands and expectations. I don't know how to protect myself without freaking out.

◆*Memory.* My mother is holding my chin between her fingers, saying, "Look at me, young lady. You will pay attention when I talk to you." My neck aches with fighting to turn my head away from her.

When I do look at her, I know she does not see anything good in me, only something evil that she must conquer.◆

When I first started seeing Jean, I couldn't look at her at all. I looked at the wall, the carpet, the bookcase, the trees out the window. I look at her more now. I have never felt cut down by her eyes.

"About the phone," Jean intervenes.

All this material and she wants to talk about the phone. "I want to take my phone and my goddamn phone machine and throw them out the window!" I say, enunciating each word carefully and glaring at her. "I hate the phone. It is always interrupting me and giving me more things to do! I would be happy if we got rid of them altogether and had the mail delivered twice a day instead. Sometimes I think my phone is a malevolent being!"

I run my hands through my hair and laugh. "I know it's stupid to have this many feelings about the phone. It's a metaphor. I'm living in the wrong culture."

"It's up to you to decide what you're willing to do," Jean

says, gently reminding me that I have to take charge of the machine age. She rests her head against the back of the chair and folds her sixty-two-year-old hands on her stomach.

"It makes me feel like I'm fighting for room. Work has always been about doing what I didn't want to do. I want to be heard but it all seems too complicated." My teeth are chattering. Inside, Sarah says that everyone else can manage their life but me.

"About the phone?" Jean repeats.

I roll my eyes at her and growl from the back of my throat. "I don't want one," I say. Jean has seen me like this before, determined to rant. She waits for me to get tired of it without the least sign of impatience. The effect is calming.

I look at the sign on her wall which says, "All you really have to do is breathe." I try it.

"It is about what you will and won't do," Jean says, when I can't find anything new to say. "It is up to you to decide what your boundaries will be. You don't have to get mad that someone's asked something of you if you've already decided what your limits are.

"Read your mail when you want to, save it up, answer it when you're in the mood. Find out right away what someone wants on the phone. You can do that."

Sometimes I hate it when Jean says I can do that. Exactly when was I supposed to have acquired these skills that I'm now supposed to have? "I just want to sit and look out a window and not do anything," I say.

Jean touches her turquoise necklace and tilts her head to the side, looking at me. I am afraid she'll say, "Stop whining and get on with it. You're lucky you get fan mail."

"See how long you can just sit and stare without doing anything," Jean says.

At home, I find the answer to that question is less than five minutes. I can sit in rebellion but not with permission. I never saw my mother rest. I never saw her stop to admire a sunset or a garden, nor close her eyes nor just breathe. It wasn't okay to stop. Sometimes I smoke just to be doing something.

I get up and start throwing darts. I feel more satisfaction than I felt with words in therapy as the darts sink their tips into the dart board.

"Just get out of my space," I yell as I throw. "I am going to be who I am no matter what." Thunk, bull's-eye.

"I am fucking tired of being told that I have created this reality. In my reality, we would have no phones, (thunk) no cars (thunk) and no money." I wrest the darts from the board and start all over again. "We would work four hours a day (thunk, thunk) to benefit the general community (thunk) and make things the rest of the time (thunk). We would garden and write and clean up and build reasonable housing and sing. We would have less stuff and more art." I throw darts for ten more minutes.

By the time I get to the phone I've made myself some tea and positioned my chair so that I can throw a dart between each phone call.

"I do not have to do anything I don't want to do," I write in bold Magic Marker. I tape the paper on the wall above the phone.

"But we want to enjoy what we are doing!" Lulu says. "And we don't want to worry about what impression we're making. How do we do that? That's what I want to know."

. . .

I am sitting in the opposite corner of the motel room, away from Marianne. She wants to walk down the street to the ocean beach, even though the wind is gusting and the rain hammers the roof in staccato taps. I am reading a murder mystery. The Cannon Beach motel is dark with the weather and the smallness of the windows.

Once in a while I peek at Marianne, but mostly I am avoiding her. I don't want to feel anything so I go away inside my skin.

She gets up and walks toward me. "It's because we're talking about living together," Marianne says.

"Is not," I declare and hold the book in front of my face.

I refuse to think about the fact that we're here on the coast of Oregon to look it over and check it out against our fantasies of living by the sea. Although I have been in relationships before, I have avoided this living together part. I couldn't imagine I'd be free to be myself if someone was there. Having someone at home would mean another critic telling me what to do or not do. She might have plans for my time and I might not have any for myself. Maybe I would become dependent on her and forget who I am; losing my wants and preferences to what she wants.

We've been together eighteen months, most weekends and some weeknights. I was never going to live with anyone. I didn't believe in it. I didn't believe in committed relationships either. What am I doing?

Is it all right to change my mind about what I want? Is play, good conversation, comfort and passion worth the loss of personal space? Is it safe to live with someone? People change in the confines of their houses. My family looked quite respectable from the outside.

We look at each other across the indoor-outdoor carpet.

"Well, maybe it's about living together," I admit. We laugh and the carpet stops looking so vast.

"But what if I don't like you on a daily basis? And what if you don't like me? I have many flaws." In my head I hear my mother say, "No one will like you if you act like that. You'll never get along with anyone!" What if she was right?

I always marveled at my friends who want a relationship more than anything, or the couples who move in together after a month of dating. There's a joke that goes, "What does a lesbian take on her first date?" "A U-Haul trailer." But for me, living with someone intimately has meant too many responsibilities and not being myself.

"I'm not going to be nice all the time when we live together," Marianne declares. From her tone, I know this is a declaration of Beth.

"Me neither," Lulu says. We're both standing now, hands on our hips and sticking out our tongues at each other.

"I was married for seven years," Marianne says. "And I decided never again. So this is going to be different. I'm never being a wife again."

"I suppose this means you'll never make me coffee in the morning, even though when I get up first I almost always make you tea."

"Maybe once," Marianne says.

"I am wedded to my writing," I say.

"You have already mentioned this one hundred times or so. I have things to do, too."

"I don't know if I can make enough noise around you. Or if I'll be able to relax with someone else in the same room day in and day out."

"I guess that's what we'll find out," Marianne says. "But I don't really think the other parts of ourselves will let us be quiet."

I hope not. But quiet is too familiar to me from childhood.

"I don't want to move to the Oregon coast," Marianne says. "It would be like living in a tunnel, with this one main road going through it. There aren't even any gardens."

"It'd be okay," I insist. I want to live by the water. I don't want to consider imperfections.

"It is not okay. In the winter it's a ghost town and in the summer it's a madhouse."

I want to ignore everything that's wrong with it, like my mother would.

"Louise, I like you," Marianne says. "We'll find a place we both want."

"I don't know if I'm ready," I say.

"I don't know if I am either, but since we haven't found a place to live that's probably okay.

"So now do you want to go for a walk?" Marianne asks.

"Only if we don't hold hands," I say, determined to make one last statement in favor of autonomy.

"What, hold your hand? No way," Marianne teases.

. . .

I am teaching workshops for incest survivors and professionals for the next two weekends and giving a lecture on the third. Sarah is having a conniption fit over all that must be done. I put off the preparation work. Sarah says, "What are you going to wear? Remember to take enough crayons. You'll never get it all done. Probably the workshops will bomb anyway and it will be your fault. Hurry up and get to work."

The workshops sounded like a good idea when I agreed to them and I always have a great time when I'm actually teaching. But preparation drives me crazy.

"I wish I was in Mexico, I wish I was in Greece. I wish I had a million dollars and didn't have to write this speech. I wish I'd had a different life, I wish I was writing a novel. I wish it was summer instead of spring, I wish I'd become a lawyer," YoungerOnes chant, led heartily by Lulu.

I look warily at the clock. Sarah yells, "You're wasting time." I smoke another cigarette.

"All right Memory," I say out loud. "Let's have a talk. You're an authority on time. Do I have enough of it or not? Does worrying if I have enough of it really help?"

"Time is a resource, a tool," Memory says. "You can do anything you want with it. You can invest it, spend it, enjoy it, fill it and kiss it goodbye."

"I'm afraid of wasting it," I say mournfully.

"The secret is to make time give you the kind of experiences you want," Memory says. "I don't mean that you get to decide what's going to happen. No, time usually doesn't allow that. Time likes interaction. Time likes to mix life up together, to cross paths and bring circumstance. But how you feel about it is up to you."

"Mumbo jumbo," Sarah says. "You're just lazy."

"Girls just want to have fun," Lulu sings, then says, "I will plan these workshops with Carrie if Sarah will shut up."

I write "Pet Clock" on a Post-it note and stick it on the clock in my office.

I feel a welcome spark of wanting to do what I have said I would do. I map out each hour of teaching, imagining a journey through childhood which includes time for songs and sound and curiosity as well as pain and Memory. I put my plans into loose-leaf binders. Then I Scotch-tape some of my favorite pictures from postcards and old calendars on the pages between the notes for my workshops. I cut out a picture of Maggie Kuhn, the sparkling octogenarian leader of the Gray Panthers. Below it I write, "I am enthusiastic, eager, alive and courageous." I add a picture of me as a baby waving my hand in the air, like I do now when I teach. I put in a postcard of a woman riding a dragon. I write, "Time for lunch. Take a walk. Good work," and "I am healing as I heal. I enjoy my work," below the pictures. I do this partly to encourage myself throughout the day, but mostly because it's fun to put together pictures and to find words that make me feel good. I am putting play into my work.

My mother said, "Why can't you just pretend to be happy? How you look reflects on me." To her, pretending to be happy was as close to happiness as we got. Work and being busy and what everyone else thought were much more important than how it all felt.

I walk up the hill to a store that sells embroidery hoops, yarn, fabric, paper and pens. I find strings of metallic beads used in crafts and attach them to the binder so that I can play with them as I teach.

# 8

---

# *Stunned in the Disaster Area*

IN THE INNER house a narrow door is set into the shadow of the grandfather clock. I open it to the room where all the disasters of the house are manifest. Socks and saddle shoes, school clothes, notebooks, pens, library books, shards of broken glass and pottery from mirrors and bowls make a dizzying collage on the small rectangle of floor. A pencil sketch of Jesus is thumbtacked crookedly to the wall next to the unmade bed. The dresser is shiny wood and too big for the small beige room.

I enter the open alcove that serves as a closet. The pillow from the bed is on the floor. I sit cross-legged on the pillow in the closet; I become eleven and twelve, hiding beneath the hanging shirts. During the day I button them up to my throat and tightly around each cuff. My favorite shirt is burgundy with a stiff collar and tails that cover me down to my legs.

Even in this closet, I hear the clocks ticking from all through the house, chiming numbers until I imagine that I am swinging from a pendulum in wider and wider arcs, suspended over a pit and holding on for dear life.

I hide from the clocks. I push myself farther into the recesses of the closet. A new monster has come and I am trying to hide from him. I take tiny fast breaths and go away to a gray land full of fog and mist.

My mind plays a song from the radio, "I am a rock, I am an island. And a rock feels no pain and an island never cries." I am practicing being a rock, a solid boulder of granite.

Every twenty minutes my mother yells: "Louise, what are you doing in there? Have you finished your homework?" Part of me is always listening for her footsteps so I can get up and pretend to be doing something.

She opens my door and walks in. The clock chimes eight times. The room is very small with both of us casting shadows on the walls from the light over the bed. "This room is a pigsty! If you can't take care of your things any better than this, you don't deserve to have any."

A chipmunk inhabits a cage on the bureau. Chipper races against the metal bars and plans escapes that take him over the living room draperies and under the dresser into the drawer where he shreds the T-shirts into a nest. I don't get to wear T-shirts under my blouses anymore, my mother says I have to wear a bra every day instead. At night I have a dent all the way around my chest from its stiff bottom ridge.

"I am cleaning it," I mutter and stoop to pick up a book without looking at her or at the floor. The floor sucks at my eyes if I look down.

"You better shape up or I'll talk to Reverend Hale about your attitude," she says.

My mother is words that wear away like water on stone. My mother sees messes and imperfections. But she can look right through disaster and walk away.

I am too big for the closet now. I'm knocking down walls and making plans for additions. I'm adding a skylight and an exit to the yard. I am putting everything I can't stand into words. I have turned disaster into constructive chaos.

. . .

I hate the city. I hate my neighbor. I hate my life, I think futilely as I storm through my apartment. It's too hot, it's too late, my downstairs neighbor has gone on too long with his piano and drummer and bass guitarist. It is his third rehearsal this week.

All week I've written notes saying, "We have to talk about this. I have a life too. I have to sleep." But he never responds to them, refusing to negotiate or to warn me ahead of time. The night before last, I called him on the phone but no one answered. Then I ran down the flight of stairs and pounded and kicked his door but no one came. I ran back upstairs and jumped up and down on the floor over his head, screaming, "Shut up, dammit, it's 1 a.m.!" I threw some darts and then dismantled my brick and board bookcase. Holding a brick high over my head, I let it come crashing with gravity to the floor, but the music didn't lower one decibel. When I ran into him on the stairwell yesterday, he told me I was being rude for making noises on his ceiling. Currently I hate his guts. Life in an artists' co-op is turning out to be a lot less romantic than it sounded.

I cannot imagine a woman making this much noise. I could escape to an all night restaurant but it's a late Sunday night in August and I want quiet. I return to violent fantasies and cigarettes, lecturing and hitting my neighbor in my imagination, sitting frozen in paralyzed rage.

Suddenly I am mad about everything I learned about being a girl.

◆*Memory.* We are each given a round white cardboard case zipped shut and told to take it to our folding chairs in this big room of linoleum at the top of J.C. Penney's. I am eleven and I'm at charm school.

The white case holds a dazzling array of cosmetics and facial cleansers, provided to us by Bonnie Bell, in miniature doll-sized bottles. Next week we're supposed to wear nylons and learn the correct way to finish our finger nails which I'm supposed to have stopped biting by now. "You will notice," the stiff-haired woman continues the tour of our cases with clearly enunciated words coming through her raspberry lips, "that there is both a bottle of clear and a bottle of pink pastel polish. The clear polish will protect your nails from dish soap and provide a luster for daily wear. The pink pastel is only for special occasions and parties."

I look at my nails. I don't like to think about my body too much. All the years of my mother's impatient upkeep tug at me and I sigh because all of this sounds like more work.

Before this, charm meant shiny medals that could be attached to bracelets or the green and pink crunchy marshmallow shapes in Lucky Charms breakfast cereal. But here it means looking like a lady so that Prince Charming will notice.

We move from hands to ankles, which we are supposed to pay attention to as we position our feet at ten and two o'clock. I feel squishy and square and sure that there is something wrong with my ankles. My body trips over itself and is spilling out in strange new ways. My mother is always yelling about that look on my face, or telling me to pick my feet up or not to slouch. Just as I knew it would, the dictionary slides from my head to the floor after five steps of my solo hideous journey across the room in front of the tongue clicking woman and a jury of my peers. "Now try again," she says, and I would rather not, but to say such a thing is unheard of, so I hold my breath and imagine that I have reached the other side.◆

I held onto those bottles until I left home for college; each one was opened only for charm school and never again. Fuckit thought that if I didn't use them, I wouldn't really have to be a girl.

"Fuck charm school," I think, as the floor beneath my feet vibrates to the rhythm of my downstairs neighbor's jam session. "I wish I'd learned firearms instead." I think fondly of making my neighbor dance to gunshots as the silverware rattles in my cupboards.

I take refuge in my writing room, which is not directly above the drummer, and stare at the funeral parlour across the road. At least the mortuary is quiet. I light another cigarette and glare at it. My body is too small for all the fierceness I feel and when nothing changes, I sit still and fume, just as I did for much of my adolescence. Outside the window a silver and blue unmarked van arrives with silent men who unload and wheel stretchers through the oversized garage doors. It's past midnight and the drummer is doing a solo, complete with cymbals.

My rage turns to despair, a familiar transition. The late night minutes pass slowly, like all the minutes of my adolescence. I worry about being tired when I'm with clients and whether I'll be able to listen to all the accounts of Memory I will hear tomorrow.

Sometimes I think I have had too much of it; too many stories of children assaulted in every opening by every device of the prurient adult imagination. But when I am working, I seem able to hear everything and feel calm and caring and full of respect for the woman before me who has survived all of this.

My eyes fall on the mountains of index cards and yellow legal pages and the smaller number of typed pages for this book. I am reluctant to go beyond YoungerOnes and take up Stunned and Fuckit, the inner voices of my adolescence. I'm good at hearing the terrible stories of my clients. I do not doubt that the world is full of terrible abuse. I know this especially from my own experience as a teenager.

"Everything got worse," Stunned says from inside the inner house.

Stunned has bangs that meet the top of her brown glasses and dull eyes that look alternatively fearful and dead. She avoids looking anyone in the eye. Her hair is cut square to her face like a curtain. Stunned is one part of my adolescence, the big sister of Tinsel; vulnerable, awkward and shy. Stunned is the part of me who was repeatedly betrayed and assaulted when I was between the ages of eleven and seventeen. I have listened to Stunned many times, but I am still reluctant to return to Memory with her. The worst things that happened to me happened to Stunned.

When I was eleven, I visited the Chamber of Horrors in Madame Tussaud's Wax Museum. I was horrified but not surprised at the rack and the hook, the guillotine and the noose. In the background a tape recorder played a man's screams and the sounds of dungeon doors being shut while across the velvet rope was an exhibit of Marie Antoinette being beheaded and Joan of Arc at the stake. Last weekend at my workshop for survivors, a woman screamed when I invited the group to make any sound they wanted. The room shook with her scream and the fear of the forbidden sound of a woman screaming. As Carrie, I could acknowledge the power of the scream, applaud its release and reassure the group. But inside of me, the part of me named Stunned, who began when I was eleven, waited for something bad to happen.

For many years, Stunned wanted to become a stone, numb and hard and not noticed. When I rock myself, I am Stunned rocking.

Stunned wanted to escape the feeling of ugly that rubbed off on me from my mother's words and my uncle's sexual abuse. But the only place to go was far from anyone else, a dull thick despairing consciousness. Stunned decided that being a girl was too dangerous. Women were victims, like my mother.

My mother used face powder and lipstick, but not mascara or eye shadow. I stood in the doorway to her room and watched her cover her freckles with a brown pad of chalk and roll her lips inward, smiling her company smile into the mirror and running a comb through her permanent. Once she showed me a picture from when she was a prom queen in college during the Korean War. She didn't say what that had been like. She didn't tell stories about parties or dates or boyfriends. I never knew that woman. My mother was hidden under layers of conservative clothing and dull make-up. The secrets of being a prom queen remained forever hidden.

Nor did my mother instruct me in the arts of beauty and they remained a mysterious secret. I was in awe of my friends who talked with their mothers about the changes in their bodies or pleaded for razors to shave their legs, and nylons to wear. My mother handed me bras and deodorant and when I got nylons, she gave me a girdle to go with them. But none of it was about being attractive. There was no hint of sex and sensuality in her apparel or mine.

At school, I discussed the obligatory boyfriends with my friends. I was assigned one who was round and wore glasses like myself. One of my friends said there was a place boys touched you and then you couldn't keep from going all the way with them. But no one else mentioned this and I wasn't sure what sex was or what it meant.

Certainly my mother never talked about it. Instead there were threats: "Those girls that wear those tight pants, what do they expect when they get in trouble. Girls make men do bad things. Men can't control themselves."

But as I reached puberty, my mother began to say, "Oh, if only I had a man. A man to protect me and to take care of me. No man's going to want two of someone else's kids though." My mother had been single for nine years and had not gone out on one date during that time. Later, when I was in college, my mother said, "I never felt sexual. I just wanted someone to hold me."

I had always wanted someone to hold me, too, but I couldn't imagine wanting a man to do it. When I was eleven and twelve, I wanted softness and something else I had no words for: an unquenchable desire from between my legs that made me want and then feel guilty.

It's 1:30 a.m. and the drummer is winding down. For a

while I have barely heard the racket, lost in Memory, adrift in the dressing rooms where my mother and I shopped for school clothes. Mirrors reflected my round shoulders and cellulite-pocked thighs from three sides of the room as my mother handed me dresses she had selected from the sale racks, with lace around the collars and lots of polyester. She favored tent dresses and jumpers over blouses for me while the popular girls wore soft sweaters and pleated skirts. When I was in high school, she took me to maternity shops and bought me pants with funny elastic panels and pregnant blouses. She said I was too fat for regular clothes at size 16. At first, I would try to be enthusiastic, because this was a mother-daughter outing, but I soon became irritable at the lack of color and style, and the shame of being in a maternity shop. So I reverted to trying to get it over with, agreeing to everything so that we could stop and have the sweet butterscotch sundae she had promised.

When I was eleven and twelve, my mother was always mad at me because I couldn't smile. She could yell all she wanted, she could tell the hairdresser how to cut my hair and make me wear the clothes she had selected. But she couldn't lift the corners of my mouth or make me pretend to be happy.

. . .

I am on an island again, nine months after beginning this book on a different island. For many years, I have visited the islands of the Pacific Northwest for writing and retreat and the feel of water on all sides of me. But now I am moving to one island, bringing my life and my phone with me.

I am starting a life which includes Marianne and our three cats. Under the circumstances, it feels like homesteading. If my mother saw the house, she'd say, "You're not going to live here are you? Why couldn't you find a house that looks like a house from the outside?" My mother's houses always looked tidy on the outside because the neighbors could see and make judgements. Her houses wouldn't have tarpaper instead of siding or get their water from a series of hoses that drip in and out of concrete cisterns.

My mother wouldn't notice the 180 degree view of Puget Sound because she would be worried about what visitors would think about the piles of chicken wire off the driveway and the wooden beams and studs visible in the interior. "You're not going to live in a house showing insulation. It's dangerous," she'd say.

It's true that the ceiling looks like someone took a large roll of Reynolds wrap to it. "Well, at least there's some insulation," Marianne says, "as we can see."

"Which will hopefully compensate for the daylight showing around the door and the window frames," I say.

We did not plan to live in a house lacking our customary accoutrements. We were housesitting for a friend on this island, and were intrigued by the quiet and the forests, the birds and the deer. We called the number on a note card posted on a bulletin board with information about renting a house.

Before we went to look at it, Marianne said, "But what if we like it."

"Oh, we won't," I blithely assured her. "This is the first house we made an appointment to see, we're just looking. We probably won't really find anything until next spring. Spring's a better time to move anyway."

Thus assured, we drove off the ferry and into a place my heart had longed for since I was twelve. It was love at first sight—not so much for the house as for the place. An island house situated down a winding forested road dotted with summer cabins and a couple of intrepid islanders who live here year round as we plan to do.

"Look at the windows," I would say to my mother. On the side of the house facing Puget Sound there are more windows than walls. Through them, ancient herons cackle in flight and the water below changes texture and color, framed by the alders now losing leaves in air so quiet that there is a sound to leaves meeting the ground.

My mother would be looking at the doormat. "All these pine needles," she would say, "you'll be vacuuming all the time."

She would be wrong; nothing could induce me to vacuum very often. Nor can I imagine her outside in a weathered cedar chair watching the lime green and bright red insects climb to the top of the long grass. My mother sat outside on concrete patios, with the bug zapper my aunt and uncle gave her for Christmas.

Nature made my mother nervous. She liked it cut short and covered with beauty bark and slug killer. During all the years my grandparents grew our food, a tradition my mother eventually continued, the ground was spread with poisons to keep the bugs away. My mother continued using pesticides; she never did understand that what she put into something affected what came out. Nor did she keep with the seasons. In the winter she planted plastic daffodils amidst the beauty bark and the sturdy, tidy perennials. There was no natural wildness in my mother's garden.

"I can't get the stove to turn on," Marianne says. I wade through our boxes, combined for the first time. We peer at the burner and wonder what happened to the pilot light.

I turn on the kitchen tap. The pipes sputter and spurt. "Uh, Marianne? I'm not sure we have water."

Further investigation reveals that we're out of propane for the stove. Soon we're going to have our first experience "blowing the hoses," which involves wading through vegetation to the stream and removing the sand from a cistern with a saucepan, then blowing the hoses free of debris, then sucking in a mouthful of mud to get it going again.

We unearth the Coleman camp stove and a can of refried beans. It is the romantic cabin of my adolescence, the life amidst nature that Stunned wished for. Almost. The whole house has only two doors. One door goes outside and one leads to the bathroom where it is possible to take a bath and stare out the full-length window at a panorama of Puget Sound. The other room is the combined bedroom, living room, kitchen and writing room. Although there are nooks, there are no floor to ceiling divisions. It's the first time I haven't had a room of my own. I never thought I would live this close to someone.

We named the house Habondia, in honor of the Goddess of Abundance. Right now all the abundance seems to be outside.

I suddenly feel suspicious of Marianne; anxious about the fact that she folds her underwear and likes fine glassware and wears dresses. We construct a division in the room with tall bookcases so that I have a nook for writing. I have never written with anyone near me. I have never lived with a lover. I wonder if I will grow easy with her presence or whether I'll be ever vigilant, afraid of her being in the house, afraid simply because the solitude of living alone has felt safe.

We announce every move we make. "I'm going to unpack this box." "I have to go to the bathroom." "I'm going to smoke a cigarette." We decide to take time out and write in our journals and not talk to each other. It's an effort not to talk, I feel self-conscious trying not to look at her. I can't think of anything to tell my journal. Stunned wishes the closet was big enough to sit in.

I sit at the picnic table and smoke, hoping we will have a long warm fall so I can escape outside if necessary. Marianne sighs largely and looks at me from her chair. The YoungerOnes want to go toward her, to cuddle and tickle and play, but Stunned keeps me seated and silent.

"I hope this wasn't a mistake," Marianne says.

"Especially after moving everything down three flights of stairs from my apartment," I say. "And I sold all my dishes at our sidewalk sale."

We chuckle as we think about the feats of physical strength and coordination we have pulled off in the last week, paring down our possessions to fit four hundred square feet. But I still can't get too near to her, nor does she come too close to me.

"I hope we don't freeze to death in the winter!" Marianne says. "I miss my garden."

"Get close again!" YoungerOnes urge.

"Time to Process," Carrie says.

Fuckit groans with the memory of long uncomfortable discussions in relationships gone by. Marianne and I have been involved with each other for two years and so far our discussions have never been grueling.

"But now we're under the same roof," Fuckit says. I see my mother standing in the doorway saying, "As long as you're under this roof, young lady, you'll do as I say." Can I be an equal under a roof with someone else? Can we both have all of what we want and live together?

We decide to have a creative consultation with our various inner characters. We tape a piece of paper to the antique cook stove and take turns writing sentences with different colored Magic Markers. "I like you but I'm scared." "Is there going to be enough room for me here?" "I'm mad at your boxes." "I'm mad at how much room the furniture takes."

"I don't like change," Stunned writes. She regards every new event with suspicion, especially those requiring assertiveness or intimacy. I wonder how long it will take to heal from the terrible unexpected changes of adolescence. Changes still bring more fear than anticipation.

Too often Sarah responds to Stunned by yelling at her because she's afraid or uncertain, which only makes it worse.

We decide to act out our sentences, to let each character speak for herself. When I'm Stunned, I become a mass with arms and legs folded, staring at a spot on the wall. I am disconnected from Marianne and seem to be at an impasse until

Carrie comes forward and says, "You don't have to do what you don't want to do, Stunned." Stunned stares at Carrie with distrust.

Marianne picks words from the sentences on the stove and starts singing them. YoungerOnes come forward. I join in with different words and begin drumming on the cardboard boxes. Suddenly I remember Marianne again as companion and playmate. Tinsel finds my fingers and I touch Marianne on the wrist. She holds out a hand toward me and in slow motion we hold our palms flat out against each other and then move them so that each of our palms covers the other's heart.

.   .   .

Uncle Kevin did not move in with us, but he took to visiting us a lot. The first time I met him, I was eleven and he was forty-five. He was the brother of one of my aunts. He'd recently moved to town and taken up residence with his elderly parents, opening a watch repair shop adjacent to their house. Like my mother, Uncle Kevin knew the power of gifts. He brought watches and clocks and Dip-it, a cleaner for silver. He offered help around the house, bearing hammers and saws and wrenches.

He came in the hour between school and my mother's arrival home with my brother. He came with nooses that he put around my neck and straight pins which he poked into my nipples. He brought Monopoly pieces which he put into my anus. He shit in our toilet and made me eat it. He bounced on me and called me "bitch, cunt, whore." He said I liked it.

I said nothing. I had no language, no reference in books or movies. My mother always gave him her company smile and invited him to stay for dinner when she got home and he was there. My mother dropped me at his house while she went to the dentist or shopped. My mother thanked him for picking me up from Girl Scouts and made me sit at the dining room table and write him thank you notes for his latest watch or clock gift. On my sixteenth birthday he telephoned my mother and said he had a present for me. He came over to our house and gave my brother a car. Then he said, "Oh happy birthday, Louise," while my mother said, "Oh how nice for Jim."

Although my mother continually made judgements about strangers, especially women, she automatically gave relatives the stamp of approval. All we knew about Uncle Kevin was that he was divorced like my mother and that his daughter had refused to see him since she left home ten years earlier. The latter was whispered among my relatives as evidence of his daughter's ingratitude. Everyone thought he was "interested" in my mother because they were both divorced.

Years later when I was flooded with memories of Uncle Kevin's abuse, I asked my mother about him and the two-and-a-half years he was so constantly around. She said, "I never liked him. He was uncomfortable with adults and seemed more at home with you kids. I was afraid of him, so I always had you kids with me when I was around him."

But what about me, I wanted to ask, not for the first time. Why did you allow him to be alone with me when you were too scared to be alone with him yourself? He liked to molest me on my mother's bed. Once my mother arrived home early from Saturday errands and stood silently in the doorway to her bedroom. Uncle Kevin was on top of me, poking me with straight pins. I saw my mother reflected in her own dresser mirror, framed by the door. Then I saw her back as she silently left the house in order to come back in again, banging the screen door to warn Kevin of her arrival.

I stop breathing and thinking just like I did then.

"Leave us alone," Fuckit says to Memory. "She was a jerk. He was a jerk. So what? It's not like it was the first time she let us down."

"Cheer up, Stunned. At least we don't have to live with

them anymore," Fuckit continues.

I leave my writing nook to stand in the rain and smoke a cigarette. Then I chop wood. Raindrops fall from my bangs into my eyes. I raise the ax above my head and feel solid and strong when the wood splits all the way down.

"You couldn't count on her, not ever," Stunned says.

◆*Memory*. This is the third time I've changed my underwear today. I roll the other ones with the brown stuff on them into a ball and stuff them in the back of my drawer. I keep thinking it will stop soon; even the things Uncle Kevin does stop after a while. What if this brown is something he did?

My skin feels hot and greasy and I just want to sit down. I have a sinking feeling this is the period that was explained in the booklet we got a couple of years ago in school. "So You're a Young Lady Now," it was titled, with a pink cover and little stars. Inside were cross sections of ovaries and fallopian tubes which I guess are buried somewhere by my intestines. There was a movie, too. Loretta Young narrated it. All the boys tried to steal the booklets, but we weren't supposed to tell them anything about the movie or show them the booklet. Todd snapped my bra strap and Jimmy tried to get in my desk to grab it, but they didn't succeed.

If we're on our period, we have to tell the P.E. teacher in front of everyone and then we go to the library. I don't like P.E. but I don't want everyone to know. I thought I wouldn't ever have to because I had been determined that it wasn't going to happen to me.

My mother is in her room. I stand in the doorway and look at the floor. "I, uh, think I started, uh, my underpants, there's stuff on them." I am getting that dizzy feeling that I can't let her see.

The Kotex comes in an enormous carton. She reaches in and hands me a thick rectangle of white and a small box with a strap in it. I finger the Kotex by myself in the bathroom and fidget with the elastic strap. I thought it would be thin like a napkin. Instead it makes me walk bowlegged. I don't like how it makes me feel that place in my body I am trying to forget.

My mother is waiting outside the bathroom. "You're a young lady now," she says. I know she passes out those booklets to the girls in the sixth grade but she never talked to me about it herself. She is fidgeting and blushing and trying to look like this is a good event.

"Sometimes you get cramps," she says. "It feels like having to go to the bathroom all the time. Grandma always said, 'Just take your mind off it and you won't notice the hurting.'"

This is the first time she has ever quoted my grandmother. I just want her to stop talking and leave me alone. We are on dangerous ground discussing the place between my legs.

"When I started, I was twelve, a little younger than you," she continues. "I was out back picking berries. Your grandma handed me a rag and told me to put it in my underpants and go back to work.

"Well you're growing up now. You better get ready for the party over at Jenny's."

But I don't want to grow up, I think. I want to fly away like Peter Pan did. But if I'm grown up, another voice whispers, my mother will have to listen to me and treat me like an adult.

My Aunt Jenny and Uncle Hank have a new house and this is a party to show it off. It has a sunken living room and a white carpet. I'm afraid to walk across it, afraid of leaving a trail of dots, afraid to sit in the golden chair and spill. I am in a long narrow tunnel and the light at either end is a pinprick far away. I lean against a wall.

The adults are talking and eating. The cousins my age are all boys and they are in a group together. Uncle Kevin comes toward me with a glass of punch in his hand.

"So you're a young lady now," he says in a voice thick with contempt and sarcasm. "Your mother told me."

I am becoming part of the wall. Inside I say, I'll never tell her anything again. How could she have told him? At least I can keep a secret.◆

At thirty-five, I've had a lot of time to get used to having a period. "I'm a young lady now," I announce to Marianne monthly. I long for menstrual huts where women of other times sweated and shared and colored the ground red. I've fingerpainted with my menstrual blood in order to claim the power of my own fertility. I have come to welcome the intensity of emotion and sexuality that comes before I bleed and as I begin. When Marianne bleeds she puts her tampons in a bowl of water and feeds the rich redness to our plants. This blood is about life and fecundity, not illness or wounds or curses.

But when I was twelve and thirteen, menstruating was widely regarded as part of God's curse for Eve. The magazines showed Twiggy and women with tiny painted tidy bodies. My body was always leaking: sweat, blood, dandruff, and mucus. There was too much of me to keep track of and I couldn't control any of it.

Emotions whirled like a cyclone, sucking and lifting me up from the ground, taking me to places my mother named "crazy," "insane," and "incorrigible." Then she would say I should be "put away," "locked up," "made to behave." I was afraid of her descriptions of me. I tried not to show my emotions on my face. But they were too big.

I have a manila folder of writings saved from the seventh and eighth grade. Pencilled poems and stories which say, "Sharon, read" at the top, from when my friend Sharon and I traded our poetry the way other kids traded notes.

It used to make me shudder to try to read through this folder. "Melodramatic!" Sarah said. "Adolescent." I looked down my nose at raw stanzas that read, "Desperation clutches my heart, but no one understands. I scream for love and care, but no one hears or cares." I wanted this teenager to be less direct, to understate, to find images and metaphor. But as Stunned, I was only beginning my quest to fit words to feelings.

"Just who do you think you are?" my mother would yell. "You just exaggerate. You've got nothing to complain about. You're just acting that way to hurt me."

Once I became a teenager, my mother had a new permission to dislike me. She could be critical and count on everyone else to understand how difficult teenagers could be. I was finally old enough to be posed as her persecutor. Not only that, but "teenagers think they know everything," she said, dismissing my visions and passion. "You just think you're so smart, but you don't have any common sense. Bad things happen to girls like you who don't respect their mothers."

◆*Memory.* Yesterday Uncle Kevin came while I was singing "We Shall Overcome" with my guitar, on the floor of my closet. He made me eat from the toilet.

This morning I am flashing stainless steel razor blades against my wrists, slicing into my skin. "I don't care. I'm too tired. Growing up is too far away," I say.

I stand in front of my dresser mirror, holding the razor blades my mother uses on her armpits and legs to get rid of the hair and make herself clean and smooth. I am far away from the blood as it rises in tidy thin lines which topple and run in bright red streams down my wrists.

I look away from the blood and meet my eyes in the mirror. I hear myself say, "Help me, help," like a little kid. Then someone else inside of me gets out white swatches of adhesive tape and straps up the cuts and gets me on the school bus. All day I finger my cuts.

My mother is informed of my attempt by the school authorities. "You just want attention," my mother says accusingly. "How do you think this makes me look? If you try something like that again, I'll kill you."

The school nurse calls my mother after I faint repeatedly in art class. "Do you want me to put you in reform school?" my mother says. "You're crazy."◆

Now I know I was mad. Furious. Outraged. Despairing.

I imagined building a wall in my chest. I closed the door to my throat. At times I could not think or speak. I was surrounded by nothingness. Movement involved pushing myself through gray water.

Stunned scuffs through the rooms of the inner house but does not see them. Sharp hot currents flood my body and make my hands want to tear away at my skin. The air is so thick that words take a long time to hear. Uncle Kevin turned me to ice. My mother followed like a blowtorch, shooting long searing flames from her throat. I froze and disintegrated. I evaporated and lost my balance until the ground pulled me under. I boiled with the silent frustration and hatred that causes poltergeists to shatter television screens into falling windows of glass and to throw vases of flowers across the room. Young ladies weren't supposed to have feelings. They were supposed to be obedient and cheerful and respectful. The things Uncle Kevin did were not supposed to exist.

But inside, beneath the despair and rage was an unquiet question that haunted me. Who am I? I asked. I knew that if I could find the answer, there would be hope.

．　．　．

"Yea, it's Halloween!" eight-year-old Tinsel says and Lulu seconds with, "It's about time!"

When I was Tinsel, I dressed up as a witch and wandered the neighborhood with my brother Jim who was a clown, until our shopping bags bulged with Tootsie Rolls, Dots and miniature Sugar Daddys. I had learned that the best plan was to eat as much of our bounty as was practical while we were on our rounds, for when we got home, we would have to put our candy in big glass jars. After a couple of days, our mother would appropriate the jars for use in her classroom, where she gave a bit of candy to students who got an A or cleaned the blackboard. Our inevitable protests of "That was my candy!" were met with my mother saying, "Too much candy isn't good for you. You had enough. Don't whine."

I still think of Jim as a clown, smiling at what's not funny in our childhood photos. But I no longer think of witches as ugly women with warts. Now I know that witches are women and men who work with ritual and honor the goddess. Witches work in harmony with the power of the seasons and the cycles of life and death. Witches raise energy and work with magic, guided by the maxim, "Do what you will and harm none." Witches honor trees and herbs and cats, the rhythm of healing and the power of intention.

Halloween marks the end of the ancient lunar calendar year. It is the night when the veil between the world of physical bodies and the world of spirits is thin. It is a time to invoke ancestors and to listen for wisdom.

Marianne and I have a pumpkin on our altar, amidst fall leaves, crystals, mirrors and candles. In the corner we have poured a glass of chardonnay for the spirits we wish to invoke. Marianne invites her grandmothers and aunts to speak to her. I invoke Virginia Woolf, Gertrude Stein, Sappho, Sylvia Plath, Zora Neale Hurston, Brenda Ueland and Vera Brittain. I imagine them writing with pen and typewriter, by candle light and kerosene lamp, taking the time to pay serious attention to themselves and their craft. I thank them and ask them to teach me from their wisdom and creative spirit.

Marianne and I drum and face the directions; east, south, west and north, meditating on the elements. We imagine a circle of light around our cabin, to protect us and to define the space of our magic. We kiss and toast each other with wine. We hold hands and breathe together. We imagine roots from the bottom of our feet connecting us with the earth and sunlight warming the top of our heads to join us with the sky. We stand with our eyes closed, holding hands, inhaling the sweet scent of incense and warm air.

We take off our clothes. Every Halloween we paint each other. Marianne circles me, holding a stick of red body paint in her hand. She paints my face with curves and moons. She draws green lines on my chest and an oval around my navel. With blue she draws a river on my thighs. I feel her painting a shield on my back. I breathe in the smell of the make-up paints and the incense as she draws a vision on my body. I think about the ancient statues and paintings of round fleshy, breasty women made before the bodies of women who had undergone two centuries of being burned, shamed and compressed. I am a fluid sculpture, yielding to the hands and designs of this woman I trust.

I stand in front of the full length mirror. I am a shaman, a warrior, an old spirit. "Wise child," YoungerOnes say. "Dear body," Carrie says. "When are you going to lose . . . " Sarah begins, but Carrie says, "Dear body," again. Marianne takes my picture to add to those of our last three years.

I follow the lines of Marianne's face with my paint stick. I circle her nipples and breasts and bless them with health. I paint a life flame from her vulva to her chest. I draw purple lines from her toe nails to her thighs. With my left hand, I stroke her.

With our hands we are loving our women bodies, filling ourselves with enough love to safeguard us as we walk through the danger and challenges of our lives as women. Marianne and I part to meditate by ourselves.

I hold my black mirror of obsidian and let my eyes go soft so that I no longer see my reflection, but focus inside myself instead, crying on this anniversary of the end of my relationship with my mother.

I return to my mother's bedroom where I am pinned beneath Kevin and my mother appears in her mirror, coming forward and then turning and walking away. In that moment

I do not feel surprise, only shame and confusion. I see Stunned on the bed looking dazed, not taking breaths, so still that she looks like a mannequin.

"It's no use," I thought then. "Nothing matters. I wish I was dead." My relationship with my mother was a series of determinations to give up on her; telling myself over and over never to want anything from her.

I stare into my mirror and feel my legacy of paralysis and inertia.

"I will never leave you," Carrie tells Stunned.

Then I have an image of a woman writing; one of the writers I invoked. How strong her face looks, how sure the movement of her pen.

"You are the writer," she tells Stunned, and I feel as if she has blessed me.

"Aw, Stunned, I love you," Marianne says when we come together to share our experiences. Stunned is still taking that in.

"Trick or treat time!" Lulu announces. Marianne and I take turns going outside and knocking on the door. "Trick or treat!" each of us yells and tells of the elaborate tricks she will perform unless she gets a treat, which of course we do.

We release the directions and open the circle. An owl hoots in the fir tree next to our cabin as we make love on our platform bed.

# 9

# *Fuckit Dances*

MEMORY BECKONS from the front door and I follow through the labyrinth of dim halls. The clocks seem deafening but Memory begins chanting, "Hope, hope, hope."

I stop in front of a door splintered on the outside as if knives had been thrown at it. My mother has painted, "No one will like you if you act like that," over the door frame in Day-Glo pink.

On the door a pointed middle finger is dominant in the newspaper photo of an anti-war protester. Beneath that is a hand in a V meaning peace from *Time* magazine. Beneath that is a piece of paper changed daily which says, "1,461 days until I'm eighteen," four years to the day. Carved into the door frame are the words, "Keep out."

There are two twin beds next to opposing walls. I am standing by the bed which is under the window. The wall beside it is decorated with a black-light poster of a psychedelic peace symbol. Love beads and a copy of the *Berkeley Barb* newspaper are on the floor next to the bed. I am staring out the window, watching demonstrations and love-ins, communes and free speech. Music, peace and people, I think. That's what I want. Not this house of hypocrisy and conservatism and confinement. I tear the sheet off the bed and begin ripping it. I am making a rope to escape from this second story window. I have to get away from here. I'm going to join those people who are talking about love and stopping war and sharing food and clothes. I have found a tribe. I am refusing to follow the narrow path of my mother's people.

I wear jeans I have smuggled home from a thrift shop and a man's blue work shirt I bought with babysitting money. These are the first clothes I have bought on my own and my mother forbids me to wear them. She'll yell when she sees me, but I don't care.

I dangle the rope from the window but it stops well above the ground.

My mother flings open the door and stands holding a handful of paring knives. She slices open my mail and then throws it at me. "What are you wearing?" she says. "You're not wearing those." She walks to the window and closes the curtain. Her nose curls at the love beads. She throws a paring knife at the poster. She seizes on the *Berkeley Barb* and begins yelling about Communist takeovers and bad influences.

"Fuck you," I say, without moving my lips or speaking above a whisper. "What do you know?"

My mother puts me on restriction. She forbids me to see certain friends. She questions my teachers and tells them I am a problem.

But I am listening hard to the whispers that come in through my window. I hear people saying that authority should be questioned and held accountable. I watch unarmed people in jeans and T-shirts bleed at the hands of police. Peace, love, and freedom are words that make me ache with excitement and vision. We can change the world, I think. Nothing has to be the way it is.

Stunned shares this bedroom. She is hiding under the other bed, writing secret poems in tiny printing. Under her pillow is a diary with a lock that my mother has broken. Stunned has a lump in her mattress so that she will always be in a state of readiness. Stunned has a candle by the bed that she tries to disappear into. On her bed are schoolbooks and the wigs and maternity clothes my mother bought for me to wear to school.

By the door is the paper bag for carrying my jeans to school.

I put "White Rabbit" on the record player and dance in my adult body in this room. I bring in drums and a synthesizer and a podium to be heard from. I write speeches and plan workshops. I listen for what resonates inside of me and pass it on in my fullest voice.

. . .

I liked high school because finally I had a choice. There was no longer just English, but Satire, Creative Writing, Drama, Literature and Debate. The school district had just acquired a batch of affordable first-year teachers. They brought what they knew of the world with them. They had not grown up in Bryce or been there a long time like the librarian, the school counselor and the football coach. They were mostly single and lived in newer apartments and neighborhoods. I tested my newly forming social consciousness in writing essays, speaking on the debate team and hanging around their desks after school.

My four year high school had four hundred students and was the largest school I had ever attended. There was a school paper and an ice cream machine and school activities which were broadcast each morning from speakers connected to the office.

I stood with my girlfriends in a cluster by my locker. I was the most political of our group. I read the newspaper and had opinions. I identified with hippies. I wanted to live in a city. A couple of times I told my friends I hated my mother. This was a far more radical act than my politics. An embarrassed silence followed. Then one of us would change the subject.

We shared records, consulted Ouija boards, held seances, talked about teachers and movies, ate potato chips and drank pop. We didn't talk about feelings or our families. One of my friends had a house with a rec room and another had a den off the garage where we could gather away from adults.

I didn't like to bring my friends home. At my house, there was no escaping my mother. She would offer my friends food and then ask them questions about school, being nice and too friendly. Then she'd say, "Louise should get her hair cut like you," or "Tell Louise she would look so much more attractive if she'd just smile instead of looking so sullen." Once or twice Fuckit broke out and I made a sarcastic retort. I was, after all, standing right there next to my friend. But when that happened I felt too sensitive and too emotional, wrong for objecting because my mother was being nice to my friend. I liked my friends' houses better.

At home, my mother fed me grapefruit and dry toast and packed lunches of hard boiled eggs and cans of Sego Diet Liquid. I weighed 130 lbs at twelve, 140 at thirteen, 160 at fourteen, 180 at sixteen. I snuck into her freezer and ate the cookies she had frozen for company and Saturday deliveries. I paced her kitchen and ate lumps of brown sugar from the box and once a can of tiny shrimp that she had bought for herself.

◆*Memory.* Bessie Salt has no skin showing on her face, only layers of powder and rouge. All her curtains are drawn this Sunday afternoon in May and there's no air in this room of old couches and chairs.

I have *Catch 22* in my hands as I stand at the doorway behind my mother, waiting to be offered a seat. I never leave home without a book so that no matter where my mother takes me, I can escape.

When Mrs. Salt sees me she says, "Well, she's a fat one, isn't she. How old is she? About twelve?"

"She is fat," my mother agrees. "I just don't know what to do with her," she sighs tiredly. "I've been trying to watch what she eats. I just read about this grapefruit diet."

My mother hands Mrs. Salt a plate of cupcakes. I am shivering in the dark.

"Well, we won't give her any of these," Mrs. Salt says.

I hate my body for blushing. I hate my fat body for wanting a cupcake. I hate my body for feeling hurt that my mother would agree in this diagnosis of fat. I take my book to the chair farthest away. I don't look up for two hours. I climb between the pages while a small part of me listens to their conversation.

When we get into the car I look out the window and ignore everything my mother says. I narrow my eyes and harden my chin and think, I hate you.◆

I was fourteen years old in 1968. While my mother held fast to all the rules she had inherited, dismissing the 1960s as the work of Communist infiltrators, I embraced it. I joined committees to begin coffeehouses, wrote songs about soldiers throwing down their guns and learned the guitar chords for "Come on people now, smile on your brother."

While Stunned obsessed after every social interaction and waited for the next disaster, Fuckit plunged forward, joining the debate team and participating in classroom discussions on world affairs. While Stunned feared consequences, Fuckit got a thrill from challenging the forbidden.

My adolescence was twined around these two parts of my personality. Stunned, the shy introspective writer, full of big heavy emotions and needy frightened eyes. And Fuckit, the Leo of my birth sign, the part of my self unable to just take it. I could not give up on spoken words or sit silent while my mother took up all the room. Fuckit is the part of myself who fought back.

She is the adolescent full of passion with a fast smart mind and no body. She is my wildness and rebellion. She hates hypocrisy. When Fuckit is aroused I can't hold my tongue. The intensity of my convictions inspires Fuckit with confidence and fiery certainty. "I like to be eccentric," Fuckit says, "I like to be noticed." She snaps her fingers and tosses her head. She scuffs the floor of the inner house with her Spanish boots. She plays the guitar and bows to imaginary admiring multitudes. Fuckit likes to be admired.

For a long time, Fuckit has been my favorite part. She helped me leave home. She kept me from getting married or selling out my creative time. She has kept me true to myself. Without her, I'd never be able to stand in front of groups of people and talk about incest and healing, citing myself as an example.

Fuckit is also the guardian of my anger. She learned to use words to combat my mother's continual criticism. I developed my own opinion of my mother's flaws. "You just want everyone to think you're so helpless," I'd yell at her in the heat of our battles. "You just make everyone owe you. You want things to look good but you don't care how they really are." Sentences would flow from the reserves of emotion, but my mother screamed over the top of them, "You'll do what I say, young lady, as long as you're in this house."

I sharpened my sentences and yelled back until I couldn't hold myself up any more and ran to my room. I believed that if I could say the right sentences, I would win, she would listen and see me. But I never had the last word.

Instead, I acquired a sensitivity to criticism and an obsession about defending myself. For many years, when anyone gave me feedback, I found it hard to breathe. Criticism meant I was wrong and bad. I was supposed to be what someone else wanted me to be. Feedback felt just like another way of saying, "You fucked up." I still brace myself for confrontation, though being a therapist and a teacher has helped me to breathe and recognize my defensiveness. I consider what is said and decide what feels true or not and then reply, at least sometimes.

But being a public person brings new opportunities to experience criticism. Faceless book reviewers distribute opinions on my sanity and style to journals and magazines. I receive these in thick envelopes from the press without further comment. They are mostly good and I feel happy for a moment before I toss them into my "to file" pile. But once in a while, the reviewer takes a dislike to me and my work, and I begin foaming at the mouth.

"So what? Big deal," I tell myself, but inside Fuckit has taken to the podium and is heading into rebuttal.

I have met thousands of people at workshops and readings and through my books. Sometimes they write me letters. I know nothing about them when I see their return addresses on the envelopes. But their words are personal and addressed to me. Usually they are words of gratitude, support and strength. I tie them with ribbons and put them away in boxes.

But today I got a letter from a woman who had attended the reading I gave on Mother's Day weekend in which I read from a draft of this book and talked about what I have been learning about healing the daughter in this last year and a half.

She begins by saying that she got six Mother's Day cards this year. She says I have to forgive my mother so that my mother can forgive herself. And anyway, I must be hate-filled to go around saying these things about my mother. She signs it, "Love."

"Hate-filled? Us?" YoungerOnes say. I feel bad that anyone would think that of me.

"I told you you'd get in trouble for saying those things," Sarah says. "What do you know anyway?"

Carrie tries to remind me of the women who stayed afterward telling stories of mothers who locked them in closets or hit them or knocked them down with words. Women who shook my hand or nodded or whose eyes filled with tears. But they seem far away and this letter is on the table in front of me.

"Well I do hate," Fuckit says. "I hate abuse. I hate that we're supposed to romanticize our childhood and not name the ways we were mistreated. Especially when it comes to mothers. We must take care of them by forgiving them. They can't be expected to take responsibility for themselves. I suppose it's better to pretend than to be mad! Fuck!

"It would be easier if my mother wasn't a woman," Fuckit continues. "It's not a surprise that men abuse children. It's pretty much the sort of thing one expects from a gender which produces such a large number of rapists, soldiers and wife beaters, to say nothing of serial murderers and conscienceless corporate executives."

Fuckit lectures and analyzes through lunch and dinner, returning to this letter far more often than I return to letters that tell me I'm doing important work.

I could spend a couple more days doing this, hoping that the letter would bury itself under the incoming pile while continuing to lecture this woman in the odd moments left for unresolved business. I know writing a letter to her will make me feel better but I grumble about having to take the time to do it.

"If only I had thicker skin and didn't care," Fuckit says. "I don't want to spend time doing this."

"But you like to be heard, Fuckit," Memory says. "It's a waste to keep all those words rattling repetitively around in your mind.

"Besides, when you feel a lot about something, then you know there's something important for you in whatever's happening."

"Sometimes I hate the timing of it," Fuckit says.

"The timing is when it is," Memory replies, "but tell me, what did this experience give to you?"

Fuckit snorts impatiently. "I would rather do what I want when I want to do it," she says.

"Fuckit just wants to be liked," Sarah says derisively.

"I think it was important because it made us think about hatred and acknowledge our anger," Carrie says. "We do hate behaviors and unfair circumstances. We felt like our mother hated us and nothing we did could change that. But the more we write about our experience with her the less hatred we feel, only anger over specific incidents."

"I'd rather feel the praise," Fuckit says to Memory.

I tell my friend Brenda about my experience as I lie on the massage table. For years, we have traded bodywork with each other. She helps me ask my body questions. When we began today, I noticed it was difficult to open my hands. My fingers wanted to curl inward and keep out intrusions.

"What would it be like if you felt the praise you get as much as you feel the challenges?" Brenda asks me as she massages my hands.

"Then I would get conceited and lazy," I tell her. "I would become insensitive." I cry because I want praise but it's not allowed.

"I can't imagine you being insensitive," Brenda says. "But what would it be like to feel that praise, to carry it around with you? I wonder if these challenges would feel less threatening if you could hold the praise more fully inside of you."

"I'm better at fighting to be heard than at being acknowledged," I say, aware of Fuckit, fists up and ready in the inner house.

◆*Memory.* This morning I announce that I'm not going to church. It's all of bunch of B.S. anyway. If there's a God then why is there hunger and the Vietnam War and racism. "You just go so that everyone will think you're a good person," I tell my mother after she says that I *am* going and she won't hear anything more about this. I am fourteen.

"God will punish you for this!" she warns and calls for Jim. They each grab hold of one of my arms and pull me to the car. At church I make my getaway up to the balcony which is sparsely settled in this early morning service. I write a poem about the sheep people who sit and stand and sing on command. I put it into the offering plate.

The minister calls the next day and talks to my mother. "He wants you to write a prayer for the congregation," she says, pleased, as if everything is settled.

"Atheists do not write prayers!" I object. "I don't think there's any God up there to hear them. Don't you get it?"

My mother slaps my face and says, "You're not going to talk that way in my house! I'm going to call Reverend Hale and tell him about your attitude. Maybe he can talk some sense into you."

My mother is always finding men to talk sense to me. She has my uncles come over to quote the Bible or to bring tracts from the John Birch Society. I am never convinced and they always end up telling me that I can't possibly understand the issues involved.◆

Fuckit developed a reflex in regard to my mother. Whatever my mother said I shouldn't do because it was bad, I did. Whenever I light a cigarette, Fuckit says, "Take that, Mom." Sometimes I think it would have been better if my mother had been a smoking alcoholic so that I could have rebelled by waving fresh air and exercise into her face. But I was allergic to my mother's wholesome ideal. It still makes me itch.

Fuckit took to coffee and cigarettes and men's clothes. They were symbols of freedom. Freedom meant being cool, articulate and sophisticated. It had nothing to do with accepting support.

So far it's still easier to accept support from nature and inner allies than from people. As Fuckit, I defined myself in opposition to my mother. If I accept someone's approval, I'm afraid I'll have to keep earning it; I'll have to give them even more to thank them for being nice to me.

Brenda tells me to meditate on support. I imagine that every good affirmative word I've ever heard is a melody that stays with me. I imagine that all of the support I have ever received is a nectar and I swallow it so that all of my cells are encouraged. I allow the support to move through me and cheer me up. I feel the solidness of my back on the massage table. "Just so I don't have to be some way I'm not," Fuckit says. "I want to be liked, but I don't want to conform to get it."

. . .

I had my first experience with the authorities when I was fourteen. Before that, the institutions of law, religion and state were an abstraction. Then I ran up against them in person. I learned that my age and my gender made me David against Goliath, but I was without a slingshot and Goliath had a thousand arms.

At that time, I thought I could slip through the cracks and find a new life of love and peace. I saw a chance to escape and I took it, plunging through a hole in the wire like the heroes of the war movies I watched on TV.

◆*Memory*. Mrs. Harding and I stop at the store so that she can do her shopping before taking me home. I don't mind because I like being with her. The only thing is, she's so nice to me that I feel sad in my stomach.

We are in the blue front seat of her station wagon. She looks at me. "Is there something wrong, Louise?" she asks. "Is something bothering you?"

She has said the magic words that I am always wishing someone would say.

The sadness rises to a heavy cloud in my chest. "I can't get along with my mother," I say. I've hinted at this to other people before, but they said, "Your mother has had a hard life. She loves you." There was nothing else to say then because adults stick together.

Mrs. Harding says, "Why don't you get along, what happens?"

I look at her out of the corner of my eye, trying to see if

I can trust her. I'm always telling myself not to trust anyone, but I want to find someone to talk to anyway.

"My mother doesn't like me. She says I'm crazy and incorrigible and belong in reform school. She reads my diary and my mail and tells my teachers I'm weird. I can't do anything right for her. She yells at me all the time. It doesn't matter what I say, she won't listen."

I don't know how to tell her that my mother uses words like a whip and she can't stop and then she slaps me when I start yelling back and I keep yelling because she won't listen and I can't stand feeling as if I am not there. I yell desperate words at my mother, words with bits of my story. The harder I try the more noise she makes, until I run from the room and eat a candy bar.

"You sound unhappy," Mrs. Harding says. Her voice is warm so that I want to keep talking, even though I hear a voice inside my head saying, "You're going to get in trouble for talking like this."

I search for a scar to show her so that she will believe me. I run my thumb over the cuff at my wrist. I haven't talked about cutting my wrists since the day I did it. I say, "I want to die, I feel so bad." I tell her about the razor blades.

Now I'm really scared that I told. "You won't tell my mother I told you, will you?" My fingers are twisting with sweat over each other. Everyone always tells my mother when I talk too much. They think it will help, but it always only gets me in trouble.

Mrs. Harding is quiet for a minute. "No, I won't tell her."

"Maybe you could come and live with me," she says. "I'll have to talk it over with Frank, but we have an extra room." Mrs. Harding has five children and it seems like someone else is always staying at her house as well.

How could anyone really want me? I am afraid to believe that this is real. But she talks to Frank and he says it's all right. She says maybe I should wait until after Christmas.

No. If I wait I might miss my chance. Christmas will mean presents and owing my mother for all she tells me she has given me. I don't want her presents. I just want to leave. I just want it all to be better.◆

I didn't understand that kids couldn't just go off and find themselves another family. I assumed that my mother would make no effort to retrieve me, especially since she said it was because of me that her life was so difficult. But my mother was not about to relinquish her authority over me. And she had every institution of the patriarchy on her side.

I tried to vanish when I should have been leaving a paper trail and collecting evidence. I should have left a note instead of just taking off after school with my biology book and my homework. The note should have said, "I can't live here anymore. I've found someplace better. Don't come after me. Louise, no longer your daughter." I should have made a Xeroxed copy so I could have produced it in defense against my mother's stories. Instead, my mother said, "She's just trying to hurt me." And I didn't leave a note because I wanted my mother to forget about me and leave me alone. I thought she would just pretend that I had never been there, the way she pretended about a lot of things.

◆*Memory.* Mrs. Harding says she told the juvenile detention center I was coming. She said I'd stay there a little while until things are straightened out and I can go to the Hardings' house.

The woman on the other side of the counter tells me to empty my pockets and my bag and give her my books. She turns me over to another woman with a ring of skeleton keys and heels that click on the linoleum. My cell has two sets of bars over the front, a toilet, a cot, a glaring light. I did not count on being in jail. I sit on the cot and stare.

Another woman comes and takes me to the day room. It is ten days before Christmas and there's a small tree in a stand. She gives me a peanut butter cookie, but my mouth is too dry to swallow. I am afraid that I sentenced myself to jail. I think it would have been better to buy a Greyhound bus ticket and go to Haight-Ashbury. What if I get sent to reform school like my mother says. It must be just like this, with bars and pale green walls.

The door to the day room is open and I hear a sudden loud screaming, echoing between the green linoleum and the high ceiling. "Where's my daughter, where's my daughter?" my mother shrieks. "Let me see her." She found me by going to my best friend's house and coercing her parents into forcing her to reveal where I am. My mother has brought my best friend along with her to juvenile hall.

The woman behind the counter comes in and asks if I want to see my mother. I say "No," sure that they will make me anyway.

There is more screaming from the doorway, "Tell her she has to come out here right now. Tell her she's coming home with me!" The matron has turned on Mr. Ed reruns on the black and white TV. I stare at the talking horse while my mother sobs hysterically in the hallway. She sounds angry, not sad.

The matron looks at me. "Troubles?" she says, as she lights a cigarette.

"I ran away," I say, looking at the floor.

No one asks if I want to see Judge Granite. He walks into the day room frowning at me, wearing his black courtroom robe. He doesn't have to ask any permissions. He's a judge. What he says goes.

"What do you think you're doing? I've talked to your mother. What do you think you're doing to her?" he says in a voice not to be questioned.

I stare at the floor. He is a friend of my aunt and uncle,

he goes to our church. I've seen him at family gatherings but he's never talked to me before. He has a son my age. His son doesn't talk to me either.

"I'm not going home," I whisper.

"Your mother has a hard life," he says. "What right do you think you have to do this to her?"

"I can't live with her," I say, but I can't look up because I'm afraid of what he'll do to me.

He leaves shaking his head hard in disapproval. The next day I am told I can stay at the Hardings' for a while, but Judge Granite will not make me a ward of the court. I still belong to my mother.◆

The Hardings' house looked onto a winter pond, with blue carpets and a piano and a kitchen with Swedish trivets and an iron for making Krumcake. Sometimes the house was filled with a soft quiet. The TV was in the basement and it wasn't on all the time, like my mother's was. The rugs were soft and good for lying on. Outside the living room window, the wind swept the grasses and bare willows sideways and ruffled the pond. In this house, the colors were blue and wood and windows, with muted lights and light yellow slabs of stone on the hallway floor.

Mrs. Harding said she had always felt funny having an uneven number around the table and it was good to even it up. I made cookies with her and went on errands. She never yelled the way my mother did and all her kids seemed relaxed and glad to live there.

I wanted to feel casual, the way they looked. But I couldn't stop being afraid. I felt tight at the very center of my body as if a time bomb were always ticking. I couldn't get away from all the nightmares and the fears I'd already experienced. Nor was there much chance to rest.

I had been there two days when my mother called to say, "What do you think you're doing? What are people going to think about you not living at home? I want you to get back here right away. I'm coming to get you."

Mrs. Harding called the social worker I was seeing and the social worker called my mother. And my mother didn't come. The next day she called again. "Your grandmother has had a stroke. Just look at what you've done! You're not getting away with this. I'm coming to get you right now."

Mrs. Harding and I packed my things and I stood in the hall waiting, but she didn't come. Instead, she called every ten minutes to threaten that she would come.

My brother Jim called to say he never wanted to grow up to be like me. I should see what I was doing to our mother, he said, she was screaming all the time. Uncle Kevin called and threatened to spank me and then haul me home in his car. The minister called and so did my uncles, all at the urging of my mother. "You talk some sense into her," she had told them.

Twenty-two years later, the sound of a phone ringing still makes me flinch.

I had run away in search of peace and freedom. Instead I started a war. My mother was in her element. Not content with her contingent of judge, minister and brothers, my mother started calling all of my teachers whom she already knew from the school district meetings. The high school librarian, my home economics teacher and my P.E. teacher made it clear that they didn't approve of what I'd done to my poor mother. They delivered their judgements in clipped sentences as I was on my way out of the classroom or standing in my gym shorts waiting to take a shower.

Some of my friends began saying that their mothers didn't want them to associate with me. My mother had had a long talk with their mothers and convinced them that I was a "bad influence." On my way to my locker, I would feel surrounded by judgements from people who never asked me for an explanation. People I had not been connected with seemed eager to tell me I was bad and had done the wrong thing.

I began walking on tiptoes and trying hard not to breathe.

I always looked over my shoulder. I could not keep all of my worries in lists; they flew around me like crows. I never knew who my mother had talked to. In U.S. history, we read three paragraphs about McCarthy and the Red Scare. I do not remember learning that McCarthy had in fact been discredited. We did not study the lives broken by his mass manipulation of fear and anger. My mother certainly knew his tactics of accusation and name calling. She used his language, telling others I was a "troublemaker," "Communist," "atheist," "bad influence." My mother knew that people like to take sides.

I hardly told anyone that I had run away. I just wanted to feel normal, to pretend that the Hardings were my real family.

At night, Mrs. Harding held me on a couch in the basement and I clung to her like a barnacle and cried. Night after night this went on for two and three hours until she said she had to go to bed. I didn't know why I was crying. I was too exhausted to make connections. After she went to bed I walked the circle driveway outside of her house, until four or five in the morning. Sleeping meant surrender. They could come and take me away at night. I had to push myself. I had to defy my body. I welcomed the world of dense exhausted fog. I was tired of trying to figure it out. All day I was tired.

I'd been at the Hardings' less than three months when the superintendent of schools became involved. Mrs. Harding had been substitute teaching in the high school home economics department when she and Miss Wibble, the ancient, prissy home ec teacher, had words about my leaving home. Mrs. Harding defended her decision to offer me refuge, but Miss Wibble accused her of just helping me persecute my mother. Miss Wibble called my mother to tell her that Mrs. Harding had gotten angry and my mother took the story to Mr. Sud, the superintendent of the school district.

Mr. Sud decided that Mrs. Harding could no longer substitute teach in the district if she couldn't get along with the staff any better than that. Mrs. Harding told me after school. I knew it was my fault. I lived under a star of misfortune and anybody who tried to help out would get hurt.

I decided I would go talk to Mr. Sud myself. I was on the debate team, after all. I knew that Mrs. Harding was a good substitute teacher because I had studied under her. He wouldn't want to fire a good teacher like her, I thought.

The superintendent's office was adjacent to the elementary school. He was seated behind the biggest desk I'd ever seen, a desk that stretched from an American flag in a stand, past the picture of President Nixon, to the green state flag of Washington. Mr. Sud was dressed in a suit and tie with an Adam's apple that bobbed in his throat and sharp severe edges to his face. There were no people my age anywhere around.

I wasn't used to suits. I didn't understand school district politics or factions or that hiring and firing didn't have to do with fairness. He said, "Your mother's a good teacher and we can't have any disturbances among the teachers. The Hardings had no business taking you in."

"But Mrs. Harding's a good substitute teacher," I protested. I could not tell him that she was the first person who had ever really tried to help me and that I needed a lot of help.

He said, "I've already decided. My duty is to your mother as one of my teachers and Miss Wibble in the home economics department."

I had had too many years of being respectful to sob or yell, "Listen to me, damn it." I didn't know if I could remain upright on the journey out of his office; my legs felt funny and I felt vacant.

Within a week, my mother convinced Judge Granite that I was too happy with the Hardings and that they had dangerous subversive ideas, being Democrats and Unitarians. If I was too happy, I wouldn't want to come home.

I was made a ward of the court so that Judge Granite could

move me to a foster family he knew who attended my mother's church. Their daughter, who was a year older than me, had been killed in a collision with a semi. There was a picture of her in the living room but neither of the adults nor the two remaining children ever said anything about her. The man was harsh and silent. The older son lived in the basement and came out only at dinner and late at night. The woman wanted a cook, a maid and a babysitter. She chatted with my mother frequently. She listened to my phone calls on the extension and told my mother what I said to my friends. I told her I hated her and that I was going to run away, for real this time. "One more time and you go to reform school, Judge Granite said so," the foster woman told me.

Fuckit dreamed of being a boy and hitchhiking to California. Stunned watched the walls close in as my foster brother came into my bedroom and chewed on my breasts.

People in uniform still make me nervous. I become short of breath in government buildings and fancy offices. I am never sure whether to challenge authority or to acquiesce. I have written letters to the IRS complaining about tax forms, all to no avail. I tried to persuade a hospital to let me work off my bill in trade for massages or writing on their newsletter. They turned me over to a collection agency instead. I tried to contest a parking ticket and raised my hand at the wrong juncture, inadvertently dismissing my own case.

I have had to learn that it is possible to make a difference.

. . .

◆*Dream.* I'm in an old house which has been turned into a mental institution. I'm here as a spy. I sit at a high table and write with my hand cupped to hide my paper. Writing makes me feel jubilant and I begin waltzing from the chairs to the couch, holding my paper close to my chest. An attendant wants to know what I'm writing; I tell her it's a letter but it's not.

A very mean matron brings in a new inmate, an adolescent with dark hair half in front of her face, who looks terrified in her eyes and tough in the tilt of her head. I want to befriend her.

The matron says to me, "We didn't establish rapport, you and I, and we should visit more later." She makes a motion with her hands toward my nose and I know she wants to put her fingers up my nose and twist. She wants me to know she's in charge here and that I'm under her dominion.

I smile falsely at her and say, "Oh, that's okay, I'm fine." I have folded my writing into a square and put it under my arm so that she can't read it.◆

Every week or two, for more than five years, I have met with a dream group. Jane, Sara, Betsey and I bring our journals of dreams and work with them together. Our dreams have touched on every area of our waking lives, giving us messages about our relationships and feelings. Our dreams provide adventures that would make us quake in the daylight. When we tell them to each other, we listen and nod and laugh, recognizing themes and patterns in our lives. Sometimes one or more of us wraps up in a blanket and sobs about how overwhelmed she feels, or uncertain, or small. In dream group there is an abundance of hugging and touching as we track our own and each other's journey through the inner and outer worlds.

We take turns leading, which means bringing a plan that will help us work creatively with our dreams. We have made mandalas and acted out our dreams without words in front of each other. We have drawn tarot cards and interviewed our inner dream characters and felt our dreams in our bodies and drawn pictures of dream scenes. We use our creativity to make our dreams come alive in the daylight so that we can look at them again and carry them forward.

Sara, whose turn it is to lead, suggests that we pick one

dream character to embody. I become the spy who is a writer. I dance around Jane's dining room, waving my journal and kissing my pen. When I get near Jane, who is being a very stiff-limbed character and marching, I move with small tiptoeing steps, for I am a spy and I have to be careful. I hide my journal under my shirt, gripping it with my right arm. This makes me think about how I hid my writing and my songs from my mother, in a house where nothing seemed my own and even my diary had been read and used against me. When Jane's not looking at me, I stick out my tongue at her, covertly defiant.

The spy reminds me of Fuckit. "I was a spy in our family," Fuckit says. "I like to sabotage the powers that be."

We move around each other, all in character. I climb up on the arm of the couch and make notes in my journal. I imagine I can see the dark adolescent in the corner of the living room. I know it is Stunned. I move toward the corner and pretend to show Stunned my writing.

Then I pretend I am in my dream, sitting at the table facing the matron. She looks like Sarah, worried that I'm breaking a rule.

I imagine her going for my nose. I remember how it felt that my mother was always going toward my face. I bare my teeth instead of smiling.

Sara of dream group comes close, looking very mystical and wise in her dream character. She smiles at me and nods approvingly at my journal.

"Why don't you take lessons from her?" Fuckit tells the Sarah inside me.

We come together as a group to talk about our movement and what we recognized in ourselves and each other as we moved our dream characters. Betsey says, "I liked how you swooped around with your journal. You looked so pleased with yourself, it was great."

"But then you hid!" Jane says and we all laugh.

"But when I saw Sara, I realized that I could have allies,

that maybe it wasn't just me alone against the institution," I say. Fuckit is still learning how to have support.

At the end we have a group hug and chuckle about the many people we have been with each other. We are our own institution.

# 10

## *Influence*

THE BATHROOM of the inner house has three cracked tile walls and rusty holes where the mirror over the sink has been removed. Now photographs are Scotch-taped where the mirror once hung. Here are Mrs. Arnold, the high school drama teacher; Miss Key, who taught debate and creative writing; Miss Meyer, the P.E. teacher I liked who looked more genuine in shorts and a T-shirt than in the wool suit she wore when she had to teach Health Ed. Joan Baez is wearing her guitar and raising a fist in a photo from *Time* magazine. A presidential campaign poster of Angela Davis, Ph.D., announces her Communist party candidacy. Janis Joplin is backlit by a strobe light. Her face is electric.

I study their eyes and the set of their chins. I am thirteen, fourteen and fifteen; I want to look like them. I turn the key on this door, the only one that locks. I try to see myself in the metal faucet, but it's too cloudy. "Fuck it," I say out loud. I practice conversations with the women on my wall. I pretend to be on a stage with microphones and applause. Then my stomach hurts and I tell myself to quit being silly, that no one would want to look at me. I cover my face with my hands. I fill the bathtub with steaming water that turns my skin red.

My mother wants to know when I will be out of the bathroom. "What are you doing in there?" she demands. My mother has me under surveillance, like J. Edgar Hoover. In high school, my history teacher wrote a letter opposing the Vietnam War and two FBI agents showed up at his house. At least he didn't have to live with them.

YoungerOnes have been stuffed into the laundry hamper. "Love me, somebody please love me," they whisper. They grab at the pictures on the wall and capture one which Tinsel presses to her chest and curls up around. I ignore them.

My mother is breaking through the door with a battering ram. I pretend not to notice.

She is yelling about bad influences. She says God will punish me for having idols. She forbids me to leave the house.

I am an adult, bringing a full-length mirror to hang on the bathroom door. I fill the bath with bubbles and floating toys and tell all the kids in the laundry basket that they can come out now. I place an offering of heart-shaped cookies on a tray beneath the pictures. I put a photograph of myself among them and add more recent arrivals, a mixture of friends and heroines from my adulthood. I stand in front of them and say, "I love you. I love you."

.   .   .

When I was twelve, I watched my seventeen-year-old cousin, Jake, wave goodbye to my grandparents at the airport. He told them to "take care," and "have a good trip." I was awed by his apparent mastery of grown-up discourse. I waited for this confidence to befall me, for the time when I would sound like an adult and treat adults as equals.

I was at least twenty-four before I could even fake chit chat. Now, twelve years of therapy have destroyed my interest in being superficial and when someone says, "How are you?" I have to stop and think about it. I'm thirty-seven years old and every year this question gets more complicated.

I complain to Jean that gaining awareness has only meant

being vulnerable and honest when it would be easier and more effective to remain manipulative. But I have to admit that speaking what feels true is more satisfying. Or maybe it's just that lying and pretending make my jaw ache and my stomach tense; I have a lower tolerance for discomfort now than I used to have.

I still agonize because I feel shy or I'm in Stunned or Tinsel and can't find words. I have never learned how to say goodbye, but mostly I haven't had to do this. No close friends have died. My brother, Jim, the only member of my family I really cared about, stopped having anything to do with me after I confronted my family about the incest. It's been seven years but I keep thinking I'll see him again. Mostly goodbye is taken care of by losing touch because of distance or time. Or by accumulating disillusionments that turn the soft place in my heart to leather so that when the person is gone, I don't feel the shock of loss. I worry about it though. When I am feeling especially connected with Marianne, I am seized by terror of her dying. I am afraid of how much I would miss her and the loss I would feel.

I've seen Jean longer than I've known Marianne. In these years I've imagined losing her more than once. It always made me cry and eventually it made me laugh, because she was still there, standing with me on this road.

I practiced because losing her was inevitable. I practiced because the thought of losing her reminded me of how much she meant to me. I thought that rehearsal would take away the shock when it happened.

Jean gave me a full six months notice that she was stopping her work as a therapist. But when she told me I still felt like a giant hand had yanked on the rug and I was falling breathless on my back, like an infant.

I wanted to leave and go cry in the bathroom. I held my breath and kept back the tears that were lining up on my eyelids. I said, "I don't want to talk about this now," and discussed an upcoming workshop I was teaching instead.

"So, eight years is a lot," Sarah says. "What did you expect, forever? I don't know how she stood you this long."

"Are you tired of me? Do you like me? Will you remember me or will you forget? Did I affect you or am I the only one who got something from this?" Some variation of these questions occurs about once a week.

I want her to say she loves me. I want her to tell me that I am important. Most of the time she just sits there when I ask. Today she said that I didn't really trust her or I wouldn't be asking that. I do not doubt her caring but I want more to hold onto.

At the time, I felt like I'd flunked therapy. Then I got mad. What's so bad about asking to hear something? "Yeah!" YoungerOnes said. But the truth is I don't want her to go.

"I'm not done yet," Carrie protests. "Asking for what I want and saying what I believe is still hard and mysterious. I need help in being so public. Talking to Jean has helped me find clarity and given me room to feel all the edges of this rapidly expanding life. And what about the mother book? After a year and a half I'm only half through. There are still so many challenges and too few experienced models."

I've cried so much that I've stopped wearing my contact lenses unless I'm teaching. Lately I've been waking up crying at about 5 a.m., feeling bereft. My life feels too large and I feel too small and ignorant to do without Jean. Sometimes Marianne rolls over and holds me and hands me Kleenex. I feel like a water wheel, going down, coming up dripping.

When Sarah says, "Enough already, this is ridiculous," Memory stops her and says, "Jean matters. Let her matter."

Now I memorize the therapy room and notice the lines on Jean's face and the stones on her necklaces. It's been three months since she told me she was leaving and three months until she will go. I stare at the painting of the native woman on her wall and the clay ball with etchings carved on it on the table beside her chair. I wonder how many Kleenex I have pulled through the opening of the wooden Kleenex box in eight years of nearly weekly nose-blowing. On her desk are spheres of malachite and obsidian that I gave her, in her bookcase there is a copy of my first book. This is a relationship contained in a place. I never worried that what I said here would leak through the walls and turn against me.

I felt every feeling I have ever known here. Jean never turned away from them no matter how loud or raw. She did not sink into them either or try too hard to let me know that she was there. She was more distant than I wanted but she was present and solid. I learned that she didn't have to be everything. I had bodywork and astrology, friends, dream group, writing group, workshops and finally, Marianne. After the first couple years I mostly stopped trying too hard to get Jean to give what she couldn't give me.

In the last three years, I finally came to value more fully what Jean did give. The questions she threw out as I was walking out the door at the end of our session followed by, "Just think about it," as she closed the door behind me. The way she applauded when I got mad at her or differed in opinion. The permission she gave me to be powerful.

. . .

My mother always said, "You're lucky you have a family like this. I see some of those little kids in my class with dirt on their faces and clothes with a hole in them and they don't have anything."

◆*Memory.* When my mother has a dinner party, I steal salted nuts and gum drops from the nut cups she puts by each plate. I always say I have a lot of homework to do and hide in my room until it's time to eat. I spend most of dinner just looking at my plate and feeling clumsy. I was going to escape right afterward tonight like I usually do, but my mother said, "Louise, why don't you help me clear the table?" in her company voice, as if she were actually asking for my compliance. In the kitchen she says, "You are going to sit with us and show some politeness to our company." She says this in a low voice and the tone of it says, Don't you dare make a scene or you'll be sorry.

She doesn't know that I don't know how to talk to adults, especially around her. I sit on the couch. One of the women she has invited asks me about high school. What about it? I want to ask, but I restrain myself and say something inane about being in band. The woman has lost interest. I get a book and start reading it on my corner of the couch which I'm not supposed to do either. I can't just sit here and listen to my mother's litany of the hospitalized, or watch people smile and make concerned noises in response. It seems I can't even pretend to do what I'm supposed to do anymore.

They don't stay very long. My mother says to get their coats. I stand by the door as they pull at my bundle of jackets. My mother comes to stand beside me to say good-bye. "Thank you very much. So nice to meet your daughter, too," a woman says and my mother puts her arm around me. I become wood and stone. I do not move even a fraction of an inch toward my mother. I cannot pretend to feel any warmth toward her. I am not like my mother, who is always very busy making life appear as it is not.◆

I don't know what would have happened if I hadn't found other women to love instead of my mother when I was a teenager. But here luck has often been with me, bringing women who inspired me and smiled on me. They didn't make everything all right, but they alerted me to the possibilities of being different from my mother. And thoughts of them kept me warm in my heart and hands.

These were women who were more than wives. They read books and newspapers. They didn't talk about how tired they were. I couldn't predict what they would say next, not like my mother who endlessly repeated herself. I listened eagerly to them, like a dry plant soaking up rain. These women taught me mysteries as I dangled over their desks and rode my bike for miles to their houses. I visited them for years after I left their classes because they were different from my mother. They were interested in 1966, 1968 and 1969. My mother still listened to Bing Crosby and never even played Elvis.

I wanted them to love me. I wanted them to replace my mother. Now I see that my relationship with them was like my relationship with Jean, offering sustenance, vision, empowerment and experience. What I learned from these women has stayed with me because their thinking resonated with what felt right to me. They are linked in my heart.

I didn't understand what they got from spending time with me. I didn't know that some wonderful rare people enjoy the company of people younger than themselves. Now, when I come home after working in the city, my neighbor, who is ten, runs up the driveway and says, "Louise," throwing her arms around my waist. When I see her, I can forget that I was tired. I think of what a great honor it is that she has chosen me from the world of adults. Maybe this is what these women felt as well about me as a gifted, scared, wanting, thoughtful and smart adolescent. But it was hard to believe then that anyone really liked me.

But what if they had not been there? What if no one had paid attention to me? What if all women had been like my mother? Would I still have gotten away?

◆*Memory.* I still hate going to church in the morning but Sunday night youth group is a different matter. I talk to Amy in my mind all week long—she's the new leader. We don't have to read the Bible, finally. Instead we see slide shows about civil rights, poverty, situation ethics and the Vietnam War. Then we discuss them. I'm twelve years old and I want to change the world.

Amy is beautiful. She has long black hair and brown

eyes and dark skin. She seems situated in her body, not like me or my mother. She talks about Summerhill, gestalt therapy and encounter groups. Maybe someday I'll show her my stories. They're about being a hippie and trying to find out what love is. The hippie is also a fugitive and is always on the run.

Tonight she tells us about how Gandhi meditated and developed nonviolence. She lights a candle, turns out the lights and tells us to breathe and imagine we are one with the flame. When I try it, the room whirls around and all the debris I'd been holding inside my skin rises up like bats and circles my head.

Afterward, I follow her down the stairs from the chapel to the social room where we have cookies and punch. "I felt like I was disintegrating," I tell her. The words come out all of a sudden, when she turns to look at me. I feel stupid because the words came from a place where there are a lot of feelings. If she knew how scared I am she might think I was crazy like my mother said.

She raises her eyebrows and waits.

"I felt like I was being shaken up," I say. "Like there wasn't anything that was just me."

I can tell she is listening from her face.

Then she smiles just a little and says sometimes teenagers feel like that. She's looking for a babysitter and would I like the job, she says.

I will be paid for being in her house!

"Sure," I say, hiding my glee, because enthusiasm is shameful. I straighten up and try to look very reliable and useful.◆

Amy has rescued me twice in my life. This first time, I was in the seventh grade. She and her husband and two children were living in a cabin on the water while their house was being built. The walls were wood with interesting pictures on them. On babysitting nights, after I'd put the boys in bed, I sat in the window seat and experienced the luxury of silence. There was no television set, only the licking of small waves on the beach. I was the oldest person in the house and all I had to do was stay awake, which was easy because Amy had shelves and shelves of books.

*Brave New World, Animal Farm, Black Like Me, Johnny Got a Gun, Summerhill, The Naked Ape.* I discovered more ideas on her window seat than I found at school. In her bookcase was hope for a new world without war or racial hatred or injustice. Surely if people were writing these books, we were on our way to a kinder world of love and nonviolence.

Amy's house was a refuge from Uncle Kevin and my mother. Thinking back, her home reminds me of this house I am sharing now with Marianne. In my writing nook, my long table is pressed beneath the window and I inhale the quiet cloud-streaked sky. My bookcase almost reaches the ceiling. All I have to do is move my arm and I can read a letter from Virginia Woolf or urge myself to continue onward with Natalie Goldberg. My mother had the same unchanging books on a shelf for most of the time I knew her, but I never saw her open one of them.

The summer after I finished eighth grade, Amy tore the tendons in her ankle and I was hired to watch the kids while she sat with her foot propped up on a pillow. When the boys took their naps, Amy and I talked about psychology, free schools, alternative communities and ecology. I was an attentive listener and could think fast. As the days passed I became brave and was able to ask questions. It was easier to talk about the pain of the Vietnamese and the change that the antiwar movement would make in the texture of democracy than it was to talk about myself. It has taken many years to find the words for my self.

Once I said, "There's things my mother won't talk about."

Amy said, "Like sex?"

I remember wanting to die of embarrassment and wanting

to know at the same time. Sex was dirty and terrible, I already knew that. But I wanted it to be different than that.

She took down a book on telling children about sex and showed me drawings of penises and vaginas. She said that sex was great, that it was important to use birth control and it was perfectly healthy to masturbate. I did not look up once while she was talking.

She asked if I had any questions. Old unnamed feelings and shadowed memories all rose from my vulva and I felt hot and dizzy. I shook my head.

But if she had not said those words on that particular afternoon, I don't know how much worse I might have felt about my sexual feelings, which came heavy and strong and felt dirty like Kevin.

I didn't know the word "needy" then, but I knew the feelings and I was always fighting them. You were supposed to have big feelings only for your family and eventually for a boyfriend. But I talked to Amy all the time in my mind and imagined telling her secrets although I did not know what they were. When my mother yelled I kept my face blank and took myself away to Amy's window seat.

I couldn't help but brighten with excitement whenever I said I was going to babysit at Amy's. Nor could I stop quoting her even though I knew it was dangerous if my mother knew that someone was important to me. At first my mother threatened to call Amy and tell her I was disrespectful. But at church, Amy was polite to my mother and friendly to me. She didn't respond when my mother said she hoped I hadn't been any trouble, but instead asked me how I was and what I had been reading.

My mother began to say Amy was a "bad influence" on me and that she was putting ideas into my head. As if my head were some kind of a breadbox. As if I weren't always asking questions already.

Then my mother came home with rumors from the church women's circle. "You're not to spend any more time with that Amy. I just heard she's having an affair with the associate minister and him with two kids and her with a family. She has no morals and I'm grounding you, no babysitting, no youth group."

"She is not having an affair, you just don't like her because I like her more than you!" I yelled back. "You're the one without any morals. You're the one who doesn't care if people starve and who thinks this war is good. You pretend that God is love and then you hate everyone that's a different color."

"I suppose you want to be like her, breaking commandments and ruining other people's lives," my mother yelled. "Well you're not going to amount to anything either if you keep on the way you're going. Now go to your room and stay there until I tell you to come out."

I called Amy and told her my mother said I couldn't babysit anymore. I didn't tell her what my mother had said about the affair. I was sure my mother had made it up. Amy told me to hold on. I did not remind her that I couldn't find anything solid.

A week later Amy's phone was disconnected. My mother came home from her church circle saying that Amy and the minister had fled.

I tried not to cry but couldn't help it. "You thought she liked you," my mother said, "but she didn't even tell you she was leaving."

"I hate you," I screamed against the sting of her words while trying to tell myself that it didn't matter that Amy was gone.

"I'll call the parents of your friends and tell them about how Amy has turned you against me," she said.

She went to the phone and began dialing numbers. In the smallness of my room I hugged my knees and tried to hold myself together.

A month later I got a letter from Amy telling me she was in love with the associate minister. I hid it in my room. But one day when I got home from Girl Scouts, my mother held up the letter and said, "I don't want you to have anything to do with her." I tried to get a post office box, but they said I had to have a parent's signature. So I circled the mailbox like a hawk and walked my letters to Amy to the corner box for mailing.

In the inner house, Stunned looks embarrassed with the Memory of making Amy so important. It was not the first or the last time that I turned to an older woman looking for the way out. I knew I wanted assurance and recognition, I wanted to be special and connected. But it was bad to want that.

"Oh Stunned," Carrie says. "You wanted Amy to keep you with her, because your need for safety and love was so great."

"It's better to be needy than to be a sociopath," Memory says. "For all the terrible things that people around you did, you were compelled to find different people instead of hiding in total isolation. You did not give up on all people."

"I just wish there had been a name for those relationships so I wouldn't have had to feel ashamed of them," Stunned says. "Like life-teacher or mentor or even just older friend."

. . .

When I was fourteen, I believed that solving major world problems was not difficult, even though nothing I tried at home made any difference. I thought then that the political and the personal were disconnected, that political acts were committed by someone other than people acting out their family and cultural mythologies. Even though nothing I said or did altered the injustice and abuse in my family, I was convinced that I could change the world.

"Fool. Optimist," Sarah says accusingly.

"Oh shut up," Fuckit replies. I pick up my guitar and start tuning.

I also believed then that the world would end before I

turned thirty, which seemed an eternity away. I figured I would probably die young. I thought I wouldn't care if I did. For years, I went back and forth about whether I wanted to die at the time of the great disaster or whether I wanted to stick around to help start the new order. I finally got mad at all the books and movies that said the planet would be destroyed before the earthlings got around to saving it.

My mother used to say, "You just think you can change the world. What do you know? Start in your own back yard."

This comment always followed an escalating argument about cleaning my room. I would say I had been writing an editorial for the school paper and that was more important. This led to her statement that I was a Communist just like all those other young people who couldn't even take baths! How did I expect to change the world if I couldn't even get along with my own family?

So here I am, in my own back yard, though I suspect my mother didn't know I would dig it up to find what was buried there.

I thought I would be able to finish this excavation of my childhood back yard in a year. So far it's been two and a half years. It's been hard to find blocks of time for this writing. It takes a day to transition away from my current schedule, a day where I can just write in my journal and walk. Memory will not come fully unless I have a sense of timelessness that is not always easy to arrange. But scheduling is only part of it. Since I hit the time of adolescence, it's been harder to find playfulness. Instead there is resistance and rebellion, responsibility, ambition, uncertainty and rage.

"Enough roots already," Fuckit says.

Stunned shakes her head and looks away from the computer cursor, which is blinking black curses on the monitor. "Stuck in my own back yard," Stunned mutters. "Who cares?"

In Sunday school, I learned the parable of the talents.

Three men were given talents; two of them buried the talents in the ground and were not rewarded. The third invested his and it multiplied. His father was so happy that he gave him even more wealth. From this I deduced that talents were gold coins and that the rich just got richer. I thought talent was different from creativity and art.

No one talked about gifts or being gifted when I was a child. Smart students were outcasts if they were a little too smart and not pretty. Gifted people were weird. Look at Einstein, he never even combed his hair.

Once in a while, my mother would ask me to sing for her or for company. She would be working in the kitchen and I would get my guitar. But as soon as I began singing, she would turn on the television and pretend I wasn't there. Singing in front of company was even worse because everyone would look at me and be politely silent. When people looked at me, I couldn't breathe or remember the guitar chords or the words to the song. My voice came out thin and strained with self-consciousness.

At high school the teachers said I had potential. I knew they meant I got good grades and would go to college. I got mad when they said that, because potential was about the future and I wanted to have an identity right then as a teenager. No one talked about the voices inside of me who insisted on writing poems and making up stories and songs. No one said that ignoring these voices felt terrible, that nothing was worse than fighting the creative impulse. I didn't learn about the muse or study the lives of writers. I didn't understand that singers are people who keep singing and writers are people who keep writing. Scientists and politicians, war heroes and conquerors were prominent in the curriculum. Ordinary people were supposed to get a job and work for someone else. Talents were hobbies, not life work.

But my talent kept demanding time. As soon as I got home from school I would go to my room and stay there. I cut pictures from magazines and wrote poems and essays about them, gluing them into notebooks. I studied chord charts and worked my way through songbooks with my guitar. I made up songs and typed them hunt and peck on the typewriter. I wrote songs about boy soldiers who came to regret killing and tunes about caring. I had a passion to express myself, but I was afraid of people seeing me. I was sure the abuse had stained me and made me unbearably ugly. If my mother could decide what was bad about me just by looking, then what would other people see? If they didn't like me, I knew they could do horrible things. My experiences with Kevin and my mother had left a deep fear about how people might mistreat me.

Once after church, Amy was telling my mother and me that she taught gifted students in a pilot program in the neighboring, more progressive school district. My mother immediately said, "Louise isn't gifted, she just works hard."

That comment spurred me to swallow hard and work even harder trying to prove myself, writing sixty-page college papers in pursuit of my summa cum laude. I learned how to douse the voice of creativity with caffeine and cigarettes, spending far too much time doing what I was told. I was learning to make uniform sentences, quoting endlessly what had already been written, afraid to sing a song or look out the window.

When I was a teenager, I read autobiographies but they were of Mark Twain and John Steinbeck. I knew that girls would never get to live like they did. Being an author is still shrouded in mystery. It is among the discouraged occupations, with secret passageways and walls. But at least it's quiet.

Not like singing. Where my mother listened to Mitch Miller and Bing Crosby in the rare moments she turned off the TV, I listened to folk music, singing along with Peter, Paul and Mary, Pete Seeger, Arlo Guthrie and The Seekers. But it was Joan Baez who most deeply inspired me. I cut out stories and photographs of her from magazines. The first time I saw her sing and talk on Johnny Carson I stayed up until 3:00 a.m. writing a song and wishing there was somewhere in my mother's house that I could sing without being heard. When Joan Baez sang, her eyes became deep and wise and I could feel her voice in my body, stirring me and lifting me up. In between songs her eyes flashed as she spoke on the crimes of governments and in support of César Chávez and Martin Luther King, Jr.

She wore jeans and took her shoes off and caused quite a stir when she said "fuck" on nationwide TV. There were paragraphs about her in the newspapers visiting Hanoi and Saigon, being banned in Korea.

I knew it was important that her singing was about the issues of our time, not just entertainment.

My mother hated her. "What's that noise!" she'd say when I played the records.

"She's just a Communist," my mother would continue. "Just a troublemaker and a hippie. She just can't get a real job."

I bought a full-sized black and white poster of Joan Baez in a head shop. Joan Baez was eighteen years old and singing at the Newport Folk Festival. It was my greatest treasure. I put it over my bed. Sometimes I would stand in my room and talk to her. "How?" I whispered. "How are you brave enough to sing and be seen and speak what's in your heart. How do girls get on stage? I want to move people like you do.

"But I live in Bryce and I'm fifteen years old. I get very scared. My mother is always telling me I'm not important and that I don't really know anything. But I do know that I would like to stand up like you and sing and teach."

I fit my voice to hers, learning to jump between notes and to memorize the verses of ballads. I read her autobiography, *Daybreak*, four times, especially the parts where she talked about singing, therapy and throwing up from anxiety. She became sister, co-conspirator, wise woman and mother. I had endless fantasies of meeting her. I would clean her car, dust her house, scrub her bathtub, or plug in her amplifier. Then one night, she'd hear me singing in the stairwell and invite me to sing with her. She would take me into her tutelage and teach me how to be like her.

Then Sarah would remind me that I wasn't Joan Baez and that I wasn't good enough. Singers were special, gifted people born with a microphone in front of them. They all knew how to play the piano and read music. Singers and musicians weren't people who made up songs and just wanted to sing them, like me.

I played the oboe in my high school band which specialized in John Philip Sousa for sports events and Johannes Brahms for quarterly concerts. I didn't like how small I had to make my mouth, scrunching my lips into the correct embouchure, squeaking with variations of lip tension. I didn't like the way that oboes always had solos, and the band teacher bore down on me with his baton as I squeaked and sweated from my too visible chair. My secret desire was to be in choir, but I didn't think I could change the instrumental decision made by my mother when I was in the fifth grade. She had chosen band for me; I didn't understand that I might have a choice for myself.

It has taken many years to call myself a musician or a singer. I did not have the requisite years of formal study. I had one year of piano in the fourth grade and seven years of band; I never learned anything about music theory or composing. But I have always been able to pick up a musical instrument and make a song on it.

Fortunately, when I was in high school, all of my friends loved to sing. While the popular girls practiced cheerleading routines and went to football games, Theresa, Lee, Sue, Margie, Sharon, Laura, Nancy and I became a jug band of washboards and washbuckets, guitars, kazoos and folk songs. I sang and played my guitar with Sharon in duets of "Where Have All the Flowers Gone" and "The Cumberland Mine." I sang her the songs I wrote. We gathered for slumber parties of munching, singing and stories. We laughed a lot. Singing and playing the guitar were even better than reading, because my voice took me to places of healing and connection.

After I left Bryce to go to college, I hardly ever went back, as if the town were contaminated. I lost touch with my friends. When we did get together, we didn't sing anymore. Somehow it was not right for grown women. I moved into apartments and a life in which singing seemed too loud and too much fun when there was a lot of work to finish. But I've never stopped missing the harmony of our voices. For a long time I hardly sang at all and came to accept longer intervals of silence. Then I realized that singing always makes me feel better. Nothing helps more than a sad song when I'm feeling terrible. Even a happy song can help, at least for a while.

Just when I thought I'd never have friends to sing with again, I found voice classes with April. I had tried to take voice lessons once before but they were boring and my voice felt artificial. In two years with April, our class has never once sung scales or learned a song in Italian. Instead, we allow our bodies to lead us and then allow sound to come out of our mouths. Sometimes I crawl and babble or stomp and growl. I rock and hum to myself, I find notes and words. When I follow my body and my voice, my emotions rise up and find sound and then melody and words as well.

We sit in a circle and share our experiences in movement and sound. Our songs are not separate from the circumstances of our lives. We talk about how our sound and movement express our life rhythms and stanzas.

Sometimes April says, "Take five minutes and find a song inside of you. It might have words or just a melody." We each find a place of our own to move our bodies and play with words and sound until a song begins within us. We find songs from both our overwhelmed inner children and our undaunted warriors. Sometimes even our critics sing or we become animals and sing songs of wolves and whales. Then we come together and sing our newfound songs. The group joins in with each woman, making harmony and exotic dissonance, enlarging the song and filling the room with sound.

In voice class, I learn a new rhythm; risk and support, risk and support.

# 11

## Stunned and Fuckit in the God Room

WHEN I FIND a chapel in the inner house I begin to wonder if
I am in a house or a castle. It's a narrow room of wooden
chairs with a pulpit and an altar. Jesus is bleeding on a cross
from his hands and forehead. He looks wiped out and
sweaty. On the wall a wispy, insubstantial Jesus pets a lamb.
Next to it, a stained glass window shows the Holy Spirit filling the disciples at the Last Supper. Judas's seat is empty.

"Bullshit," I say. "God is dead. Forgiveness is the least of
what needs to happen." I sing "With God On Our Side," a
satirical song by Bob Dylan about all the atrocities that various world governments have sanctioned in the name of God.
"He couldn't even find twelve good men to help him out," I
say and throw a hymnal through the stained glass. "Thanks
a lot for the mess, God!" I yell.

Then I see big monster shadows on the wall and they fall
across me. "Protect me, take care of me. Father. Father," I
pray. "Here is my worthless soul. Save me. Send an omen.
Send an angel. Make me like those popular girls in Young
Life. Make me fit in." I am fifteen and sixteen.

My mother is praying loudly from the front row. "Please,
God, please. Please God, send me a man."

The shadow on the chapel wall belongs to this man. It is
the shadow of another monster.

I want to break all of the furniture. I begin to smash the chairs against the wall. But then I freeze like a statue. I suck on a bitter root and bow my head. My mother says there are no shadows or monsters, only goodness and righteousness. She says God will punish me for my ideas and my disrespect. Now I need this room. I take down the art and put a picture window where the Last Supper was. I arrange the chairs in a circle and put herbs and sweet wine on boughs of cedar on the altar. I call the four directions and speak to the spirits of the land and sea and sky, the spirits that lived before God became so jealous. I say the words of power, "Do as you will and harm none. Blessed be." I separate truth from lies with an athame, slicing the air with this knife. I touch my heart with salt water and bless its loyalty. I stand as a priestess and petition the Goddess. I feel my spirit and feed it with my breath. I visualize my dreams. I no longer plead. I find my authority and speak in this room of peace and power.

·    ·    ·

My mother always called herself a Republican, but she was really an Authoritarian, not that there's much difference between the two. According to *The Concise Oxford Dictionary*, an authoritarian "favors, encourages or enforces strict obedience to authority as opposed to individual freedom."

Authority is primarily defined as "the power or right to enforce obedience." An authority is a person with power and rights. Authorities like to be in charge, love to make people do what they think is best and vigorously resist any examination of their own motivation. Authority loves institutions, where there is a bottom and a top. Adult over child, husband over wife, minister over flocks, employer over employees, teachers over students.

"Down with the authorities!" Fuckit says. I am a person who argues with news commentators.

In 1967 and 1968, when I was fourteen, radio stations

banned the song "Society's Child," by Janis Ian because it was about an interracial relationship. There were race riots in New Jersey, Detroit and Los Angeles. The government kept files on citizens and harassed political dissenters. The term "generation gap" was coined.

◆*Memory.* We always watch the nightly news with Walter Cronkite while we're eating dinner. I am supposed to be on a diet, so what's new. Jim is having more mashed potatoes. I stare at the salad of iceberg lettuce and shredded carrots that my mother has put in front of me. It is afloat in diet Thousand Island dressing. I have a hidden carton of malted milk balls in my bedroom. I ate half of them after school, putting three or four of them at a time into my mouth. I like to feel them pressing against my cheeks, then my jaws don't have to work so hard to keep my mouth closed. No matter what I eat, I always have a gnawing buzzing feeling between my stomach and my rib cage.

On TV there's a special report about the Haight-Ashbury Free Clinic. A man with long hair and a beard says that people bring things there that they don't use, like clothes and furniture, and the stuff will be given away free to whoever needs it. Pictures show twenty-year-olds with long hair and jeans making selections from cardboard boxes. Then the camera flashes to a house called a commune.

My mother says, "Can you imagine living like that? In that filth!"

The camera is showing mattresses on the floor and a woman and a man smoking rolled cigarettes on the porch.

"I just don't know what's wrong with young people today," she continues. "It's not like they had to live through the Depression. They've just had it too easy. They don't appreciate the value of a dollar."

The lettuce in the salad has brown edges. "Just because they don't want to sell their soul to buy a frame for the bed," I say, disgusted. "You just don't like them because of the length of their hair."

Daniel Berrigan has been arrested for pouring blood on the files at the Pentagon. "Out now, out now," a group of people chants in front of the White House, holding signs against the Vietnam War.

"The news media is just full of Communists, look at that!" my mother says as I scatter strips of shredded carrot with the tines of my fork.

I see a picture of a bag that looks like the ones hanging in my mother's closet, but I learn there's a dead soldier inside it. "We're killing people, don't you get it?" I say to her. "The home of the free and the brave is sending its own citizens over to be slaughtered, only it's mostly the poor citizens that end up dying. At least the Communists care that people have enough food which is more than in this country."

"You just calm down," my mother says. "Why do you always have to spoil dinner for everyone? I don't know where you get your ideas. This is the best country in the world and you should be grateful to live here. Now finish your dinner and let's not hear any more about this."

I roll my eyes and sigh audibly. I turn toward Jim half-hoping to find support. But in the last couple of years Jim won't even look at me when I argue with her.◆

It's 1991 and we're at war again, a new fast war with the name "Desert Storm," as if it were a weather condition. There are no visible body bags and only a few protesters in the news now that the war has begun, only daily Scud missile counts.

I am sure that my mother is in favor of this war. She probably has a yellow ribbon on her car antenna. I was always afraid there were more people like my mother than like me and my friends.

I have rented a tiny summer house next door to our island cabin for my writing studio. I do not allow myself to listen to the news here but I cannot put this new war out of my mind. The day is full of the suffocating blue-grays of sky and water and bare-limbed alders. I hear a throbbing boat engine on the waterway and when I look out I see a naval destroyer from the nearby base.

This is the same fear I felt when I was hiding under my grade school desk during the Cuban missile crisis. And it's the same rage I felt arguing with my mother and being given judgement and labels in return. Sometimes I felt like I was pleading with my mother to think, to engage in real discussion.

"But she had sold out before I was even born," Fuckit says. "She liked to be told what to do and how to be. If she'd ever had a questioning mind it was gone before I knew her." My mother gave away the jewels of her desires and dreams and abilities in order to possess the security of authority's mandates. She never questioned what she had been told about right and wrong. Patriotism was good, dissent was bad. Obedience was good, change was bad. People on welfare were bad and lazy, but working people were superior, if they were white.

As a teenager, I wrote songs and poems about racial equality and pacifism. I fasted with the Quakers at the nearby state capitol and read Mahatma Gandhi. I argued with my mother every night as we watched the news. At the end of the show I felt ravenous. I ate candy bars and began smoking to quell this need of my mouth to talk and to be acknowledged.

Like I'm smoking now, one cigarette after the other. "Fuckit and Stunned," Carrie says softly inside of me. "We don't have to plug our mouth up anymore or become paralyzed. We can let our feelings lead us into action."

I climb the steep trail down the cliff to the beach and look for whitened bones and magical rocks along the shore. I feel heavy with the war. I watch seagulls fly and know that thousands of miles from here, my tax dollars are paying to cover someone else's beach with oil and the number of lost birds is not even considered significant. I think I want to cry but I can't find any tears, only a desire to throw rocks. "Damn, damn, damn!" Fuckit says as they break the surface.

I return to my studio and begin writing an essay to send to the newspaper, just as I wrote letters to the editor when I was a teenager. I do not stop to smoke as I write. In this writing I feel strongly seated in my body and deeply satisfied by the act of finding language and image.

The second definition of authority is "a person or body having authority." My mother's authority was based on her role as a parent, a scaffolding stronger than her own knowledge.

"Listen to me," I say as I write my essay. "I feel an authority that comes from my body. An authority based on conviction and inner knowing. This authority does not need to call names or lessen someone else, but it does impel me to speak."

I'm still learning about wielding the kind of power that says, "This is my way, this is a way, tell me what do you think and why, be powerful with me." This is the authority of truth speakers, healers, teachers and gutsy women. The authority that says, "I know, I see, I think, I feel, I want, I don't want." This authority says, "My rage is clean and with reason."

. . .

My stepfather was crowned King my mother's wedding.

◆*Memory*. My mother wears a turquoise satin dress with a new pearl necklace and a high neckline. With sweating white-gloved fingers, I pull at the dress the foster woman picked out for me. I am watching my mother get married.

The foster woman said I would regret it later on in life if I didn't attend.

The small gathering of relatives is seated in wooden chairs in the chapel of my mother's church. This is the third time I've seen Don. The first time I only caught a glimpse of him at the front door, handing my mother a salmon that he'd caught. They didn't date until after I'd run away. I met him for the first time last night at a dinner in the banquet room of the Tyee Restaurant. All my uncles and aunts were there and a bunch of people I didn't know who were his relatives.

My mother sat next to him at the long table and smiled. I felt so dizzy I couldn't talk. She didn't say anything to me. "This is my daughter Louise," she told Don and his relatives. My jaw hurt from smiling and trying to stop my teeth from shaking.

Today I had to get here early for the pictures. My mother holds onto his arm and smiles up at his face. He nods at me. So far we haven't said anything other than hello. My mother looks at me and gives me the same smile she gives everyone else.

I wish I weren't here, no matter what the foster mother says. I haven't missed my mother since leaving home. I am not curious about this bald man in a brown suit. I have no feelings about him, no opinions yet. Just a sense of awe that my mother dated, got engaged and is now getting married four and a half months after I left home.

The social worker, Mrs. Field, said that my being gone had given my mother an opportunity to meet someone. Until I left home, my mother had had three dates—and those came only after we'd moved out of my grandparents' house. It confuses me that I somehow prevented my mother from going out.

I'm not surprised she's getting married, though. When we moved next door she started talking about needing a man to protect her and take her out to dinner. If she had a man, she could have married friends, she said. "But no man will ever want someone else's children," she would finish.

I used to wonder what it would be like to have a dad. But I'm not sure that this man at the altar whose cheeks are moving with grinding teeth is a dad.

There are more people at the reception than at the wedding and there is a long table of presents. I try to act happy for my mother. No one is talking to me very much and I wonder who my mother has told about my running away and living in a foster home. No one mentions anything about it. I can tell the people who don't know when they say, "Do you like your new father?" I smile and look at the floor and if they keep talking, I say, "I just met him last night."◆

The foster woman and the social worker, Mrs. Field, began pushing me homeward within two weeks of my mother's wedding. "Everything will be different with this new man and all," the foster woman said. "You should go home now so that you can all settle in together as a family. You've been gone long enough now."

Mrs. Field said that my mother wouldn't be so focused on me now that she had a man so things would be better.

No one mentioned that I would be having a relationship with this man myself. I was gaining a stepfather who was a total stranger. But I never had had any choice over who my mother brought to our house.

The foster home had been a lot like my mother's house. The foster woman was cold and determined to help my "poor" mother by making sure I didn't enjoy my stay with them and returning me home.

I figured I had three choices: I could go back to my mother's house. I could run away and be put in reform school. I could kill myself. I told myself that maybe this man really would make a difference. Maybe my mother wasn't really so bad either and I had just exaggerated. I'd be eighteen in only three more years. I could stick it out. I tried not to think about the only time I'd tried to talk to my mother in the four and a half months I'd been gone.

Mrs. Field had said the three of us should meet together. I remember being terrified beforehand that my mother would convince Mrs. Field that I was crazy and that they would commit me to an insane asylum. I knew if I ended up there I would go crazy listening to people scream and mutter.

Mrs. Field said, "What have you been thinking about your relationship with Louise, Mrs. Smith? It seems that Louise thinks that you and she don't get along."

"Well, she's just been around people with bad ideas. She just wants attention. She's so ungrateful for what I've given her. She ran away just to hurt me," my mother said.

Mrs. Field held up a hand and said, "Let's have Louise explain what she thinks the problem is."

I was surprised to be given a turn to speak. How could I explain the bad way she made me feel? Or the way I hated her?

"She yells at me," I began. "She doesn't like anything I do or anything about me."

"She's always talking back," my mother said, "and she doesn't appreciate what I've given her. She has absolutely no respect for the church or the family. She has Communist ideas and hangs out with the wrong crowd."

"I do not," I erupted, caught by the same old phrases. "She's always blaming me for everything. If someone likes me, she hates them or she tries to win them over, she doesn't want me to have friends."

"She's always interrupting," my mother objected, looking to Mrs. Field.

Mrs. Field said, "You interrupted Louise, Mrs. Smith."

My mother looked at her watch and said, "I have to go meet Don. He's waiting. We're going to pick out flowers for the wedding. I'm not going to ruin my day with any more of this." She left without saying goodbye after fifteen minutes.

When I moved back to my mother's house, my mother turned to face me in the dining room and said, "We'll just forget about everything that happened. We're going to be a family now. We'll just be nice to each other. We're so lucky to have Don."

Don filled the house with the horns and heads of elk and deer. They had marbles instead of eyes, stuffed and mounted into perpetual motionlessness. The buffet housed a new set of china and a sterling silver coffeepot and creamer. A fake leather recliner was delivered to the living room so that Don could put his feet up after work or eat in front of sporting events on TV.

We had meat more often, because men have to have meat. My mother complained less about money. At the wedding, I watched Don put his hand on top of my mother's on the knife as they cut the cake. His first act was to chop my mother's credit cards in half with the scissors because he did not believe in them. Later he burned my mother's boxes of school handouts and bulletin boards. He thought my mother was a pack rat, so he took it upon himself to remedy the situation with a unilateral bonfire. It was supposed to be a joke, this burning of my mother's boxes. I remember my mother giggling and saying, "Oh, he just says I have too much junk."

She gave him power. He assumed it. I never heard them argue. Don was a nonverbal king. From my mother, I learned to ask him questions like, "Who's ahead?", "Getting ready to go hunting, huh?" or "What a great tasting fish you caught!" He did not ask about me. But Don never was about asking. He just took whatever he wanted.

My mother began watching football and basketball so that she could share his interests. She was always home to make him dinner, she got up to cook him breakfast, she packed his lunch, tidied his house, did his laundry and arranged married social life. She was becoming a wife out of a magazine. She even talked for him.

"Don wants you to call him dad," my mother began, but it was never clear whose idea it really was. Jim and I had several secret conferences over what we were going to call him. Jim tried "Dad" and I tried not calling him anything. We eventually both settled on calling him Don. "Dad" suggested an easygoing good nature. Don was too tense for that.

"Don wants to adopt you kids," my mother announced. This time, Jim acquiesced. I teased him, chanting his new name back at him and adding insults. I couldn't tell Jim that I was mad at him for giving in and for learning to hunt and talk like Don. I flatly refused this adoption. "I'm not going to change my name now, I'm a junior in high school."

"It hurts his feelings that you don't want him to adopt you," my mother said. "And after he bought you a new guitar. You just can't ever go out of your way for anybody, can you?"

But I knew it was not affection but possession that lay behind her request. It felt right that my name was different than theirs.

.   .   .

Now I'm home at last after four days of teaching and seeing clients. Marianne meets me at the door and says, "Your brother called."

"Who?" I say, after trying to place him for a minute. "You're kidding. Jim?"

After eight years of silence from my family, it seems phenomenal that my brother is suddenly reappearing. Between *The Obsidian Mirror* and this book about my mother I have been writing about my childhood and my family for nine years. For most of that time I haven't seen my family in person. It's easier to remember Jim in Memory as a toddler holding my hand, as a little boy with a frightened smile, as a hail-fellow-well-met teenage cheerleader, who never fought back or did anything controversial.

"How did he get my phone number?" I ask. I have changed my name and moved.

"He said he wants your help," Marianne says.

Taking care of Jim had been my job, but that was a long time ago. Although he periodically confided in me when we were teenagers, he never challenged the adults. Although I hardly knew my cousins and never socialized with them, Jim worked with one cousin in his business. He never seemed to dread family gatherings the way I always did.

I'm accustomed to not having my family around. I have long-standing friends and my relationship with Marianne. I have chosen to be around people who want me to speak and be myself, people who make me happy. I don't have to keep anyone's secrets anymore and I haven't regretted it.

I want to pretend he hasn't called and put my feet up, drink a beer and tell Marianne about my workshops.

I look at the phone. The last time I talked to Jim it was by phone, too. It was the day after I confronted Don with the fact that he raped me at the ages of fifteen and sixteen. When I first told Jim about my incest memories, he said he believed me. But then I confronted Don, and Don said he hadn't done it. Then Jim started acting like Don was the victim instead of me. The last time we talked, he said he didn't know whom to believe.

I try to expect nothing when I dial the phone. He answers on the first ring.

He says he's had two sessions of therapy and when he was telling his therapist about the last time he talked to me, his therapist said he should try to find me and listen to the rest of what I had to say. He tracked me down through my high school English teacher I'd kept in touch with. I remember old warmth. I remember betrayal. I don't know how to feel now that I hear his voice once again. He wants to see me.

I am shaking all over after the phone call. I stand outside

and smoke many cigarettes, staring at the moon path across the water. I tell Marianne what he said. He still lives next door to my parents, with his wife and two small children. He still works with our cousin and goes to our childhood church. I keep feeling dizzy as if there'd been an earthquake.

"But he's in therapy?" Marianne asks.

"Can you believe it?" I say. My teeth are chattering. I try to stabilize them around a cigarette. What if I see Jim and find out I was exaggerating or misguided about my family? Maybe I've made it worse than it was.

Memory jerks me back to my body with several successive waves of nausea. My chest is small and tight with the weight of Don's body. I have a cold fear down the middle. I remember how he brought his hunting guns into my room. I remember my fear of not knowing what he would do when his massive restrained body sought release. Marianne puts her hand on my back and breathes with me. "My fear is about what happened. I didn't make anything up, I know that in my body." Neither did I know how much safer I felt not having contact with my family. Despite Jim's promises not to reveal my name, location and phone number, I feel scared. What if he slips because he wants to deny the seriousness of the situation?

I tell myself I am being melodramatic to imagine Don coming with his guns and shooting me. "But people do get shot," Carrie says. "Lots of them. The story behind the killings usually does not make the newspaper." My stepfather has always reminded me of the silent men who one day shoot everyone in their families and then turn the gun on themselves.

A barge hums on the water, lit with blue and red lights. I lean against the pine tree and look back through the lit windows of our house. The walls are full of paintings and prints of women with bowls and round goddess bellies. Bookcases reach to the ceiling.

"Jim sounded so grateful that I called him back," I tell

Marianne. "Maybe I'm scared to want something from him and end up disappointed again."

I smile at Marianne. "One thing is for sure. Life is sweeter than it's ever been."

"I don't know what will happen with Jim," I tell the inner voices. "But I'm going to take care of you."

No one looks more like me than Jim. Our hair is the same definite brown, thick and straight. We have the same full lips and eyebrows. I always wanted his eyes, which are brown, like our long ago father's, where mine are hazel, a shade darker than my mother's.

I had forgotten how tall he had become or even the fact that he's a thirty-five-year-old man now, an adult. He hugs me. I hug the middle of his chest. "Louise," he says, "It's been too long. Every day I thought about you and wondered how you were doing."

We're standing on the bluff, watching a seagull circle and squinting at the sun straining through the sheets of clouds. I am standing apart from him.

Eight years have passed. The reason we have not spoken is that I told my side of childhood and my family kicked me out. "Jim, you're the one who didn't want anything to do with me," I remind him. I'm the one who sent the last unacknowledged Christmas card eight years ago. On it I said, "Call me when you're ready." Now that he's here, I need to let him know that I have not forgotten.

"I'm sorry," he says, "I should have said that right away. I'm so grateful that you'll see me. I'm sorry that I turned away from you. I believe you about Don's raping you."

Eight years ago Jim had said, "Why did you have to call it rape?" I said, "Because that's what it was." Maybe Jim paid more attention eight years ago than I thought he had at the time.

"I have to say this first," he says. "I'm a sexual addict. I have to keep saying it out loud. I've compulsively had affairs for the fifteen years of my marriage. I've harassed the women I worked with. I've lied and put on a good appearance so that no one would ever know this truth. Then another man recognized what I was doing and confronted me about it. Cindy said we were through unless I changed.

"I hit bottom. I started in a Sex Addicts Anonymous group. Cindy's going to the Co-dependents of Sex Addicts Anonymous. We're both in therapy, too. It's been rocky."

We've moved inside. He's sitting on the couch across from me. His voice is shaky. "I know I have a long way to go."

"Do you have any memories of being sexually abused?" I ask him. I never really thought of the incest touching him. He got along without arguments or endless interrogation, unlike me. He went hunting and fishing with the men. He couldn't have been vulnerable like me. Or could he?

"I hardly have any memories of my childhood," he says. "That's one reason I want to talk with you."

He has a clipboard with lists of questions. I have memories of being sexually abused and thousands of abusive moments with my mother. But I only know my own story. I do not remember him being sexually or physically abused; it was all I could do to cope with the violence that landed on me. I thought then that being a boy gave him protection. He was called the "man of the family" from the time he was six. But he was also sent off with my grandfather, Uncle Kevin and Don. Like me he was quiet and now, in Memory, I see a younger Jim, scared and trying too hard to do the right thing.

"I'm glad you're getting help," I say.

"I've been numb for a long time," he says.

Then I ask the question I've wondered about for eight years.

"How is Mother explaining my absence?" I blurt, unable to contain my curiosity any longer. I knew from experience she would be bothered not by my absence but by how it looked to others. My mother was never an adherent to the literal truth. I figured she had married me off to a faraway man or maybe even killed me in a car accident in one of the Xeroxed letters she sends to relatives and acquaintances. The year after I quit graduate school, I received her Christmas letter, in which she said, "Louise is doing well at school," instead of, "Louise is serving pizza in downtown Seattle." Once I started therapy, my mother omitted me entirely from her letters, though she mentioned all of my cousins and uncles and aunts as if she were putting out a family newsletter. Still, I was sure people asked about me, since grown children are a small town topic of conversation.

Jim says, "I got mad at her because she tells everyone you accused Don of abusing you and then she lies and says that you decided not to have anything else to do with them. I told her, 'Why don't you tell the truth that you didn't want anything to do with Louise?'"

Jim looks puzzled and polite when I break out laughing. I had never even pictured this as a possibility. "You mean she's telling everyone what I said Don did? She's telling my story for me? That's fantastic!

"Oh, I know that she probably thinks that everyone will think I'm crazy for saying such things," I continue. "But a lot more people are talking about incest than ever before. Hardly a week goes by without someone on TV talking about it, bless Roseanne Arnold, among others."

Jim nods his head and looks a little lost. We aren't used to each other.

"A couple weeks ago I took her out to dinner, just her and me at the Clam House. I wanted to ask her two questions. I wanted to know what she knew about our real father and I wanted to know if she thought there was any truth in what you said about Don."

I sigh impatiently at the thought of Jim asking our mother for the truth of something.

"All she said was that I should know Don wouldn't do anything like that. Everything was very cordial and she thanked me for the dinner and said how nice it was to spend time with me.

"The next day I get this seven page letter from her." He holds up a thick envelope. "I want to read it to you."

I am all ears.

Her words weave a familiar pattern. She begins by telling Jim how happy he was as a teenager because Don took him fishing and hunting and taught him to drive a tractor.

She writes of Don, "He never did an unkind act. That is why you must understand the hurt he must have from Louise." Then she gives the familiar litany of Girl Scout camps and trips I am ungrateful for. How Don gave me a guitar. The way I always exchanged my Christmas presents from them for cash. She goes on to detail my dropping out of graduate school and how I left behind my grandfather's desk "without a care or a sentiment."

On the subject of Don, she writes, "But when I look at this very special man that I am most fortunate to have, who gave his all to raise another man's sperm children—I can't see him hurt anymore.

"I shall never forget that look on his pale face and his shaking body as I read that made up Hollywood movie story the drama etc. If Louise wanted to hurt me again she would do it to Don and destroy my lover. I talked to Judge Granite and Reverend Hale. Both think she was on drugs . . .

"I'm really hurt to think you even think Don would touch anyone but me!! He is still one of the old-fashioned kind. Thank God. He is a better Christian than I."

It is all I can do to listen to Jim read the letter without making growling noises and interrupting. What about my pale and shaking body, the one our mother had plenty of years to notice? It's been eight years and she still uses exactly the same phrases she used when I was fifteen years old. And they still bring Fuckit to my throat.

Jim stops reading to tell me how mother bought basketball

tickets for Don's birthday and signed Jim's name to the card assuming they would go to the games together. When we were growing up, our mother always bought presents and signed cards from us. It was embarrassing to be thanked for gifts we didn't know about and never would have chosen ourselves. Jim told her, "I don't want to go. I don't have time. The tickets weren't really from me."

In the letter, my mother writes about this incident, "Well, I guess this mother is too busy planning how to make old folks have fun in life and thinking what they would like instead of how I might like to have spent $100 other than on a ball game. I am hurt almost as much as what Louise has done to him.

"Can't you count your blessings and set down on paper the goals you want for your family. . . . Don't dwell on the past or what you did or didn't get as a child. Be happy and be the kind of person others look up to for strength. You have a wonderful personality and are very very handsome. . . . We are not trying to run your life.

"I am trying not to talk and listen more."

The last sentence is my mother's mantra. She's gotten about as far with it as I have with quitting smoking.

My entire teenage experience with my mother has flashed across my mind as he was reading. She is quoting the same judge and minister, saying the same phrases I heard a thousand times, reciting her list of what she has given and calling in the chips: loyalty, gratitude, obedience.

I take some deep breaths. At least the letter wasn't sent to me.

Jim says, "My therapist says she's the most controlling woman he's ever heard of."

I am beginning to feel good about his therapist.

"It's been hard living next door to them. Whenever mother has company, she just brings them over. We were going crazy cleaning our house all the time. She calls me at work or just drops by when I'm working. The last thing was over the church photograph. The first one didn't turn out so everyone was supposed to go to the studio and get it redone. We don't have time. I mean I'm in two twelve-step groups, therapy, I call square dances on weekends and I have two kids and I think I want to get to know them now.

"So she goes on and on about how the woman putting together the booklet is a friend of hers and Mother would be so hurt if I don't take my whole family back to the studio in their Sunday best and get their picture taken.

"I feel like I don't have a life of my own," he says. "I'm thirty-five and I don't know what I want to do, I'm so busy doing what she wants."

I feel a familiar resentment that Jim stuck around until he owned a very expensive house built on land given them by Don and a retirement plan of $50,000 a year at the relatives' business. The sibling comparisons continue. My mother never told me I was pretty or that I had a good personality.

I look out the windows and watch a robin land on the picnic table. The sun has delivered a patch of robin's egg blue over Puget Sound. Marianne makes tuna fish sandwiches and slices an apple for us.

"So what do you remember," he says.

Now, I used to pretend that someone in my family, maybe a cousin, or the next generation of nieces and nephews would start therapy and look me up wanting to know what I knew. And I would hand them a copy of *The Obsidian Mirror* and say, "I just happen to have written it down." I never thought I'd really get to do it though.

He holds my book reverently and turns it over in his hands and says, "This is wonderful. I'm so proud of you."

I smile from ear to ear.

I say, "I'm glad to hear you say that because for the last three years, I've been writing a book about our mother."

He says, "I can hardly wait for that one."

.  .  .

I am teaching a three-day workshop on Healing the Daughter, for women who were emotionally, physically and/or sexually abused by their mothers. I invite the circle of twenty-four women to travel with me through Memory and visualization and to explore what we carry and how we heal. I invite them to make noises and move their bodies, to tap the floor with the rhythm of their healing symbols, to find words for incidents and feelings that have never before had language. I hear stories of scars from being beaten with hoses and plywood. I hear of vulvas splayed open by prying mother hands that left nothing for the daughter to call only hers. I read from my book. We write.

Sarah is very loud after the first evening group. "You're not doing this right. People were subdued. No one thinks you know what you're doing. Did you see that woman looking at you critically? Who do you think you are, some kind of authority?"

First thing the next morning, I lead everyone in the making of inner critic puppets. We draw them on white lunch sacks and name them. "What do they say?" I ask. "You're not good enough," says a prim critic named Martha. "I don't know why you have to act like that," says a critic who looks feeble except for her big teeth. "You should die!" says another critic who is a black cloud.

We put the critics outside now that they've had time to express themselves. I help one woman find a rock to hold the self-destructive aspect of her critic. Together we create boundaries and make safety.

We stand in a circle and say our first names exactly the way we'd like to hear them said. Then the group repeats each name with that inflection. Some women cry as they say their names with love and tenderness or boldness. Some women say their name in a solid way, others with an open gesture of their arms. We go around and around the circle saying our names.

We sit in a mineral pool and recount the lies our mothers

told us about our bodies. One woman said her mother ridiculed her because of the smallness of her breasts. Another was humiliated because she was full-breasted. I talk about being fat. Hips, hair, eyes, posture, genitals, we name the curses that keep us from standing as free women. Our lips name lies which leave our muscles, pulled out of us in the hot sacred pool.

We meditate on the powerful perfect woman inside each of us. We pass a stick around the circle and proclaim what is true. "I am beautiful." "I am lovable." "My breasts are perfect." "I am my own." The voices of the daughters ring like a bell with authority and greatness.

# 12

# *The Parlour*

ALL THE WINDOWS are open but the room is still full of cigarette smoke. The curtains are long and thick; they narrow the windows and block some of the breeze. A burgundy velvet Victorian lady's chair is dimly visible through the haze.

I sit in a love seat in a corner of the parlour of the inner house. I play with my split ends, catching a tiny forked hair and splitting it into two weak strands up the side of my head. I stop to light a cigarette.

I like the way the smoke stings the back of my throat and gathers like a tangible force at the top of my chest. I like the solidity of the cigarette between my fingers and the long cloud that materializes in front of my face. I like the lifting dizzy sensation that lightens this heavy stuffy room. I like how I hold my head when I smoke. I am mysterious and exotic and tough. I am sixteen and seventeen and I know more than my mother. I have these cigarettes and she can't take them away from me. They give me something to clamp down on with my teeth, like biting on a bullet.

My mother is sitting across from me in a straight back chair in her best clothes. She has company. She's pointing her finger at me and saying, "Just look at her, see how bad she is, sitting there and smoking. I've done everything I could. I just don't know what's wrong with her." She is inciting them to riot against me.

I light another cigarette. I like the way smoking helps me not care. I look out the window. I tap my fingers on the coffee table.

The company leaves. My mother mutters derogatory statements in my direction. I roll my eyes and exhale a long cloud of smoke.

The monster is still here. His shadow covers me up completely, suddenly, taking my breath away. I am speechless when he leaves. I turn my chair to face the corner. I fill ashtrays to overflowing. My fingers shake as I light another cigarette from the embers of the one before it.

I fume. I gather strength. With it, I stub out a half-smoked cigarette and say, "I'm leaving," out loud.

I collect my passport and stand at the door.

My mother blocks the exit, cutting the light into small triangles.

I crawl outside between her foot and the door frame.

On the outside, I'm like something that has just hatched, wet all over and so uncertain that I wobble. I have habits of ducking, flinching, smiling and smoking. I go on a long trip. I find good allies. I try to outgrow my mother and this house.

I return of my own volition. It's my house now. I hold salons in the parlour dressed in costumes of green silk and long shiny earrings. I say aloud everything I was ever forbidden to mention. I speak without any shame. I come and go from this room without interference.

. . .

◆*Memory.* My mother and I are arguing in the kitchen. Don's at the table reading the newspaper. I can see his teeth grinding as he reads. Mother is threatening to sic the minister on me because of my attitude, as usual.

I say, "Right. All we need is a little more prayer," in my most sarcastic tone of voice.

Don leaps from the table and pounds his fist down on

the kitchen counter next to me. "You will not talk about the church or to your mother in that way!"

My mother and I both stop. Usually Don leaves when we're arguing.♦

My mother used to say, "Don doesn't talk much, but when he does, it's important." From the beginning of their marriage, my mother began mythologizing Don. She made him flawless, like a god, attributing unquestioned virtue to his behavior. When I remember this, it isn't his voice that makes my shoulders flinch, though, it's the sound of his fist coming down on the counter.

Jim called today to tell me that Don agreed to go with Jim to see Jim's therapist. Eight years ago, after I confronted him, Don had agreed to go to therapy with me, too. I haven't heard from him since.

This news comes several months after Jim attempted to set limits with our mother and stepfather. He told them he did not want them to come over or to bring anyone else over without calling first. He said he did not want mother dropping by his workplace or calling him there. He also told them he believed Don had sexually abused me and that he did not want his kids left alone with either one of them.

Incest is another form of sexual addiction. Offenders rarely limit themselves to one child victim. So I was very glad when Jim said he wasn't going to leave the children alone with our parents. But as I walk down our driveway to my writing studio, I feel a twinge of guilt. This limit was set because of my memories. I have to remind myself that Don is the reason a limit is needed, not me. In every other phone call to me, Jim worries about depriving the kids of their grandparents or the grandparents of their grandchildren. Yet one of the few things Jim remembers is that he was terrified of our grandfather. I have to remind him that I for one would have been infinitely better off without Grandpa. We agree on this and yet we were teethed on "Honor Your Parents and Especially Your Grandparents."

"Sometimes I wish the damn incest would just go away," Stunned says. I sit at my writing table and stare at a blank page of my journal.

Every time I talk with Jim he tells me how important *The Obsidian Mirror* is to him. He says he believes my memories of Don sexually abusing me. He says he supports me and my work and that he does not want to discount me in any way or fall into denial. Jim has said most of the right things to me, but I still feel shaken at the image of him, his male therapist and Don in the same room. On their agenda are my memories of Don sexually abusing me. It makes my stomach ache.

I sit at my long writing table and watch the water. My studio is set in a valley, between the folds of a hill. The trees lean toward me, revealing a patchwork of water. At our house, I can look far over Puget Sound. In my studio, I am brought back to the immediate, the heaviness in my chest, the revisitation of Memory that Jim's phone call left with me.

◆*Memory.* I am fifteen. My mother s away at summer school. We're living in the house where Don lived from his adolescent years until he married my mother; his aunt's and uncle's house.

We moved here because Don is building us a new house nearby. Jim and I are supposed to take care of Don while mother is gone. I am supposed to iron his underwear and his shirts. Mother made dinners in advance and froze them. She said Jim and I are supposed to be good for Don and take care of him. I did not hear her tell him to be nice to us.

I am sitting on the floor next to my bed, propped against the wall. I crawled down here a few minutes or a long time ago after Don's eyes became cold boring flint and I was trapped on my bed under him.

I am staring at blurry far-off shapes. I can't remember

the names of anything.

There's a line at my throat between my face and my chest and everything I swallow is stuck in that split. My face is losing form. My mouth dangles open. My eyes don't blink.

I am waiting for whatever happens next. I sniff the air like a deer and freeze at his scent. I don't know why I am hunted by him but I suppose deer don't understand it either.

If I were dead I could stop. Waiting.

Some other self has a fiery tongue but she leaves when Don is here because I am too frightened of what he would do if she talked. I clench hold and keep us still.

"Write. Write. Write," a far-off voice whispers.

My pens are across the room. I crawl over to them. I write a poem about a walnut broken open, soft flesh picked by a sharp instrument. The mists that seemed to rise in my forehead settle back down as words return.◆

On the edge of sleep, when Don's hands pulled me over in my bed, there was no Fuckit or God or any other sort of intervention. There was only Stunned, holder of sensation, explorer of the land between the inner eyelid and my eye, willing herself to disappear into the black limitless land away from the body.

Stunned is the writer. She is the me who has felt every emotion before, who has drowned and floated to the surface. She is the part of me with the patience to sit for hours and let sentences come from a mind in trance. She is the one who allows me to stare out the window and go slowly enough to write and revise. She is the one in my body as I sit in this chair and type. YoungerOnes are too active for sustained concentration. Fuckit likes to read aloud and sing. Stunned lets the feelings finger her again, mining them for words, familiar with their pull. I survived because Stunned wrote.

In my journal I write, "I just wish Jim would move away

from them!!!! For a long time Jim has tried to play peace-maker. He is more practiced at avoiding conflict than at being firm."

A week after Jim set his boundaries with Mother and Don, Don called Jim at work saying that Mother was having a nervous breakdown because of what Jim had said and Jim had better leave work right away and come talk to her. Jim left work and went to their house to find Mother with another repetitive letter to give him, sobbing and yelling. She said Jim had no right to deprive them of their grandchildren, and asked how he could say such things about Don. "You just don't care what you do to me," she sobbed.

Jim got mad and yelled back at Mother, like I did for all those years. This is new for him. "You just can't talk to her," he tells me.

Our mother represents everything men are taught to despise in women: manipulation, guilt and displays of emotion. For a daughter to hate her mother is a betrayal. For a son to hate his mother is a defense of his masculinity. Although I agree that communication with our mother is impossible, I am uncomfortable with Jim's suggestion that Don is actually easier to talk to. She is verbal but he's a coiled snake.

I have to remind Jim that it's Don who violated his boundaries by calling him at work. I notice Jim did not tell Don "No," or refuse to come at his call. I am afraid Jim will not stand with his own truth in the face of the unquestioned authority we were taught to give to Don.

I can also see that my stepfather and mother are perfect for each other. They are so busy defending each other that neither can take responsibility for his or her own actions.

I remind myself that this is between Jim and the parents. I have no desire to have a relationship with Carol and Don. I have not been impressed with their response to him as he has challenged them and set boundaries. And I have vowed that I will never be Don's victim again.

Can three men in a room not side together when they discuss the sexual assault of a woman? I recall the Senators who interviewed Clarence Thomas for the Supreme Court and his accuser Anita Hill. They were so stupid and insensitive that it was obvious they had never thought about their own treatment of the opposite gender. I have seen men humiliate women in the company of each other, in bars, on sidewalks, in institutions and courtrooms. I have not seen them challenge each other.

But Jim is saying things I don't usually hear men say. "I went to this twelve-step retreat," he said. "I felt like people really cared about me there. It's the first time I've ever hugged another man. It felt so good."

He said that he and four-year-old Noah are learning to cook together. "There was so much role work in our family," he said. "Why should Cindy have to do all the cooking? She works, she's busy. It's this idea that women should do everything in the house. It's ridiculous."

He tells me that his sexual addict group talks about all the ways the media supports sexual harassment of women. He says they talk about how the macho portrayal of men is disgusting and unhealthy.

I have been waiting to hear sentences like these from the mouth of a man for a long time.

• • •

When I was sixteen, Stunned filled my head with scenarios of suicide. I imagined holding rifles to my head and pulling the trigger, jumping off bridges with weights on my ankles, walking in front of oncoming cars or inhaling carbon monoxide in our garage. "If I were dead," Stunned said, "then nothing else would happen. I would really be like a rock then."

But Fuckit was not about to allow me to surrender to Stunned's catatonia or even to die in such a boring way as Stunned envisioned. "If I'm going to die, I'd rather die in Greenwich Village," Fuckit reasoned.

Getting to Greenwich Village was the problem. Nonetheless, from the time I was twelve until I left home at seventeen, Fuckit said, "We have to get out of here."

◆*Memory.* I yell back at my mother with fiery words that come to my lips fast and in complete sentences. I can think faster than her; it's the way I win debates at school. I know what my mother will say in her next sentence and I refute it before she has finished saying it. She hates my hair, the look on my face, my clothes, my friends, my politics and the way I walk. The feeling is mutual.

"As long as you're under this roof, young lady, you will do as I tell you." She almost always ends up here, after she's put me on restriction for another ninety-nine years.

This time I walk toward the door. "I'll find another roof then," I say.

"Go on, just get out!" my mother says, opening the door.

I feel strong and certain in my legs as I walk closer.

My mother stands in front of the opening with her hands on the frames. "You're not leaving and embarrassing me like that again! Now go to your room."

I burn her with my eyes before I surrender.◆

When I was losing hope and Stunned seemed to be gaining the upper hand, Fuckit met a compatriot named Paul. We shared an above average grade point, rounder than popular bodies, glasses, large vocabularies and a love of eating. He had a car because his father owned a wrecking yard. He was interested in the theatre, elegant restaurants and poetry.

He was Fuckit's best friend, bolder and wilder than my girlfriends. He taught me to inhale cigarettes. I tasted hard liquor the first time under his tutelage. I made him hold hands with me. But we did not explore sex, even though Fuckit wanted to do that as well. Paul knew he was gay before he had language to explain it to me.

He persuaded me to try out for plays and to join nearly

every school club outside athletics that it was possible for me to join. We belonged to Future Business Leaders of America which was filled with typing and shorthand students, and Science Club, which had good field trips. We even attended an occasional meeting of the Future Homemakers of America. I prevailed upon Paul to join the debate team and to enter speech contests. We won trophies and spent hours refining political arguments.

Paul had a casual style that I lacked. He was very polite to my mother so that she was hard-pressed to find fault with him beyond her wonder that he would want to hang out with me. His pie crusts were so flaky that the home economics teacher asked him to teach the senior girls to make pies. Even now, twenty-two years later, Paul cooks spontaneous feasts in his extensive kitchen, reeling off recipes he has just invented. As teenagers in Bryce, we explored the exotic cuisine of Taco Time and The China Clipper.

I stopped asking my mother if I could go out and just told her that I was going. I stopped paying attention to being on restriction since I was always on it anyway. What I wasn't was home. Paul introduced me to bingo at the American Legion, where we smoked and drank 7-Up amidst the long tables of middle-aged and elderly Bryce residents. We wore jeans and love beads. Following in Paul's footsteps, I ate raw eggs because he had read about their health benefits. Together we put Sun-In in our hair, which turned the palms of our hands orange.

We engaged in political activity, protesting the dress code and the right-wing offerings of the high school library. When the garbage on the floor of Paul's car was knee high, we drove to the local John Birch Society bookstore after it had closed and emptied the garbage on the lawn. Occasionally, we'd dress in our moccasins, love beads, peace symbols and headbands and wander inside the John Birch Society bookstore, just to make them nervous. Paul took me to see *Hair* and *Tommy* in Seattle.

But there were still too many hours of being home. Fuckit could not always cast off my growing depression and despair. Thoughts of suicide intensified. I felt dirty and numb, angry and despairing.

Stunned chanted, "Everyone hates me. I hate my body. Nothing is ever going to change."

Then I learned about exchange students who were allowed to leave home early and go to other countries and have adventures. This suited Fuckit just fine. I wrote and rewrote applications explaining why I would be a good representative of the United States and of the Bryce Rotary. I went to interviews where I had to eat standing up, balancing a tasteful amount of food and talking to the other candidates. We were then scored on social graces. I was interviewed on the matter of the Vietnam War, civil rights and my favorite books. Because of debate, I could quote a variety of sources and opinions in my answers. Because of my mother, I was very good at being polite and smiling even though my jaw was so tight with apprehension that I could hardly open my mouth. But Fuckit saw a way out and I went for it like a moth to light.

After the first interview, the Rotary wanted a statement signed by parents about their willingness to pay for airfare in the event that their child was accepted. That was the only required money, since the host family would provide food and shelter and the local Rotary gave a monthly allowance.

"How am I going to do this?" I asked Paul.

"Just kind of act like you don't care," he said. "But mention that it's really an honor."

When my mother was mad, she yelled, "You and Paul just want to be famous. You're just ambitious." It was bad to want that, just like wanting attention was bad. But she approved of getting good grades and winning awards because these accomplishments reflected well on her.

She signed the form. I will never know why she said I could go in the first place, although the fact that several of the Rotarians attended our church probably helped. At home, though, her signature became the cornerstone of what I now owed her.

"How can you be an exchange student and treat your mother this way?" she would demand when I walked in the house after spending time with Paul.

"But I told you this morning I had a debate this afternoon," I would say.

"You did not," she would insist. "You can't just go off anytime you want, young lady."

"But I told you," I would repeat. She just didn't pay attention when I talked.

"You better watch your step, or you're not going anywhere," my mother said.

At school, a couple of months after I filled out my first application, it was announced over the loudspeaker that I had been selected to be the exchange student.

But my mother had decided I wasn't good enough to go. She assembled a committee to blacklist me. At the time, it was like a fist falling out of the sky and landing right on Fuckit.

♦*Memory.* It's the last period of the day when a pink slip is brought to the door instructing me to see the school counselor immediately. The last time I saw the school counselor was when I ran away from home two years ago. I feel my heart beat in my stomach. I stop at the bathroom first, bending over and holding myself in a stall. I don't know why I'm so nervous.

Miss Turk purses her tight lips and looks down her nose at me when I enter her tiny office. She says, "There has been a meeting about your being the exchange student and serious questions about your suitability came up."

I am trying to understand what is happening, checking through my mind to find something I have done in the last week that has caused this. I feel like my body will fly apart. Inside I am holding on tight, waiting until this is over to find the sense in it. I passed every interview and application. I have letters of acceptance from the Rotary on my dresser. "Just don't lose it," I say to myself.

Miss Turk says, "You did run away from home, after all. There's no evidence you can get along with your family. If you can't get along with them, then how can the Rotary count on you to get along in another country?

"Your mother says you are disrespectful and that you don't help out around the house. We've met with some of your teachers and Mr. Mason of the Rotary.

"At school, you've been involved in that underground newspaper, you've worn a black armband and you were seen holding hands in the hall with Jerry Harmon. We decided at the meeting that we're just not sure that you should get to go."

The breath I was holding is pushed out in crying, which I don't want and can't stop. Jerry Harmon is my boyfriend and an artist. Just because he doesn't get good grades. . . . My rage is flames like a house on fire, making my skin red, burning my fists.

Miss Turk continues to list my inadequacies. "You are too opinionated. You see everything in black and white. You don't love your mother and you are not responsible at home." Now the fire is ashes, leaving a hollow in my center. My mind goes blank like the TV screen with little gray buzzing lines.

Miss Turk goes on and on about my attitude and who I hang out with and my poor mother and what about God. How does she know these things about me? I swallow the tears and nod but I am not really even here. Finally Miss Turk says, "The Rotary is still undecided. We'll talk more about this later."

I return to the bathroom and sit there for a long time. My head feels like I don't have a skull to hold my brain. I wander the empty hall like a wounded animal. I know those metal containers lining the hall are lockers and that the door to Mrs. Arnold's room is open which means she's inside. But shapes and facts seem unreal, a mirage.

Mrs. Arnold teaches drama and literature. She is lively and funny. Paul and I play tricks on her and have even visited her at her house. I turn into her room where I've spent a lot of time after school hanging around her desk. I tell myself to be cool, but the first thing I say is, "I might not get to be an exchange student."

Mrs. Arnold says, "I know. I was at the meeting. Your mother organized it."

My head is too big again. What did I do? How many people were at this meeting? What did they all decide about me?

I try to act like it doesn't matter, but I leave her room as fast as I can. So what? I say to myself but I feel like I have footprints on my forehead. I thought she liked me. Why was she there? Does she believe all those things Miss Turk said about me?

I want to throw up. I am outside, walking through the football field. I wonder how far I could walk if I just kept walking and never stopped.◆

I gave my life to Jesus instead. In those minutes after school I totaled the trends of my sixteen years and decided that since I didn't have control over my life, I might as well give it to him.

"I just wanted God to take over," Stunned says. "It seemed like Fuckit only got us punished."

I only told three people what had happened in Miss Turk's office: my friend Sally and her friends Jane and Harold Lint, the local Young Life leaders. Sally was a Christian and also the new elementary school music teacher. I hung out with her a lot, cleaning her apartment and doing errands just to spend time with her. She had been trying to "save" me for a year.

I stood in her classroom and told her I might not get to be

an exchange student after all. Her first response was to be mad at my mother and that felt good.

I said I couldn't go home yet.

Sally took me to the Lints's house. On their wall was a trivet that said, "God is Everywhere," and pictures of Jesus. Their house was warm and they listened as I sat on a barstool in their kitchen and told them about Miss Turk.

Jane Lint said, "Let's just pray about this and ask Jesus for help."

Included in the prayer was an opportunity to ask Jesus into my heart. Sally and the Lints were sure that this would make everything better. Stunned discovered that if I prayed long enough and focused on the inside of my forehead, I could see a calming light.

Miss Turk, who was a born-again Christian herself, was delighted to hear of my conversion. The Rotary decided I would be a good exchange student after all, provided I lost twenty pounds before leaving. It would be better for me if I was thinner they said. They had decided 165 pounds was too fat for my own good.

I prayed to Jesus to help me lose weight. I lost fifteen pounds.

Sarah found a new permission in Christianity to tell me how bad I was. I was nothing, only God was important. His will be done, not mine. My true self was sinful and ugly. Christianity fit perfectly into the shame and abuse I had already experienced. Masturbating, hating my mother, talking back, having unkind thoughts, wanting comfort from older women or feeling proud of myself were forbidden by Scripture. I was always trying to be good enough and failing to control my impulses.

I wrote religious poetry. I sang Christian songs. I learned that astrology, UFOs and tarot cards were of the devil. I stopped reading fantasy books. I stood on street corners and passed out booklets on converting to Christ. I witnessed to my friends. For Christmas I asked for a Bible with a fancy concordance system in the margins.

I left Christianity three and a half years later, after a steady progression that began in a conservative church, passed through a Pentecostal congregation and ended in a Christian cult whose members gave up personal decisions to a hierarchy of men called prophets. At the head was a male apostle. Women were "handmaidens." We spoke in tongues and the homeowners stored barrels of grain for Armageddon in their basements.

Still, Fuckit survived, though much less flamboyantly than I might have otherwise. I failed to quit smoking or masturbating. I felt guilty and prayed for forgiveness and divine assistance. Because of Fuckit I never quite became a wholesome Christian young woman. The dress I was supposed to wear to church never quite fit.

Nor could I sustain myself on faith alone. At nineteen I decided I'd rather risk being struck down with lightning than to continue with a God who thought everything I did was bad. I couldn't be a sheep or keep my head covered and my mouth closed. My mother's ways of memorization and subservience would never fit me.

I used to be mad that I had spent so much time praying when I might have been untangling myself instead. I discounted the genuine yearning for spiritual experience that Stunned felt. Now I see that my work with self-awareness, ritual and healing has led me to the realm of spirit that I was seeking then.

Looking back now, I can acknowledge that Christianity did save me, at least briefly. It allowed me to leave home, even if it did nothing for my self-esteem.

. . .

"This is fantastic," Fuckit thought, as the stewardess handed me my first glass of complimentary champagne and I lit my fifth cigarette on the plane to Australia. Glorious bub-

bles of freedom rose up in my chest. I was happy for the first
time in years.

Not that the Rotary exactly encouraged me to have a good
time. "You are there to go to school," they stressed. I was
supposed to act serious and mature, like a grownup, not excited and full of adventure.

Girls were sent home if they became pregnant, although
the Rotary didn't address the subject of sex. Memory shows
me all the ways I re-enacted the sexual abuse of my childhood during the year I was an exchange student and the
years after that. My craving for sexual stimulation and touch
had been escalating since I was twelve. My desire was
wrapped in shame, forbidden by God and entirely separated
from genuine affection by Fuckit. I ping-ponged between
prayers for abstinence and heavy making out, for which
Sarah scolded me. Several times I got into what I would now
consider perilous situations. "Want to see the city?" a man
I'd met asked me while I was on a tour of Melbourne.
"Sure," I said. "Want to eat some prawns?" another man
said. I went off with them each time, refusing to believe they
just wanted sex. I would be aroused and return their kisses
and then freak out and begin preaching about Jesus. Each
man stopped in the face of my preaching, eventually.

I didn't know what falling in love felt like. I lived on the
surface, being polite, burying myself in foreign schoolbooks
instead of taking long walks on the glorious beaches right
next to where I lived. My host families were kind to me, ar-
ranging a continual stream of teas and barbecues.

I learned to adapt in a way that has served me many times
since. I became an expert at fitting in. As long as I could
eventually escape into solitude for writing and hidden cigarettes, I could conceal the inner shaking that was ever present. Sarah castigated me for every moment of uncertainty
and shyness gone by and worried over every one that would
come. "You're not doing it right, God is going to punish

you, you'll get sent home. You have to prove yourself. You're not good enough," she said. I had learned it was not polite to refuse whatever was offered, and rude to ask for what I wanted. For all that I didn't like my mother, her ways were the ones I knew. Her voice was already firmly planted in my head.

Sarah told me I ought to be happy, but I felt isolated and full of squished thick feelings that had no names and too little outlet. I was pretending, playing the part of the exchange student—friendly, cheerful, and more than anything, polite.

A Rotary exchange student stays with several host families. We were instructed to become a part of the family and to call them "Mom" and "Dad," a suggestion that made me uncomfortable. I didn't call the adults of my first host family anything.

But it was the third family that changed my life, because I met May. She was totally unlike my mother. The way she was gave me hope. It was in her house that I relaxed a little, for the first time. I felt liked and accepted and smart there.

◆*Memory.* It's the end of October and the weather is hot and clear. May's house has colored plastic fly strips hanging over the door, unfinished ceilings, concrete walls and an upstairs that looks over the Shoalhaven River. Inside there are flies and huge hairy legged tarantula spiders to eat the flies and a lizard that eats the spiders, and Tully, May's terrier.

"Everyone calls me May," she says first thing, brandishing a cigarette. "This is your room here," she opens a door, "and up these steps is the kitchen. Chuck is a carpenter, he started this house ten years ago, I hope to see plaster and walls before I die. My grandson, Bob, you'll meet him—he has promised to grow up and become a carpenter and finish the house! He's thirteen now, so it will be a while.

"Outside here is my studio with my kiln. I teach the neighbor women pottery. This is my wheel, I'll teach you to throw pots if you'd like. Now tell me what you like to eat and what you don't."

"I hate tripe," I venture, shyly, having failed in my earlier attempts to swallow the soup full of gravy and intestines.

"That's Chuck's favorite—we'll just find something else for you. Do you like red peppers? I love them myself. Just don't starve and do make yourself at home."

She gestures with her hands as she speaks. She asks me what I think of the village and what about school uniforms, did I think they were better or worse than wearing anything you wanted. She looks at me and listens, then gives her opinion, puffing on a cigarette and laughing as we drink tea and eat biscuits.

"Do come bring your guitar and sing to me," she says. "I'll trade you that for your job of drying the dishes."◆

May was everything my mother was not. In the seven months I lived with May she never once voiced concern about what someone else might think of her. She was, however, fascinated by other people and energized by her relationships with her grown children, her grandchildren and her neighbors.

She asked what I thought about politics, marriage and art. She said she thought marriage was overrated and that the government was full of crock. Although my room was strewn with clothing and notebook paper, May never told me to clean it up. She did not yell or make me feel bad about myself. She had flecks of clay beneath her fingernails and bare legs and short salt-and-pepper hair.

We went into the local pub on occasional Saturday afternoons. May gave me quarters for the slot machines. One day, as we were drinking a full-bodied Australian beer and talking, the bartender came over and said one of the villagers had said that I wasn't eighteen and therefore had to leave. Not only that but I was supposed to be twenty-one to play the slot machines. "Sorry, May," he said.

"Finish your beer," she said to me, "It's that cranky old Mr. Nesham who's just getting ready to move away from the village. Never you mind," she said, as we left.

The next week she said, "Get your coat, Louise, we're going to the pub."

I was speechless since it was still a good four months until I would turn eighteen. At the pub, May walked right up to the counter and said, "Today is Louise's eighteenth birthday." And everyone wished me Happy Birthday and bought me beer.

She tried to teach me to drive, and drove me to camp over a mountain pass so thick with fog that I had to lean out the window the entire journey, scanning for taillights or bends in the road. When my boyfriend broke up with me and I was crying, she said, "Don't pay any attention to whatever he told you." Once, she took my hand and studied it and said, "You will be a writer. Dedicate your first book to me."

"You don't have to get married," she said. "Have a wonderful string of affairs instead. Do what you want."

I stopped rotating families and stayed on with May. She encouraged me to travel, she wrote me notes so that I could skip school on sports days, and when I left she and Chuck organized an enormous party in my honor.

It took many more years for me to believe in myself. But for seven months, May affirmed everything that was important in me. Now I am thirty-seven years old and she is seventy-eight. I haven't seen her for twenty years, though we continue to exchange letters. But for these years afterward, when I have felt depressed and silenced, I write or reach for my guitar and sing, compelled by my nature and inspired by the Memory of May, the first artist and free-spirited adult I ever knew.

# 13

## A Fearful Light

ALL THE WINDOWS in the inner house are wide open. I sit on their ledges and dangle my feet far above the ground. I can stay up all night. I can eat whenever I want. I smoke in every room and drink pots of coffee. I never wash the moldings. I don't do the dishes until I run out of them. I have no plans to get married. I can put the past behind me, just like my mother always said.

I consume No-Doze and cram for a test in Economics 201. I drink Cold Duck and play pinochle. I lock myself in Stunned's room and listen to Joan Baez for eight hours while sitting perfectly still on the edge of the bed. I am eighteen and twenty-four wearing clothes from a trunk in the attic. Knit blouses and jeans, turtlenecks and bulky overshirts, polyester castoffs from the Salvation Army. None of these clothes fit but I wear them anyway.

I am twenty-five and twenty-seven. I pull out vests and berets, colorful flannel shirts and black jeans. I strut through the house and admire myself in mirrors. I take all the desks out of the schoolroom and dance. There is still fear in my eyes, but also a light, so small it could fit on the head of a pin, but bright.

My mother doesn't live here now, though I swear I can

hear her voice. In the morning I always wake with a familiar pain in my stomach.

My mother comes to visit bearing frozen peas and corn and wedges of meat brown from being kept in her freezer too long. My mother's voice comes through the shrill ringing phone. "I've been waiting for you to call or write," she says.

"I've been busy," I say.

"I worry," she says. "But you just can't be bothered to let your poor old mother know how you are. All you do is take; gimme gimme gimme is all you've ever said."

I do not understand why I am angry when we hang up.

Whoever I am when I go to her house for holidays is not who I really am.

There's a bad smell coming from the basement, where I put everything my family ever gave me. I burn incense to cover it up. But it gets in my clothes and goes everywhere with me. I wear sweet perfume. I try after-shave. A voice comes up through the heating vents, from the basement, and says it's me and not the basement that smells so bad.

Sometimes I think I hear other voices in this house. Muffled kid voices saying something like, "Let me out." I can almost hear another voice humming, a woman's voice. But the most striking thing is that I feel drawn to that basement, even though it stinks.

When I first descended to the basement, I took rocks, a flashlight and a journal down with me. I handled unspeakably gross decaying matter. I found valuable treasure. Now, fourteen years later, no trace of that bad smell lingers.

I've hung brightly colored fabrics on the walls. A well-used punching bag hangs securely from the ceiling. I come down here to write. Here I am hugged by the earth as I get to the bottom of things, cheered on by my treasures which fill the ledges of the daylight windows and overlap on the large cork bulletin board.

. . .

Perhaps it was the contrast between May's house and my mother's house that made me begin to doubt my experience when I returned home, to lose hold of the teenager who had traveled halfway around the world. Then again, I didn't know that more independent self very well. My mother alternated between saying I should act grateful because she and Don sent me to Australia and telling me that I was no longer some important exchange student and what would the Rotary think if they knew how I really was. At night I sat in the rec room holding the koala bear that May's pottery class had given me, eating passion fruit jelly with my fingers and crying in tight silent unsatisfying shudders.

My first visit to the university caused me to quail in my shoes with the sheer volume of students and the overwhelming mysteries that lay threateningly ahead. All my life I had heard that cities were evil and dangerous, especially for girls. Even in Australia I had lived in small towns. If families were supposed to be safe, then how much more scary would the outside metropolitan world be?

I understand women I have known who never moved away from their abusive families. In my mother's house again, at eighteen, I was afraid she was right about me when she said that no one would really like me, that I would fail for want of common sense, that I was bad and crazy and didn't know anything.

"Maybe I should go to the community college instead," I told my mother. I'd gotten a scholarship to the small nearby school. I was convinced I would fail at the university.

"No, you should get away and go to the university," my mother said decisively. "You'll be happier there."

Perhaps, this once, she really saw me and knew this was true. Maybe she remembered her own time at college with happiness, or she was finally tired of fighting with me every day and was willing to give up control for peace. Whatever the reason, she was right; I was happier at the university. Now, all these years later, I am grateful for these two things from my mother: my physical existence and this needed push to leave home once and for all.

Ultimately, my mother did not become a different person when I left home, the way some mothers become more reasonable or thoughtful or tolerant once they no longer have the dailiness of childrearing. She continued to be critical of my body, my hair, my friends and my ideas. She chanted lists of all that I owed her, adding items when she and Don helped me move, or gave me money, or brought me their castoff furniture. "All the ways we've helped you out and this is how you talk to me," she'd say. "And the food I've given you." She could not stand to throw away food. I became her repository for freezer-burned meat and corn, for vitamins and canned soup from her cupboards that were past the expiration dates. She called this "helping me out," because I was a student without much money. My mother had a remarkable ability to give what was never requested and then act as if the receiver owed her something for it.

I was grown up though. My mother's customs were not supposed to bother me any longer. Family was supposed to be benign. As a grown daughter, it was expected that I would go to the mall with my mother and bring a potluck item to holiday gatherings. It was expected that I would want to call and write her and ask her the appropriate questions. "What was the food like at the new restaurant?", "How big was the fish that Don caught?", "So you're going away for a few days? Isn't that nice for you." I was supposed to be cheerful and "fine." "How are you, how's school?" she would ask and then not pause long enough for my response. For all my childhood, she had spied on me, prying into my diaries and relationships. Now I was supposed to protect her from my politics, my attraction to women and my depression.

My mother told me about one of my cousins who was overseas with the Navy, like his father before him. He'd written a letter to my aunt and uncle thanking them for being such fine parents. "What a good son he is," my mother said. Now that I was grown up I was supposed to appreciate how hard it was to be a parent. I was supposed to participate in rewriting my childhood.

◆*Memory.* My mother is visiting today. I spent all Friday night cleaning my dorm room and I got up early to buy fresh flowers but she didn't even seem to notice. I am trying to be nice to her and not say anything controversial, but I can't help saying I do not want this shirt she says she's going to buy me. "I hate pink," I say.

"I don't know why you have to be this way," she says.

I wish this was over with and I was back in my dorm by myself. I am dying for a cigarette.

"It's almost over," I think to myself in the car, when my mother suddenly out of the ozone says, "You had a happy childhood, didn't you?"

I start coughing. Even though I never think about my childhood, I know that happy is not an adjective I would ever apply to it. I know I shouldn't be surprised by anything my mother does, but after all those years of arguments and suicide attempts and running away . . .

For once, I am out of words. "You've got to be kidding," is all I can find to say. I really need a cigarette now.

"Well, I gave you everything," she says.◆

Now I wonder if she gave me what she had been given by her mother: criticism, castoffs and guilt. Although I was never going to be like my mother, my twenties found me becoming who she said I was and in that way becoming like her. Now I see that what my mother and I had in common was an enormous fear.

Outwardly, I was much different than my mother had been. I wrote letters to free political prisoners. I was a member of the university's experimental "residential program," living in the only co-ed dorm on campus in 1973 and taking interdisciplinary seminars. I thought I was escaping my roots by becoming an aloof, critical intellectual, dedicated to the noble realm of ideas and the mind. But I was always waiting for punishment and censure. I got straight A's, but the more of them I got, the harder I worked for the next one. I could make myself read boring unimaginative textbooks and spend hours writing papers. I never took walks or lit candles. I always did homework on my vacations. I dreamed of majoring in music, but I dropped out of music theory for fear of getting a B. Instead I majored in Society and Justice. I had a vague notion of going to law school and emerging as a public defender or a civil rights lawyer. I needed a role to be important, just like my mother had leaned on being a teacher and a parent. If people asked me how I was, I was "busy," just like my mother had always been.

I believed in caring and social justice, but I felt scared and bad. I didn't know how to be caring any more than my mother knew how to be the perfect mother she saw in magazine ads in the 1950s.

"This is where it comes full circle," Memory says. I see images of myself at twenty and twenty-three, trying to be good enough, trying to please, terrified by other people's opinions of me. I replayed conversations endlessly, sure that I said the wrong words or made the wrong gesture. In those years, my mother's judgements surrounded me and my fear grew like a shadow coming to life, assuming flesh and form.

Like my mother, I lied about what I felt. I pretended to be happy when I was not. Like my mother, I did not really believe I could live without a man to protect me.

◆*Memory.* The hamburger casserole is turning white with grease at the edges. Every time I hear a car outside the apartment building I go to the window and look out. I know that John doesn't always show up when he is supposed to come to dinner but I can't stop waiting and thinking he'll be here any minute.

We've been going out for a year. He's forty, I'm twenty-one. He takes me out on his motorcycle. I'm learning to fix cars so we can work on them together. I hate the smell of motor oil so I try not to inhale too much. He's a campus cop. I met him in one of my classes.

I told my mother I was going out with a nice quiet man, just like Don. I didn't tell her he's black and about the same age as Don.

Sometimes John says I'm too dependent, but that I have a lot of potential. I say he's smarter than me and I love him and don't ever want him to go away. When he doesn't come over like he said he will, my stomach hurts. Once when I wanted him to spend the night, he said he didn't want to. I got panicky about his leaving and threw myself on the windshield of his car to stop him. He said, "Get in," and then he wouldn't talk to me.

The phone rings and I hurry over to it, but it's only my friend Jan. I tell her I'm waiting for an important call.◆

My mother used to say, "You just use people. You only think about yourself." I did not know how to treat people, only to be afraid of them or to scramble for their approval or affection. Just like my mother.

I am glad John was wary of my dependency, for if I had married it would have been much more difficult for me to alter my legacy. I did not know how to get what I wanted. Like my mother, I mostly hoped that it would just fall at my feet on the ground in front of me.

Unlike my mother, I could not appeal to men in authority because I had suffered too many years in terror of them. In my senior year, after a distinguished but previously unrecognized four years in academia, one of my political science teachers noticed me, offered me a position as his research assistant and steered me toward graduate school in political science. Even though he was very kind to me and a good mentor, I was too frightened of men in authority to make use of his influence.

When I was with friends and they said, "What do you

want to do?" I always said, "Oh, whatever you want to do is fine." At the same time, I was afraid my friends would betray me. I compared myself to other women and was always either better or worse. Women intimidated me. I still longed for an older woman to take care of me. But I was tongue-tied around women I admired.

By the time I was twenty-four, I was in dubious shape, but I was pretty good at looking like nothing had ever happened. I had graduated summa cum laude and dropped out of graduate school, but I didn't tell many people about that. I had a job, although it was unskilled labor; I could remember my address; I was not mumbling aloud to people no one else could see. But inside Sarah was mean and threatening. I was suicidal but it didn't show. I felt distant and desperate, reckless, self-hating and lost.

I had never learned the art of self-examination, only the dark arts of self-condemnation, guilt and shame. I did not know how to find the meaning of my feelings or to consider the effects of my actions. My mother did not know these things either, although they are basic to morality. I had not learned at home to honor honesty, gentleness and respectfulness. I lied and even stole money from my workplace for a while because I did not call it theft. Like my mother, I did not know how to observe my own behavior. Change cannot happen without this skill. But at twenty-four, all I knew was that I thought I would never have enough courage, money or luck. I felt trapped.

Fourteen years ago, when I was a graduate student at Stanford, I stripped my grandfather's desk in the back yard, applying poisons to the surface until the dark Protestant paint yielded to strips of mahogany. But I couldn't get rid of the poison I had ingested growing up.

Behind my increasingly thick glasses, on the other side of my eyes, I was having the inner voice conflict of the decade. Of course, I didn't have any idea then that the inner voices were there. I only knew that I smiled when I didn't mean it, but I didn't seem to have control over what I did. I knew that I canceled dinners and movies at the last minute because I was unable to bear the thought of being with another person, and then sat in front of my journal and tried to think my way out of the bad feelings. After I quit school, I began drinking wine at two-thirty in the afternoon and continued into the evening. I went to bed with men I didn't know. I would leave them the next morning or the next month, not returning their calls, never saying goodbye. Picking up and using. Always feeling hollow, but unable to stop dreaming or looking for another way.

I was born into a time of more choices for women. I do not know if my mother ever had a yearning to know herself. I do not know if she dreamed of becoming more than a wife. But I could not live any longer in her world of pretend and pretense, where the rules and images had been created by someone else.

"Now wait a minute here," Fuckit objects. "Are you excusing her, after we've come this far holding her responsible? Are you subtly changing sides?"

"No, Fuckit," Carrie responds. "We're just realizing that our mother became the way she was over time. She was also reacting to how she was treated, passing on the legacy of abuse and oppression. In making us her problem, she did not have to face the places she felt troubled within herself."

When my mother was twenty-four years old, she got married. When I was twenty-four, I started therapy.

I wanted to like myself. I wanted to be brave but was frozen in terror. I wanted to write but didn't think anyone would read it. I felt guilty at the thought of taking myself seriously. I wanted to play but didn't know how. I wanted to love but didn't know what it felt like. I chose to stop pretending not to have a past and to stop leaving my furniture behind when I moved. As it turns out, I would rather be an eccentric lunatic full of inner voices and unusual ideas than repeat my mother's folly.

. . .

I broke up with John after my second therapy session. We were walking and holding hands and I said, "I don't need you anymore."

I didn't understand then that in my quest for protection, John had taken the place of God, just as my mother had anointed Don. Although I did not come out as a lesbian for several more years, breaking up with John was the last time I ever worshiped a man, human or divine.

In 1978, when I began therapy, twelve-step programs were limited to issues of alcohol, the odds of finding a therapist who didn't believe anything you said about your own life were higher than finding one who did, and massage was still widely considered to be another name for prostitution. In retrospect, I'm glad I started when the emphasis was on human potential instead of recovery. It was good for me, given Sarah's tendency to make rigid rules, that I began my work when growth was considered more exploratory and less formulaic.

I was in therapy for four years before I had much Memory of my childhood. I spent that time meeting the inner voices and learning that crying, raging and fearing were parts of joy and laughter. I became committed to this journey of feeling. But I still longed to be held when I cried and soothed when I was scared, a child wanting a mother. I wished my therapist Kate would hold me and stroke my head. I wanted her to exclaim over my writing and listen to my songs. More than anything, I wanted her to like me. I thought that if she liked me I would be safe, as if her liking were a magic wand. All the child wantings for a mother who could be big on my behalf, rose and circled inside of me as I saw Kate. I thought I wanted her to erase my past and tell me what to do.

I did not want to hear that growth was a journey. It was not reassuring to be told the answers were inside me and that Kate didn't know how long the whole thing would take.

"What do you mean I have to feel the pain? I don't want there to be pain!" I objected, making one last grab at my mother's belief system. I thought I preferred the plastic daffodils my mother planted to the changing seasons.

Fuckit adamantly denied that my feelings about Kate had to do with wanting a mother. Mothers were "disgusting, unnecessary hypocrites and everyone would be better off without them," Fuckit said. At twenty-five and twenty-six, I smoked and walked in dangerous parts of the city alone and refused to admit needing anything. As Fuckit, I denied my fears by sticking out my tongue at them.

But my relationship with Kate was also about having a body. She was always directing my attention to the emotions that lived there. She held me when I cried on the floor of her office. She put her hand on my back and used gentle words like someone trying to coax a wild animal out of hiding.

Kate's office is where Carrie first learned gentle patience. Still, it took at least six years for me to feel as nurtured crying by myself as I felt crying onto Kate's shoulders. At first, the inner voices felt that Carrie was inferior to other help from outside. But the truth was that Carrie needed a lot of teachers. Mothering myself had to be learned by feel.

Unlearning my mother's curses and blooming in my own unique way required more than hugging myself. It was, as Kate had said, a journey. It turned out to be a journey of women who guided me to important doors that I had not even known existed.

◆*Memory.* The tide is in on the beach across the street from the house where I'm living in Seattle with Amy and her thirteen-year-old son, Ben. Amy and I are sitting at the wooden table, on the benches I helped her strip the paint from last summer. The phone rings. Amy answers it.

"Who are you living with?" my mother demands after Amy hands me the receiver.

I am twenty-five but I feel thirteen. "Amy," I say defiantly, "and her son, Ben. He broke his leg in a soccer match, so I'm taking care of him in exchange for rent." I had looked up Amy after I quit graduate school, compelled to see her again even though we had been out of touch for seven years. "So I'm babysitting for her again after all these years," I say nervously. I knew my mother would disapprove. She hated Amy.

"So that's why you never call home or come to family gatherings anymore," my mother says accusingly.

"You just don't like Amy because she's different than you," I begin, in familiar escalation.

"Just because I care about you and worry about how you're wasting your life. The way you didn't tell us about graduate school, sneaking around."

"It's my life!" I yell, not for the first time.

"You just should be more careful of the company you keep. I tried to raise you with the right values . . . "

I am shaking when I hang up. If my mother doesn't matter, why does what she says still bother me? I would ask Amy about this but I can't explain how roiled up I feel after talking to my mother.

Amy says I'm a good listener. Partly it's because I'm shy. Mostly it's because Amy talks about ideas and books that are new and exciting to me. I don't know enough to talk, but I am an avid listener. She talks about her work in gestalt therapy, about John Lilly and states of consciousness, Ram Dass and meditation and encounter groups. We take turns cooking from a cookbook she got from a vegetarian restaurant. We make eggplant lasagne and tofu Parmesan. She is teaching me transactional analysis and affirmations.

At night I work serving pizza. I go to bars and twenty-four-hour restaurants and write. Once in a while I read Amy something I've written but I don't want to impose on her. I'm just as happy to listen to her.

She is learning to play the flute even though she's forty

years old. It never occurred to me that adults could take up a musical instrument. Just living here makes me feel very hopeful and creative.♦

Human relations remained an unfathomable mystery, however. I joined Amy's leaderless therapy group. I was the youngest and most silent member as week after week I sat there unable to find anything to say. I watched the other members cry or get mad and then talk about how they felt. They asked each other questions that I would never have dreamed could be asked and the person who was "working" would maybe cry or yell and then say, "Oh, I see, it's about this or that." It was like auditing advanced calculus without having taken the prerequisites.

Still, I sensed the possibility that my life was neither a punishment nor a random meaningless unfolding. I began to think that everyone I met and every experience I had was significant and existed to teach me. Fuckit saw that the inner journey involved adventure and unorthodoxy. Stunned waited heavy with secrets and unexplored Memory, but even in this most frozen part of myself, there was poetry and a compulsion to write down as much as I could about this new life.

I had a sense of being led by a wiser part of myself, led into massage school, into psychosynthesis, jin shin jytsu, tarot and astrology. A new world outside of both graduate school and Bryce opened up before me. I went from resisting the journey to becoming devoted to the quest. I kept thinking that any day I would find the teacher who would tell me how to do it right. Instead I found I was compelled to honor my own feelings and listen to the truths they offered. I also began to realize that this journey was going to take a while. Following my feelings eventually led me to Memory, but Carrie had to become stronger inside of me first.

I first noticed Carrie when I began massage school. Touching another person in order to practice a healing art opened up a new feeling of centeredness and caring. In massage, Carrie learned through intuition, silence and touch.

While Sarah never liked anything about me, Carrie liked and respected each inner voice. Carrie stood with YoungerOnes when they emerged with pain, fear and Memory. When Tinsel and Tayla and Stunned began speaking, ten years ago, it was Carrie who helped me stop and listen. "I believe you, I believe us," Carrie said. Still, for a long time, Carrie was much better at nurturing clients and writing inspiring lectures than at tending myself. "True service comes from feeling full, not from feeling martyred," Carrie says, "but I am still learning this."

A lot of Carrie's work has been in trying to re-educate Sarah. When I was twenty-five and twenty-eight, Sarah said things like, "You're stupid. You deserve to die. Everyone else is better than you. No one likes you. You're bad." YoungerOnes believed her, because this was a familiar explanation for the way my world worked. Carrie learned to say, "Wait a minute, Sarah, we feel uncomfortable right now. Let's listen a minute and find out why."

Carrie says that Sarah can say anything she wants, but if it's not true, Carrie will challenge her. Sarah has grumblingly agreed to this though she is ingenious about coming up with new lies and I have to catch her at them before I can make her stop. Carrie is not the leader though, as Fuckit is quick to point out. I have harmony only if there is consensus among the inner voices. Nor do I have any desire for Carrie to take over and quiet every one else. I prefer a committee to a dictator.

Carrie is one part inner knowing, one part lessons and insights from workshops, therapy and clients. When I was twenty-six and twenty-seven, I had a good friend, Bonnie, who was also a masseuse. She taught me to meditate, read the tarot and throw the I Ching. We went to the ocean and did yoga and cooked with brewer's yeast and sesame oil. We dropped acid together and I heard the trees talk for the first time then. Gradually, I found that the Great Spirit was not above me like God had been, but was the essence of life, the difference between a tree and firewood and between a person and a corpse. I experienced my first moments of feeling a part of this earth and her people, instead of set apart and disconnected. I learned that I grow experientially; that my body, my personality, my mind and my spirit are not separate but intimately connected. I began learning from my peers and valuing the wisdom of my friends.

Carrie has helped me define what I value: growth, honesty, communication, creativity, compassion, humor and empowerment. She did not decide upon these values because they sounded worthwhile, but because they were tangible feelings that I learned to cherish and express.

Fuckit has joined with Carrie in performance and teaching but she is currently wary about how often Carrie is suddenly talking about "responsibility."

"I just have a sense that responsibility is about power," Carrie says. "It's the ability to respond to many different situations. To say 'I think, I feel, I did, I want, I don't want' without ducking afterward. It's taking on projects and standing for what we believe. I think there's room in it to honor both our power and our mistakes. Responsibility says that we matter."

"I want to matter," Fuckit says. "But I want to be wild. Responsibility sounds stuffy, like dusting. There's commitment and obligation and, 'did I do it good enough' that goes with it. Shit. Then that sneaky Sarah starts to compare us with someone else or says that we have to do even better. It's no different than having to do what someone tells us to do. Goodbye free spirit."

"You just want to be twenty-six forever," Sarah mutters.

"Fuckit, this is exactly why you are important," Carrie says. "You let us know when we're in danger of abandoning our vision! Just speak up if you don't feel free and we'll figure out how to liberate ourselves."

Carrie stands straight without straining. She doesn't look like my mother at all. She looks a little like Amy, Kate, Jean and a lot of other women I've known but she looks mostly like me when I am teaching. Her eyes are light and deep. She never stops me from crying or being mad or having fun. She likes tea and long walks.

I did not hear a voice like Carrie's from my mother. She did not seem to have a mood of introspection and quiet, or a part who listened deeply for what is true. Carrie helps me pay attention to my other inner voices, to Memory and to the current of healing. Carrie puts her ear to the ground of my being and listens for my way.

.   .   .

My mother used to say she had wanted a boy first and then a girl because the boy was supposed to be older. It was the boy who was supposed to cause mischief, like my eldest uncle who ran away and joined the merchant marine when he was sixteen by lying about his age. Eventually, a son would outgrow this foolishness though, getting a respectable job, sending money and airplane tickets for the folks to come visit. The daughter was expected to marry, but to stay in town and be available for transportation, Sunday visits, daily phone calls and the hands-on caretaking. This was how it worked for my mother and her brothers. But it was Jim who had ended up living next door to our mother, not me.

My mother never figured out that most people have limits, even if she didn't. My mother told me, "Guilt is good for you," and organized her life around obligation and duty. I learned that children have a biblical duty to their parents. But parents had no duty to care well for their children. My mother thought, I'm sure, that since she had taken care of her parents, she would be rewarded with Jim to take care of her.

When Jim calls me every week, he gives me more than an update on my mother and stepfather's theatre, which has lots of drama and no innovative action. As he tells me his unfolding stories, I am reminded that it was our family and not me, the "crazy daughter," that was the problem. Theoretically, I know that how I was treated is one case in generations of abuse suffered by women and children in my family. But it's hard to get over thinking that if only I had done something different, my family would have stood with me instead of against me.

When Jim first called me, I thought he might be listened to in the family because he is a man. Now I see that the crucial factor has always been acceptance of our family's system, to ride in the boat without rocking it and never to point out that it is sinking.

As I listen to him, I feel my blood pressure rise and fall with my mother and stepfather's failed promises and predictable avenues of revenge.

Don saw Jim's therapist and offered to take a lie detector test about the incest. The therapist told Don that the penile test for arousal was most reliable because it tests for physical responses to images. Don did not offer to take that test.

"I had hoped that Don really wanted to listen to me," Jim says. "Instead he acted like all he had to do was say I was hurting Mother and you were a liar and everything would be fixed.

"This part really hurt me," Jim continues. "Don said that because Mother was battered by our biological father, it was natural that she would not love this other man's sperm children."

I forget that Jim has believed in this love. Still, this is the first time I hear so clearly that our mother doesn't think of us as her children.

When Jim calls the following week, he says, "So much for the idea that Don was easier to talk to. The last time I saw him, he pushed back at me the book I gave him to read on sexual addiction and said, 'You're not a sex addict. That therapist has just talked you into it.'"

That's the same thing he said after I confronted him about raping me. "Right," I tell Jim. "You just want to be a recovering sex addict so much that you were talked into it. Just like I really wanted to have incest memories," I say sarcastically.

Jim adds, "And I got another letter from Mother, which I guess is better than hearing her rant and rave in person. She says it's Cindy's fault that I had all of those affairs. Can you believe it?

"The thing that really gets me is that I'm so used to taking it I don't even know when they're threatening me or discounting me," Jim continues. "Right before Don pushed that book back at me I started yelling back at him. I said, 'You want to fight about it or what?'"

I sigh. Men. It never would have occurred to me to say that.

"So he said," Jim continues, "'I can beat you up any day, boy.' Then he grabbed my arm, really hard. I tried to pull away a little and he squeezed and I tried to make a joke out of it. Then he let go.

"I had bruises on my arm afterward. But it wasn't until group that one of the men pointed out that it was a bizarre interaction."

I see being a male isn't as big an advantage as I thought. Neither fistfights nor a sharp tongue is going to change our parents. Don uses his body, while Mother sticks with her familiar phrases.

Listening to Jim, I understand again that my mother was never really interested in who her children were. Knowing us was never her motivation. To her, relationships are not about appreciating the uniqueness of someone else or enjoying someone's company. Relationships are about the advertisements in the fifties magazines, families in black-and-white photographs in spotless kitchens.

Jim's voice is shaky the next time we talk. "I just got another letter from Mother," he says. "She says she's going to tell everyone about me. I'm scared even though I don't know exactly what she means. But then I got a phone call from Uncle Robert saying all the uncles wanted to have a meeting with me and find out what was going on."

"She used to get the uncles to talk to me, too," I say. "I don't suppose she and Don are going to be at the meeting so that they'll have to answer for their behavior in front of everyone."

"That would be a first," Jim says.

Unlike me, Jim thinks he can get the uncles to understand his point of view. I gave up and withdrew from all of them. But Jim has had more experience with them, more right to expect loyalty.

He doesn't get it. I suppose he's like a long-time employee who turns into a whistle blower, naively expecting respect and instead getting told to go back to being good and mute.

Jim does not go retrograde, however. "I told them I have my own problems to work on and that I didn't know if I wanted to have a relationship with those people as parents. I told them they had to work on their own problems before I wanted anything to do with them. And even then I'd have to like them which I don't right now.

"I said I was mad they didn't bother to find out what happened by talking to you. It's been nine years since you confronted Don and they never asked you to a meeting; they just let you disappear. I also said I couldn't imagine ever abandoning my daughter like Don and Carol did."

No one in my family has ever taken my side before. I am used to "family" being a bad word. Jim may not be getting anywhere with our parents, but he is changing me. He is the first member of my family who has valued me. As I let him come closer to me, I find the pain I denied at his absence.

I feel new hope for the lives of my cousins. But I don't feel hopeful about my mother. Even though her birthday is August 26th, the same day women were granted the right to vote, I cannot imagine her coming to terms with her own choices or her life.

Marianne and I meet Jim, Cindy, Noah, age four, and Ruth, age eighteen months, at a park on a sunny spring Sunday. We eat chicken and lie in the sand and throw balls. Next to the park is "Never Never Land", a collection of plaster-of-paris scenes from fairy tales. We read them to Noah and Ruth and point out the painted figures of Jack Sprat and Robin Hood. Marianne knows all of the rhymes, but Jim and I agree that most of them are new to us.

Noah begins to get tired and scuffs the ground. "How are you doing, Noah," Jim leans down. Noah is fine-boned and tiny; Jim is lanky and large. "It's okay to feel tired." Noah comes closer and Jim wraps him against his chest. Ruth runs toward me and I light up like a beacon which makes her giggle and wobble on her toddler legs. She puts sand, the plastic shovel, crackers, balls and toy trucks in her mouth at various times. Cindy and Jim watch to make sure that she is not ingesting a lethal substance, but safe items, even if unorthodox, are not impatiently yanked out of her mouth. They do not slap her hand or yell at her. She does not flinch or cower or wear a nervous smile like Jim and I do in our childhood photographs.

"We have a ways to go," Jim and Cindy say as we exchange farewells in the parking lot.

"But you're bringing new ways to the next generation," I remind them. "Anyway, who knows what kind of large changes we are setting into motion through our own small discoveries."

# 14

## In the Company of Dragons

I HAVE GONE from being a hermit to being a woman who knows many more people that I ever would have thought possible. The walls of the inner house are full of snapshots of me and Marianne and friends both past and present; of dream group, writers' group, voice group, island friends, tai chi classmates, clients, students, Marianne's parents, Jim and his family. I have become a groupie. Me, the woman who was never going to trust anyone.

It has taken most of my thirties to make this house comfortable. I am still getting rid of walls that make the rooms too narrow. I am replacing the collection of harsh abstract paintings bolted to the walls in the parlour. I have added skylights and generous windows, favorite books and savory food.

I used to keep people out of this inner house. Now sometimes people come by invitation and other times they just drop in. Once in a while they wear masks that remind me of my mother. This makes me nervous in my stomach. Once I overheard one of my visitors saying that I was a terribly bad person. She said that Laura had told her and she had heard it from Zoe. The speaker licked her lips as if she'd just eaten something delicious while shaking her head just the way my mother had done. The mists of jealousy, competition and scarcity took on exotic colors and swirled before my eyes.

For a minute I was afraid this was still my mother's house. I smoked a cigarette in a dark corner. I felt a disturbance in the air, a draft. That was when the first dragon spoke to me. "I can teach you to breathe fire," the dragon said. The dragon exhaled a long curling flame and studied me. "You don't have to go around hiding in corners, everything you need to know about keeping yourself safe is in your stomach."

I am thirty-four and thirty-six. Occasionally an author passes through the house and I get so nervous that I can't think of anything to discuss with them. I want to reach out as a peer but I do not know how to network. I end up feeling too vulnerable, like a hick from Bryce. I become obsequious and overly generous, ignoring my own interests and desires in an effort to impress. The dragon says to knock it off, that I don't have to smile all the time.

I notice groups of women collecting in the kitchen. My stomach takes me there, to the spices and herbs and the voices flavored with humor or sadness or straight unvarnished anger. I join groups where we read our writings, make our dreams real and find our songs.

We are women of all ages and all circumstances. We have come together to perform an experiment.

We have vowed to live as if we were important.

We have decided to be bold about what we think and feel and know. We say, "I'm great! I'm great!" out loud like a cheer. We say, "You're great, you're just great," to each other. We are always clapping or crying or creating.

We take turns being teacher and student and dragon. We gather in circles, holding hands, laughing and sharing the recipes of our healing.

We are planning an uprising, seated around the kitchen table. We begin with ourselves and with each other.

.

I am a lesbian because I love women; I am at home in the intimacy that women share in emotion and language. I am inspired by breasts and circles and soft skin. Women are my lovers, teachers, friends and hope.

But women are not generic. I used to believe that leaving home would end all mother-daughter conflicts. It was my mother's right-wing patriarchal submission that made her so mean and manipulative, I figured. Surely I was safe among feminists. We could tell each other secrets and hug and get mad at the same Supreme Court decisions. Our talk was deep, not shallow like my mother's. We were sisters.

When I first realized I was a feminist and a lesbian, I did not know how intensely I would love and want approval from women and how painful our impasses and failures of communication could become. The task of my thirties has been to take care of myself in the company of women. At first it felt like being at a dance contest, dancing the same dance over and over, afraid to separate, waffling between anger and guilt. It has taken me these thirty-eight years to come closer to speaking what I feel when it's in the air instead of waiting and wanting to pretend everything is fine.

At first I couldn't talk directly to the women with whom I was having a conflict. My confusion and frustration went into music. Singing my songs was an antidote to the familiar powerlessness I had first felt with my mother.

The first of my people songs was called "Human Relations." It began:

> Well it's true that human relations can be very weird in-
>     deed,
> The lessons come and knock me down then roll right o'er
>     my head,
> Till I'm sure that I am bleeding,
> And I'm staring at the floor,
> And I just don't know if I can take it, one long moment
>     more.

Singing gave meaning to the layers of feeling inside and soothed me. When I was thirty, I wrote, "The Dance of the Innocents Flight from the Intimate, Annual Masquerade Ball," about my relationship with my lover and the endlessly repeating waltz we danced each time we sat down to talk.

*The guests that come are often uninvited,*
*Statements dress as questions*
*Discussion clothes a fight*
*Sentences arrive as innuendos*
*We are hard*
*Each wearing dusty costumes of loving mixed with shame.*

It's been seven years since the woman who inspired the song and I were lovers. Now when we meet for breakfast or I hear her voice on the phone, I feel affection in my heart. But for a long time, all I could hear was the tune to that dance.

I used to worry because there were situations that I couldn't resolve, that dangled without mutual clarity. I was ashamed because I didn't know enough. I have had to learn when to continue with women and when to let go. But Memory shows me that important lessons repeat themselves.

"How else could you identify patterns from the past and try new responses?" Memory asks. "The school of human relations is experiential."

I have had to give up the notion that everyone will like me. I have touched my anger and been kept awake at night by my sense of outrage and betrayal. Over and over I learn that I am child and mother and healer and so is every other woman I meet. There is more to being friends and partners than I ever guessed.

I did not grow up with a model for conflict resolution. I did not learn from my mother how to go inside and feel my feelings and name them. I was not trained to sort through the present situation for its resemblance to unresolved problems of the past. Confrontation of even the most minor sort seemed terribly risky.

What I didn't know for too long was that even the advanced among us were still groping to be autonomous and strong and honest and vulnerable and connected. Each year, I notice that I am better at communicating and so are the women with whom I remain in relationship or the new women who come into my life. I have exquisite moments of being in a group of women and feeling our power, aware of the strength and importance of each one of us.

Yet, there is also anger and envy and the bitter taste of unresolved events.

"Those are the ones that teach for years after they happen," Memory says. "They call the dragons and make you stand up for yourself."

◆*Memory*. I'm at Marianne's communal house, awake in bed next to her. I try to tell her what happened in my six hours with Zedra. "It was like we were trying to get to some place where everything was okay, but all of our power struggles and competitiveness became cement and the more we talked the heavier it got.

"We talked about stupid things, in a way," I say. "She said I didn't know anything because I didn't have a master's degree. I said I hated the short stories we read in her class. I got frustrated because when she talked about the class she always said 'we' instead of 'I'. I felt like I just wanted her to take some responsibility for what was going on in the class. Then she said I was giving her anxiety attacks, which pissed me off.

"I didn't feel heard and my stomach hurts." I feel younger than thirty-three. Marianne put her arms around me, but I don't find peace. I can't sleep trying to understand what happened.◆

Now I know that lying awake at night means a major lesson is unfolding.

I had been in Zedra's classes for four years. She and I had become friends, but were never equal in our relationship. I looked up to her because she was older and the teacher. She had a good sense of play, she was well-read and she was a writer. At first the classes felt magical. I was exhilarated with the experience of writing with other women in workshops free from arrogant male poets. I loved speaking and hearing women together.

But just as *The Obsidian Mirror* was accepted for publication, I noticed that the dynamic between Zedra and me changed. I felt irritated, as if I had to be small to be around her. I was tired of playing the subordinate, of giving her strokes in the hope that she would return them. My classmates congratulated me, but Zedra tightened whenever my book was mentioned in class.

I felt guilty talking about my success. I didn't know how; it felt like bragging. My dreams about my writing were finally materializing and I could hardly talk about it. I longed for Zedra's approval and assistance in this strange new public land I was entering.

Now I know that I was trying to get approval that Zedra could not spare. She did not know the secrets of being powerful in the world. It has taken six years to see my wanting and Zedra's envy.

My mother was jealous because I had the future she was daily losing. I would escape the child-rearing she had found stifling. I would find a way that did not involve selling my soul. Zedra was my mother's age. She had achieved more than my mother, but she still had not fulfilled her dreams.

Zedra began telling the other women in the class that I had psychically abused and battered her during our conversation. She said they could not be her friends if they had anything to do with me. I wrote Zedra a letter acknowledging the multi-faceted nature of our relationship, expressing appreciation for her classes and saying that we both seemed to feel misunderstood. I said I was rude and colder than I had been in the past, that in trying to have different boundaries I had expressed myself imperfectly. Zedra wrote back and said I was toxic.

When I was a teenager I was always surprised when teachers or my friends' parents believed my mother's claims that I was disturbed or crazy or a problem. I was a good student, I was the star debater, I was not obnoxious at school. It was a mystery the way my mother drew a picture of me by pointing to her pain and saying, "Look, Louise caused this great pain that I can hardly bear or cope with. I don't know what to do about her." Like my mother, Zedra used her pain as evidence that I was bad, instead of mining the pain for understanding.

Neither my mother nor Zedra could have done so much harm without a group of people being willing to bite into the sweet taste of hating. As the rumors continued to circulate I became Stunned. When I ran into women from class, I smiled extra hard so they could see I was nice. But I resented my fear of them. Just as I never confronted my mother's co-conspirators about their malicious gossip, I once again held silence and waited for everything to die down. I sought safety in disappearing and looking innocuous.

Repetition being what it is, I received a letter from a friend of Zedra's, thirteen months after Zedra had talked to me directly. This friend of Zedra's accused me of "psychically raping" and "emotionally battering" Zedra in that long ago conversation, informed me that she was sending a copy of this letter to everyone from the writing class and signed off with, "Good luck in your continued healing." Like the adults of my childhood, this woman had never talked to me about what happened between Zedra and me. The letter writer said she was sure I was abusive because I had been abused as a child, never mentioning her own childhood or Zedra's. Beyond calling me names, she gave no specific example of what I had done or what I should do to rectify the situation. The letter writer just wanted people to know I was bad. Once again, I understood the Red Scare: One person wants other people to join in discrediting someone else.

"What did we do to cause this?" YoungerOnes asked.

"No one likes me. I want to die," Stunned said.

"Not again," Carrie said, softly. I called my friends and read them the letter. They were kind and validating.

Then I heard a loud noise and looked up. It was a group of dragons, circling over my head. They said, "You can't control what other people say or think, but neither do you have to leave a blank for them to fill in." Then I heard a powerful hot hissing sound that made me grab a pen and begin a letter to my classmates, to Zedra and to her letter-writing friend. "Defend yourself, speak up," the dragons urged. "A gauntlet has been thrown to your feet, respond, my dear. Lay out the charges against you and tell your side of the story."

I wrote what I thought had happened between Zedra and me and how I felt about it. The letter was an opportunity for me to create meaning from my pain and anger. Writing helped me articulate the lessons of this experience. I wrote that I had learned to question emotionally exciting words like battering and abuse unless they were accompanied by a description of exactly what had happened. I wrote about how this incident had taught me to be more careful and responsible about reporting on what I heard about other women. I said I knew that fear makes us want to find objects among us for our anger. I invited anyone who had a problem with my behavior to confront me directly. I said I realized that these events made me think about how I wanted to act, that it was healing to me to acknowledge and affirm my ethics.

I took this letter to my friends and Marianne. One of my friends went over all the drafts with me, gently telling me when she still heard defensiveness or blaming between the lines. The most challenging part was getting past the desire to say that she is all wrong and I am all right. My friend told me that the power of nonviolence was that of "standing on the mountain without defense or self-denigration." In my family, I did not learn that relationships might require days or months or years of work and reflection or that this work between people was important and worth the time. The letter took a couple of weeks to write. The dragons circled until I felt cleared.

I never heard from Zedra or her friend again. The women who had remained my friends from class were still supportive and mostly I didn't hear anything from the others.

I no longer lecture Zedra or her friend in my mind, nor do I want to punch Zedra in the face anymore. But sometimes I meet someone who's a friend of Zedra's and I feel afraid that the person might dislike me without knowing me. Then I wish we had a mud pit.

I imagine an arena with thick soft mud and bleachers for the witnesses. I picture Zedra and her letter-writing friend and my mother one by one standing in front of me in the mud. I feel satisfied imagining the weight of mud in my hand, my arm flinging back, the plopping sound of mud hitting each of their faces. I imagine them one by one, engaging with me, throwing mud back, standing on their own feet, using their own muscles as we claim our emotions without shame. Each of us would stand in plain sight in this arena where no one is a victim but both women are angry.

At the end of my fantasy, I am spent of my anger, earthy and intact.

· · ·

My stepfather raised cows for beef. Every once in a while one of the cows would get loose and stand in the front yard ripping up the perfectly watered lawn and staring with unblinking eyes at the house. Once, when I was a college student visiting, my mother put down a steak and announced we were eating "Louie," the cow she had named after Louise. She named all the cows after relatives. I didn't eat any.

Last year I went to a Halloween party as a holy cow, dressed in black and white splotched pants, a black shirt and a white clerical collar. I made X's on people's foreheads and blessed them by mooing. Although I am normally very shy at parties where I don't know many people, blessing people was a good icebreaker and being a cow was a calming experience. Since then cows have been important to me, reminding me to slow down and chew things over. They are allies in contemplation. I wonder if without the meditations of cows the world would dissolve into the frenzy of the two-legged beings.

In my healing work, I often ask for assistance and teaching from animals or angels or aspects of the Goddess. I notice the animals I see in nature. Once I saw two raccoons climbing over a metal road guard. One of them held up her paw to help the other over, with an air of gentle grace and affection. When I'm teaching, an image of a raccoon often appears when I close my eyes and ask for an ally. She points the way with delicate hands. My raccoon ally is good at finding the path and making me laugh at her costume and behavior.

Like tribal people who take on totems, I have imagined myself as a snake shedding skin, stepping out of old ways, blind as the skin passes over my eyes, then new. In a voice lesson with April, I became a brown bear, singing and moving from fall to winter to spring, learning from this bear about the seasons of busyness, rest and stretching. I have been a roaring lion, stable on my legs and commanding with my voice. I have been a giraffe who can see far and is most vulnerable when she stoops down to take a drink of water. I have returned to play-acting and the power of imagination.

But what I've grappled with most these past few years is how to get along well with my fellow beings. The thing is, I want to do it right. I don't want to continue my family's abusiveness and disregard for life. But I also don't want to pretend to be nicer than I am. I want to be respectful and honor the teachings of the wise women before me, but I don't want to feel less than them or afraid to challenge them when I disagree. Nor do I want to feel guilty about setting limits with people who want something from me.

I first read of dragons in books. The *Oxford Concise Dictionary* says they are "mythical monsters like a reptile, usually with wings and claws and able to breathe out fire." These are the dragons I see in my imagination, with eyes like black opal showing flashes of red, blue and green, many times larger than myself so that when we talk, I am the same size as the dragon's head. A dragon holds her head with the effortless grace of a green snake. But unlike snakes, dragons are not quiet.

They like to get attention and to show off their treasure of which they are fiercely protective. They like to gather in groups and have discussions. Some dragons are scholarly, some are whimsical and some are philosophical, but all dragons are opinionated. They appear to be fractious because they never shy from disagreement, but they are, above all, dedicated to the art of communication. They never cease trying to persuade each other, because sometimes they succeed. They are perfectly proud of themselves in all ways and yet unendingly fascinated by the thoughts and behaviors of others. "In short," one of the dragons informed me, "we are just who you've been looking for. We know what your mother didn't about relationships. We intend to help you when things come up."

"Wow," Lulu and Tinsel said, pleased with this development.

Stunned looked fearful. "I don't want to have to deal with any more than we now have on our plate," she said. "Dragons are very big. Knights try to slay them. I don't like it."

The pressures of daily life being what they are, I didn't pay too much attention to the dragons in between crises. I was walking like a dragon and I didn't even notice. I dyed my hair half yellow and half brown and stuck it up with hair glue and told myself, "I am becoming a dragon," when I looked in the mirror, but I didn't think twice about it. I even quit smoking and practiced "fire breathing." More and more

I was involved with groups of women in collaboration and performance. I learned we could disagree but as long as we got what was most important to us, we could work together. But I did not pay attention to the fact that I was now in the company of dragons.

Perhaps I am better at noticing my allies when I am in full-blown agony than when I feel I can handle things. Still, even when the sky fell I didn't call on the dragons right away. Instead I wanted to pretend nothing had happened, like I did in the old days.

What happened is that a well-known nonfiction author had used a portion of my life story to make a point and further her argument in her own book. She bent the facts of my history so they suited her purposes, making it sound as if I were a victim instead of a creative woman claiming her life. She used my name and referred to my book.

Before this, she had been my heroine. She had called me from overseas after reading *The Obsidian Mirror*. I was so awed that this great person had called me that I felt stiff and stupid on the phone. Still, she was very positive toward my work. I thought she was the big person I had been waiting for, the one who would help me, the mentor.

So I felt wretched when I read her words about me in type.

"You have to do something about this," the dragons said, outraged.

"Right," I told them sarcastically. "It's in a book, it's too late. She's an expert, I'm a nobody anyway."

I became YoungerOnes, ashamed of the letters I had written to her after we'd talked. I felt guilty for having been so trusting and vulnerable. I castigated myself because I could never figure out how to network and be cool instead of confessing everything.

"I'd like to punch her in her face," Fuckit said. But the other voices were so heavy that I didn't have much energy for imagining that.

Sarah was relentless. "You're just making a big deal out of

nothing. Stop having so many feelings about this. You did it wrong or this wouldn't have happened. That's what you get for having heroines."

"No one will ever want to read my books now," Stunned said. "Everyone will believe her, no one will believe me just like with my mother. I give up." I spent a lot of days staring at the sound out our window. It was winter. I wanted to hibernate; being a dragon was too much work.

"This is an opportunity," the dragons said.

Their urging made me hot so I went to see an attorney. On her wall was a signed picture of the 1937 U.S. Supreme Court and in the corner of the room, on the thickest carpet I've ever seen, was an antique letter writing table. She said she couldn't help me: What the author had done wasn't precisely illegal, just sloppy. It would cost a lot of money if I wanted to go farther with it.

I sat in my car afterward, smoking cigarettes, feeling unimportant. It was the same feeling I had had as a child.

The dragons circled over my head. I told them to leave me alone. I started smoking again in earnest.

In dream group I acted out a dream I'd had. Jane played a threatening black dog who was barking at me and showing fangs. I was in a boat with a goddess on each side of me, played by Betsey and Sara. The dog was in the same boat in front of me. I wanted the goddesses to make the dog go away, but they said, "We're here by your side, but you are the captain of this ship." I begged them to take action against the dog but they continued to insist that they would be right by my side no matter what I chose to do.

Suddenly, I threw myself at Jane and we began to wrestle. I was astonished at the transformation of my lethargy into furious energy. As I pinned the dog, I realized that the dog represented the author's book.

When I looked at Jane, Betsey and Sara again, they looked like dragons. Jane said, "I feel strongly that you need to act on this, now, not holding back like you do sometimes." It seemed like her eyes were black opals.

I stayed up late that night breathing fire and writing a letter. I told the author my objections and asked her to rewrite this section for future editions. I felt purified at the end and energized by the dragons who had been chanting, "Speak up for yourself, be bold." When I was finished, I knew that every time I stopped ducking and spoke, I was healing myself, mending my spine.

The author responded that she did value my work and had rewritten that section and would I tell her if it was all right, quickly, for the new printing. The rewrite remedied each of my specific objections.

"Treasure!" the dragons shouted in unison and there was a commotion as all of them gathered round to see.

"Where will you keep it?" they inquired, being fascinated with the subject of storing gems.

"In here and here and here," I said, pointing to my breast and stomach and then to my ears. "I take it inside my body where the inner voices can see it. I was heard. She admitted her mistake and honored my challenge. She responded to me because I spoke.

"I feel the muscles of my jaw lengthening and my heart beating strong, encouraged. I learned powerlessness with my mother. I fought her for years without her ever acknowledging a mistake or changing her mind. I learned to be another way with the author's response."

The second dictionary definition of dragon is "a fierce person, especially a woman."

· · ·

My mother did not have an easy circle of girlfriends. She was too worried about appearance and what other people thought of her. She traded loyalties instead of confidences. She made friends into work.

My astrology says that my life path travels from a south

node of individualism and seclusion to a north node of community.

When I was in my twenties, I spent more time with strangers than friends. I remember telling someone that the more time I spent with people, the less I trusted them. I felt safer with people I didn't know whom I could easily leave. I was not taught to value genuine relationship. I did not know that the sustenance of friendship is sharing and keeping in touch.

Now I am astonished that I have known so many different people for five or ten or fifteen years. I have new and old friends and affectionate acquaintances. We met by chance and circumstance. We became larger than we were because we met each other. We have words for our feelings and courage in speaking. And scars. My friends are less interested in how things look than my mother was. We are fascinated by the synchronicity of our experiences and the journey of our changes. None of these relationships has stayed the same; our friendships have traveled through tragedy, lovers, birth, childhood Memory and triumphs. The only rule of people is that whatever is between them is not static, but fluid or shimmering or close or surprising.

I am living the truths I suspected when I was Tinsel and Lulu and Tayla. Honesty is easier, more interesting and more organic than trying to make someone else feel a particular way so that I can get what I want. What is important is how I feel when I'm with someone. What is magical is that speaking can change us.

When I was young, I said I didn't want intimacy. I thought it meant sacrifice. I didn't know that love could feel like a hammock or a round endless possibility. I didn't know I could be with someone and never run out of things to talk about or tire of kissing and hugging. I didn't know time can make everything deeper and more textured between people. I never imagined that my greatest treasures would be in relationships and in the company of my friends.

My mother insisted on perfection. People were good or bad instead of a mixture of light and shadow. A good person would never do a bad thing. Good people were hardworking, church-going and white. This is how she denied the poison in our family. She erected boundaries that included or excluded based on the wrong criteria. She never revised.

Dragons are more pragmatic. They can fling themselves into motion with astonishing rapidity, able to move from ground to air in one continuous serpentine movement causing a vast wind that flattens grass.

I am learning from them to brood less and to take action more quickly. So that when Marianne stood in the doorway to the bathroom and said that Paul had called to warn us because he had just given my mother my phone number, I rose like a dragon from the bathtub. Steam formed on my skin as I wrapped myself in a towel and dialed the phone to talk to Paul, angry with a hot, clean fire.

When Paul answered the phone I said, "Paul, I can't believe you did that. I'm so mad at you. I thought you understood how violent my stepfather is, that my parents are not trustworthy people. You have known me longer than anyone."

"Oh, Louise, I'm so sorry," he said. "I knew as soon as I did it, that I shouldn't have. You know how terrible I am at saying 'no.' Your mother called up being really nice, the way she was to me when we were in high school, kind of simpering. Then she asked if I had your phone number like it was the most normal request. I was standing there looking at the refrigerator where your phone number was written and I just gave it to her. If I had needed to leave the phone for a minute to go get it, I'm sure I would have come to my senses, but she caught me off guard."

"I want you to call her back and tell her that I don't want to hear from them," I told him. "I also want you to tell her that it was wrong of you to have given her my number. I have no desire to talk to them after what I've been hearing from Jim." I felt strong in my body telling Paul this was what I wanted to happen.

"Absolutely. I will call her right now. I'm sorry, Louise," Paul says. He sounded miserable.

After we hung up, the reality of being a phone call away from my parents sank in again. I felt sick, threatened. The last time I had talked to Jim, he said his babysitter had caught Mother leafing through his Rolodex. She had snuck in after he and Cindy had gone out. He thought she was trying to find out where I was, even though he had told her that I didn't want anything to do with them unless they had had some therapy first. I suspected that my mother wasn't calling to say she was sorry.

When Paul called back, he said my mother's only response was, "You've been a good friend to Louise, Paul," in a smug, non-repentant voice.

Marianne recorded a new answering machine message without our names on it within a half-hour. The phone rang, followed by the sound of someone holding a phone and waiting. We looked at each other and said, "Shit."

The phone rang again. But it wasn't my mother, it was Don. She turned me over to him, again. His voice filled the room like a sick joke. "Hey Louise," he said, "I listened to you eight years ago and I think it's only fair that you hear my side of the story."

Let me get this straight. Eight years ago when I confronted Don, I said, "You raped me and brought your guns into my teenage bedroom."

Then he said, "Only a bad person would do something like that."

After all these years, the first thing he says to me is that I should listen to him?

No. The first thing he should have said was, "I'm sorry. I've been thinking. I've been working on this. I'm ready to listen. I want to make things right."

I did not go and vomit after his phone call as I might have five or eight years ago.

Instead, Marianne and I drummed, a sound stronger than my stepfather's voice. We burned sage and cedar for cleansing. I found a picture of Carol and Don and folded it inward. I tied it into a red square with red thread and sealed it with wax. I visualized them restrained from harming me or Marianne or Jim or Cindy or Noah or Ruth or any other child. I pictured them circled with mirrors. I imagined that the mirrors held whatever compassion they needed in order to really see themselves.

Marianne and I buried the picture outside in the mud, with the aid of a flashlight and a shovel. We got a new unlisted phone number. I confronted again the reality of the violence of my childhood, a violence steadfastly denied by my mother and Don even as they practiced it. I jumped awake at the sound of cars on the road late at night, holding my breath, listening for footsteps. I invoked the dragons and memories of my ritual. Still I knew that violence is real and happens all of the time in ordinary houses, committed by ordinary people. Knowing my own story and thousands of others did not reassure me.

"Be fierce," hissed the dragon.

I wrote my parents a note, for the first time in almost nine years.

*Don and Carol,*
1. *Keep out of my life.*
2. *Tell your story to a trained professional therapist.*
3. *If you attempt to contact me in any way, I will call the police.*
*—Louise*

As I wrote this, I understood that I had reached the bottom line with my parents. I trusted my own distrust of them. If they are enlightened in this lifetime, I won't be the one who got through to them.

I didn't call Paul for another month. I had some weeks of being pissed at having to devote myself to protecting myself from my parents, something which would have been unnecessary if Paul hadn't given them my phone number. But I kept meeting many memories of Paul, one of the best of my friends, helping me when I was stranded, driving me through blizzards, listening to sagas of relationships, cooking me exquisite dinners, buying me terrific presents, always willing to cheer me up, always being on my side except for this one time. And even this one time, Paul called to give me warning about what he had done. He acknowledged his mistake and moved to make things right without delay.

When we do talk, I believe Paul when he says it will never happen again. We talk more deeply than we have for a while because of what we have learned together in this incident, another event in our twenty-three years of friendship. We go forward because we found resolution.

My brother calls to say he has put his house up for sale. His dining room faces Carol and Don's driveway. One day he was paying his bills, and heard a gunshot. He immediately hid under his table. "I was afraid Don was going to shoot me," he says. "But it was just a noise on the television.

"But it let me know I can't take this constant spying and feeling tense when they're home."

After he moves I notice that his voice sounds relaxed for the first time.

I recently returned from visiting a new friend with whom I am beginning to collaborate. She is a gifted teacher and musician who wants more recognition for her work, which she deserves. She said, "I'm envious of you and your work."

I said, "Sometimes I feel too vulnerable and separate." I said, "I believe in your work."

She said, "I value you."

We were not pretending or hiding or cutting down. We played music together. There was a lot of room for both of us.

Yesterday I was soaking in a hot tub at a spa. A woman there was talking about what would be needed for people to get along with each other. She said, "Everyone just has to forgive everyone who has hurt them."

Quick as a flash, I knew she was a fellow dragon. "I disagree," I told her. "I think it would work better if we all named every way we had ever been hurt and everyone who had ever hurt us. Then we would name every way that we had hurt ourselves and each other and the planet."

The other woman stopped to consider. "I like that," she said.

"Hear, hear," said the dragons.

# 15

## *The Optimistic Homemaker*

THE INNER HOUSE is no longer beige, but covered with cedar shingles and climbing plants, painted with forest green trim. The steps leading to the front porch are nailed solidly together. Tinsel and Tayla play Amazon warrior on the hanging porch swing and gather fistfuls of daisies, lupine and cosmos from the yard.

"Remember when everything in the garden had thorns?" Memory asks.

Stunned nods yes with vigor.

Carrie says, "From thorns to words," smiling at the sign on the path to the house that says, "Louise's Place."

Inside the house there are words everywhere. Signs, banners, index cards and posters; the inner voices are having their say. "Play is the Way!" "A Day Without Fun is Flat!" proclaim glittering banners made by Lulu, Tinsel and Tayla. "I am led by my inner knowing to true safety, pleasure, self-expression and comfort," says an embroidered wallhanging. On every mirror a sticker says, "I love you, Louise."

On the wall of the basement, Stunned and Fuckit painted a mural of calligraphied names of important women. In the center they painted these words from Deena Metzger, "It may be inflated to think we have been called, but it is more inflated to resist the call when it comes. Better, perhaps, to err on the side of foolishness, to look pompous or absurd, to irritate or annoy one's friend with arrogance than to miss the opportunity to carry something we are called to carry." On the ceiling a mural of Spider Woman looks down on the computer and in a circle around her is a quotation from Paula Gunn Allen, "The one who tells the stories rules the world." In the kitchen, the living room, the halls and the attic are index cards of affirmation and words of wisdom as well as pictures and crayon drawings to encourage, remind and move me.

The closets are full of clothes for playing dress up. The schoolroom holds drums, guitars, keyboards, microphones, amplifiers, podiums and a clear place to dance. Tables are strewn with projects in process: scissors, paper, glitter, glue, magazines, stacks of books, manuscript drafts, my journal, stationery, a pile of correspondence and a tarot reading for the day. Stunned is writing the words for a song and passing them to Fuckit who is finding the tune. Lulu is helping.

Carrie burns incense with powers of purification and wisdom. She gazes into a crystal ball. She reads palms. She wears long skirts and has a dragon tattooed on her wrist.

I notice for the first time that her face is lined. This adult I have been creating inside of me is no longer a young woman. She is less tentative than she used to be. She is kind and gracious in her bearing, easier with her body than when she first entered this house. She has caught up to my aging.

Tinsel comes in from the porch to blow a whistle from Guatemala which is in the shape of a shaman. The whistle is called, "She who makes things happen."

The inner voices gather around the altar, in an alcove of the fireplace. Even Sarah comes. Sarah has her own office now filled with calendars and day-, week-, and month-at-a-times. Sometimes the voices have to blow the whistle more than once to stir her.

On the altar are statues of women, collected by me or received from friends. A goddess from Thailand holds a sculptured palm outward in a kudra, a handsign, which means peace from fear. She is in the act of walking, with one leg ahead of the other and one slight breast exposed. I honor her by taking ten long breaths. A painted porcelain figure of Kuan Yin, the mother of mercy and compassion, stands on the lotus flower. I light a yellow candle and incense and chant her name. Next to her is a papier-mâché curandero, a singing healer woman from Mexico, black hair going gray and holding a guitar. I sing her my new song.

Fuckit feeds the fire. Carrie holds Clingbaby. It is quiet as it never was in mother's house. I watch the flames. On the altar, Carrie has written, "This nurturing of myself is more important than any task, for this is the experience of life, the savor of being, the liberty to say, 'I take space now, I am free to take ten or fifteen breaths whenever I want.' I follow my heart."

The wind rattles against the shutters and causes the fire to dance wildly in the grate.

"It's the wind of change," Memory says. "It's at home here."

. . .

Breathing is the individual creation of breeze.

My mother used to tell me to "quit breathing so loud," when I was little. I became frightened of the sound of my breath, afraid someone would hear me gasp in my exertion or pain or panic. I taught myself not to breathe too often. I did the bulk of my breathing hidden in doorways, inhaling silent streams of smoke.

Smoking was a sin. My mother used to say my grandparents knew smoking was bad for you before the surgeon general issued his report. I was the only woman who smoked in my extended family.

Smoking was an activity that Stunned and Fuckit could do together as it combined my need to rebel with my petrified terror. As a teenager, I snuck outside my parents' house at night to smoke on the back steps, relishing the initial dizzy moments of floating. I stared at the sky and wished a spaceship would pick me up. It would take me to a planet of wise and kind people. I wouldn't feel alone there. These other people would understand me and I could ask them questions. We would sing and dance and write all day long. They would find me by the orange ember of my cigarette.

So over time, I looked to cigarettes to lift me up and get me out of this mess, or at least to shield me from whatever was going on here.

I was determined that in the course of writing this book, I would quit smoking. This didn't mean just going without cigarettes; I'd done that many times already. Every time I clean out my papers, I find remnants of past efforts to give them up. But I always returned to burning myself. I wanted to outgrow that.

My mother was not a good model for giving up habits. One New Year's Eve she explained that resolutions were rules you made for yourself. One of her resolutions was that we would "get along and be more like a family." As it turned out, she meant that I wasn't supposed to cause her any trouble. Year after year, she resolved that she and I would lose weight. Then she would make cakes and cookies and invite me to "cheat" as if some kind of Diet Police was keeping us under surveillance.

This was exactly how I approached quitting smoking. I forbade myself to have the object of my craving, then began cheating and before long I was smoking again. Each failed attempt only reinforced Sarah's conviction that I was a weak-willed nincompoop. The more Sarah yelled at me, the more I wanted a cigarette.

I began working with a creative hypnotherapist named Sara Deutsch. She helped me realize that the only way I could quit cigarettes was to pledge faithfulness to my true desires. It's ironic that I learned this from a woman with the same name as my inner critic, minus the "h".

Unlike the other hypnotherapists I had consulted, Sara did not put me in a trance state and tell me I didn't want to smoke. That approach only made Fuckit head for the convenience store right after a session. Instead, Sara said that stopping smoking involved a change in consciousness, an inner shift of awareness about who I was. She invited me to find the fear and desire in my body and to let the inner voices speak. She worked with me in the same way I wrote this book, calling the inner voices forward, listening to their concerns and asking me what I needed.

Stunned said she was afraid of my mouth, paralyzed by the strong feelings and opinions that live on the tip of my tongue. She said smoking kept the controversy inside, at least sometimes.

Sara said, "I notice that whenever you say something painful you cower and smile at me as if you're pleading with me not to hurt you."

I practiced not smiling. Stunned began to feel the power in my jaw. As I worked, my face became less like my mother's and more my own.

The dragons said I had a right to show what I felt. They said they would teach me how to be bold and visible.

Sara the hypnotherapist chuckled when I told her about the dragons: "It's funny that you inhale fire, but dragons exhale it."

Like myself, Sara had an absolute belief in the transformative power of creativity. "Draw a picture of that dragon, use your nondominant hand, just take five minutes to do that when you get home and bring it next time," she would say. I have pictures of Carrie riding a dragon and Tinsel, Stunned and Clingbaby peeking out from behind the dragon's tail.

Sara taught me breathing exercises and meditations she had learned in an extraordinarily adventurous life which had taken her to exotic countries and through many different spiritual practices. She showed me how to tone, a simple method of healing through sound. It involves making a long

"Ee" tone, then moving the mouth into an "Er" sound, playing with the shape of the lips until the sound resonates in the upper palate and throat, creating overtones. The harmonics feel round and powerful in my mouth. The vibrations of the tone penetrate my tight muscles and release my fear. Practicing toning rejuvenates me and clears my mind when I'm overstimulated and tired. I began to notice that toning felt more comforting and comfortable than smoking did.

"Get an image for your power," Sara suggested. I saw a mandala of white light edged with silver. I could hold it in my hands and twirl it like a wheel or a shield. I could wear it on top of my head like a crown. I drew it on colored paper and filled it with silver glitter. I put it on my wall and toned into it.

"But smoking is wild," Fuckit told Sara the next time we met for hypnotherapy. "Not like healing."

"Well I don't think smoking's very wild, it's just doing the same old thing over and over again," Sara said sarcastically, sounding like a teenager herself. "I do a lot more wild things than that. Try hiking up a mountain at sunrise, going on after you want to stop. Feel the release of breaking out of an old limitation. Tone through a sunset. Try riding your bike to new places. Or dancing or painting on silk.

"Once I was at this retreat center in Hawaii and every day we went to this big auditorium and did the 'chaotic meditation.' For the first ten minutes we did fire breathing, taking short breaths and exhaling forcefully through our nostrils while moving around." Sara demonstrates. "For the next ten minutes we did Sufi chanting, saying 'huu, huu, huu,' and moving around with that. Then, for ten minutes, we did any sound or movement inside of us, that's the chaos part. The last ten minutes you just sprawl and listen inside yourself. Believe me, Fuckit, that was pretty wild."

Just how wild it was I discovered when I tried it, starting with five minutes instead of ten.

"I've been thinking that I need a practice; something I do first thing in the morning," I told Sara. "I want to replace my current ritual of two cups of coffee and five cigarettes. 'Just one more cigarette,' I tell myself, as if I'm stealing time from someone else! But when I think of having a practice, it feels rigid like rules and never works."

"Why don't you take the first two hours every day and do whatever you want in it," suggested Sara, the hypnotherapist.

"Oh sure," Fuckit said, eyeing Sarah, the critic.

"I think that sounds possible," Sarah said, surprising everybody.

The next morning I woke at seven and leapt from bed. I took a walk and found myself delighted by the scenery and the feeling of moving my body for as long as I wanted. That first day, I ended up making music for six hours, a luxury I had not allowed myself for over a year. I then sat down to work on this book. Writing came easier and with less resistance. My diverse projects seemed less tedious. I continue to wake up early, absolutely astonished at the possibilities of beach walks, drumming, throwing darts, chaos meditation, toning and acting out the inner voices in an inner theater.

In my practice, I am giving myself permission that my mother never gave. I am reveling in the luxuries of time and sensuous pleasure. I am legitimizing play. I am standing firm in taking care of myself first. I do not have to look farther for meditations or practices; I know hundreds of them. I only need to take the time to consult myself and play and revel in self-expression.

In my mother's houses, I learned to interrupt myself, not to persist into the ecstasy and absorption that comes with focusing on an activity. I continued this pattern of interruption by smoking, afraid to trust my own rhythms. Now, I find that when I can get past the place of stopping myself from doing what I want, I feel expansive and excited. In my body, the sensation of going on past my mother's interruptions is like being on a swing and pumping, lifting myself higher, free from the usual limitations.

I am still practicing having a practice. The two morning hours shrink to one hour, or even thirty minutes sometimes. But intervals of caring for myself have become part of the fabric of my day. I tone in my car and make up songs in the shower. I do mini-chaotic meditations between paragraphs. I have stopped smoking and fallen in love with my breath.

Every day I remember to close my eyes and ask what I need or want right now instead of reaching for a cigarette. I invite each part of myself to speak and want and have. Carrie has become as loud as Sarah. But even Sarah is nicer now.

.    .    .

"I'm going to start looking at houses," Marianne announced one Saturday morning last April. "We need more room. I need my own dirt! I want to plant a Celtic tree grove and have a pond with frogs and many plants."

I wanted Marianne to have what she wanted, of course. In the abstract, I'd always agreed it would be nice if we had our own house—someday, in the far-off future. It is one thing to have an imaginary house which never needs an actual plumber, electrician or carpenter, and quite another to enter the mysterious adult world of homeownership. I realized I never thought I would buy a house, just as I didn't believe I'd be in a committed relationship. I remembered anxiously how grateful I was supposed to be for the new house that Don built for us. If we bought a house, we would have a more permanent location. That had always seemed dangerous.

I looked around the ancient waterfront apartment we had moved into last year after the owner of our rented cabin decided to live there himself. Our apartment, built as a motel for the early steamers that supplied the island, had three tiny rooms plus a bathroom. Like the cabin, there were no inside doors. The view was spectacular but the narrow aisles between the bed, tables, desks and bookcases required us to move single file. I had to admit that lack of space was affecting our relationship. I also knew that Marianne needed dirt.

But even as we sat down to make a list of what was important in a home, I didn't believe the change would happen. "Garden space, trees, a making room of her own for Marianne, a writing room and office for me." "A kitchen with real counters," Marianne said enthusiastically. "Then we wouldn't have to keep our dirty dishes on the stove," I added.

"As long as we're dreaming, what about the school?" I asked. Marianne and I had created this school in our minds three years before. We even had a name for it: The Habondia School for the Creative and Healing Arts. For years we had talked about offering workshops on play and relationship and ritual. I was already teaching workshops for abuse survivors and artists. "An excellent space for teaching," I wrote optimistically on our list. I figured we wouldn't find anything that we liked and could afford; the list was only a dream after all.

Within two months, however, we found a home with healthy land and proud trees and a good feel to the rooms. Actually, we found two houses; one for living in and an adjacent smaller pine-paneled guest house. "It's the school!" I whispered in disbelief to Marianne when the owners showed us the second house. We found exactly what we had imagined. It didn't look like we thought it would; it was not a peach-colored Victorian. Still, it suited us. We made an offer.

The ups and downs of buying a house directly from its owner soon became apparent as Marianne and I huddled in conferences and negotiated in thousands of dollars. I had never talked about so much money in my entire life. I fretted about it, just like my mother always had, even though Marianne had changed jobs and doubled our income. Still, for fourteen years I had lived in inexpensive places and saved as much money as I could to buy time for writing. I was not willing to stop working on this book, after spending most of my free time for four years working on it.

"I suppose now we'll have to spend money on microwave ovens and curtains and gutters," Fuckit said. "We'll never get to write or travel. We'll have to stay home and pay for the house! This requires legal documents, just like some kind of marriage. We'll owe you because we don't make as much money as you do."

Marianne listened patiently to my misgivings. "I think we can do this," she said. We wrote our income and expenses on paper, including what I needed for writing. I had never seen my mother problem-solve or write out a budget. "I should pay more because I'm making more, but this is still something we're doing together," Marianne said.

Over the five years of our relationship, we have taken turns initiating change. It was Marianne who led us through the jungle of home acquisition. I watched with awe as she talked the strange language of ownership with Paul, who is a real estate agent, asking him questions and practicing our negotiation. Half the time, it looked like the deal would fall through. We were obsessed. Would we get the houses or wouldn't we?

As we have done many times, we lit the candles on our altar and sang songs to the air, earth, fire and water. We invoked the fates, honoring the unfolding of our lives and our work. We spoke to Diana, friend to tribes of women; Hestia, goddess of the hearth; and Habondia, our patron goddess of abundance, round bellied, full breasted and vital, like Marianne and myself.

We drummed for a while and made lists of our homeowning fears on separate pieces of paper. Fears of responsibility, scarcity, making mistakes, marriage, stodginess. Fears of consumerism, conservatism, and being envied. I was used to envying those who had houses or more means. What would it mean if I had enough? Was it all right?

We burned our fears, catching the papers on the candle flame until they turned to ashes.

We meditated on our intention of having a house. I visualized the houses we had offered to buy. The tall old firs and pines standing in the front yard, like a park, and the spacious open back yard with one enormous pine where I hoped to build a treehouse. I saw the cluster of cedar and fir trees by the driveway. I imagined parting the branches and standing in the circle beneath them. I promised this acre of land I would walk with good care upon it and respect everything living there. I entered the building where I envisioned the school and imagined song and movement and powerful women coming together, teaching and learning. I walked through the house in my mind and told it I would love it and make it as energy efficient as possible. I dreamed of my studio, of room finally for making music as well as for writing.

"It's all right to have enough," I heard from the dragon who had landed in the back yard of my visualization. "The challenge is to allow your treasure to support your service. And to enjoy it." Dragons never feel guilty for having treasure nor do they let it gather dust.

Marianne and I came together again and burned Good Luck incense and shared our experiences meditating.

We have been moved into our house for almost two months now. In the early days it resembled a war zone because we had decided to have a Russian stove built after Marianne discovered that this heating system emitted less pollutants, and required less fuel while delivering radiant heat through a series of vents and bricks. Another advantage was that trained artisans of this stove lived on our island. The only drawback was that they were members of a conservative Christian community, and we try to be conscious of who we support when we hire people to help us. "I'm not sure I want to give so much money to their cause," I told Marianne.

"There's no one else around who does this work," Marianne said. Finally, we agreed that environmental benefits had to take precedence.

Each morning, I walked through the plastic they had wrapped around the walls and floor of the living room, striving to ignore the three cheerful workmen who had arrived at 7:00 a.m. and were busily mixing mortar and cutting bricks. Each night when I returned I would note their progress and wish they were done so that order could be restored. At first there was a gaping hole in the living room floor, then a concrete pad in the crawl space, next a steady spire of fire bricks laid in a hidden maze to recycle the hot air, and finally a frame of used red bricks which would absorb and radiate heat.

One evening Marianne told me she had talked with the workmen over lunch about incest. One of them had asked what my books were about and she had told him. "You won't believe what happened next," she said. "He said he was an incest survivor too, that having a son had triggered his memories and that he'd brought it to his community as an important issue." Because of that, and the arrests of two members of the community for sexually abusing children, the community members educated themselves about incest and resolved to respect the bodies of the children.

"This is why there is always hope," Memory says. "The wind can shake loose old ways that you thought would never respond to the power of air. It is a wind that carries seeds and watches them grow in places that you might have thought hostile."

Jim and his family came to visit us in our new house. He continues to heal. For Christmas he wanted an erector set. I have re-known him for two years. It is rich and validating and interesting to talk with him, this other survivor of our childhood. I cheer for him and with him. We compare memory and insight. We play with the kids.

"Hey Memory," I say, "I can't help but notice that I started out with this image of an inner house and I ended up a homeowner. Is this a coincidence or did I actually create my own reality?"

"It helped that you were willing, my friend," Memory says.

"I will tell you something else," Memory continues. "As long as you're true to what you want to do and who you are, you will be a happy person. I don't mean that you'll be happy every moment, because when pain is present, it must be honored. But I promise you that you will know more joy and satisfaction than you ever believed was possible because you know yourself."

I notice that no inner voice shivers with fear at this or disputes what Memory says. A dragon hovers by my right shoulder. I feel solid in my torso. I take a couple of minutes to practice fire breathing. It's been a while since I felt frantic or paralyzed. "Well I'll be damned," I tell Memory. "I have gotten somewhere."

I have been told that it is important to be clear about what you want because eventually you end up getting it. As a child I looked through the windows of other people's houses and wished I lived there. I wanted to live in a warm house full of gentle voices and people who liked each other.

Ten years ago I spent more time in cafes than I spent in my own apartment. Home had become a place filled with the whispering shadows of incest and emotional abuse. Housekeeping and cooking were women's inferior work. I didn't like to have anyone visit for fear they would ask something of me I didn't want to give or that they would see that I was flawed. I called myself a loner. I tried to not really live anywhere.

In these ten years, I have recovered the lost knowledge of my childhood. I have remembered the crimes against my body and my spirit. I have wailed and screamed and strongly objected.

In my wounds I have found my power. I have claimed my stories. I have freed my self from lies and shame. I know in my center that I have an endless capacity to learn and to create myself. My hands are magic wands. My mouth holds words of power. My ears can discriminate between truth and illusion. I have retrieved my senses and sharpened them. They tell me not only of the outer world, but also of the inner: my inner sight and hearing, the moment-by-moment knowing in my bones and muscles. When Carrie holds Clingbaby, I can feel it in my body. Healing involves finding what feels nurturing and soothing and wise and becoming devoted to it. Healing through rituals has given me the opportunity to experience what I did not receive from my mother.

I walk through our houses, past a vase of dried flowers, a blooming Christmas cactus, and housewarming cards Scotch-taped to the back of the bookcase. "Home," I say out loud, touching the walls, the bed, the tables, the stove, the windows, the picture of Marianne and me on the hearth. I walk through the school with its assorted chairs and windows, the drums and the dart board. "I am at home with my work," I say. I put crystals and dragon's blood oil, made from palm resin, on this manuscript. I touch my chest, my belly, my arms, my vulva, my toes and say, "Home. Home."

Marianne gets home from the store and we hug before carting in the groceries for our house blessing and party tomorrow. Together we unpack the last boxes and hang pictures. "Look, look," we say to each other as we steadily cook and clean and prepare. Between us words are soft and strong, playful and wise. Outside our window is an old pine tree, one hundred feet tall. The trunk grows up thick and straight from the earth and then splits into two trunks growing side by side. We are grounded in our love for ourselves and for each other. We have room to grow tall and to dance wildly with the wind.

The woman I am becoming walks with dragons and speaks with a growing confidence and authority. I am glad for her, for the voice of Carrie. But she is not all of who I am. I am the children who pop up from bed to go play in the snow or who decorate the pages of my workshop outlines  I am the critic, revising my beliefs, no longer deaf to my inherited mutterings. I am the teenagers who refuse to be told how to be.

I am a daughter of life and a teacher. The mother I carry now is the voice who is always on my side, encouraging me to express each facet of my self and to remain perpetually curious.

*Photo by Tee Corinne*

Louise M. Wisechild is a writer, musician, bodyworker, teacher and lecturer specializing in work with adult survivors of childhood abuse. She is the author of *The Obsidian Mirror: An Adult Healing From Incest* and editor of the anthology *She Who Was Lost Is Remembered: Healing From Incest Through Creativity*. Information on her workshops and lectures for survivors and professionals may be obtained by contacting her care of Seal Press.

# Selected Titles from Seal Press

THE OBSIDIAN MIRROR: *An Adult Healing from Incest* by Louise M. Wisechild. $12.95, 1-878067-39-7. This stirring memoir by an adult survivor of incest explores the author's ongoing process of remembering and recovery from abuse at the hands of her male relatives.

SHE WHO WAS LOST IS REMEMBERED: *Healing From Incest Through Creativity* edited by Louise M. Wisechild. $18.95, 1-878067-09-5. This collection presents the work of more than thirty women visual artists, musicians and writers, along with essays by each contributor on how she used creativity to mend from childhood abuse.

NO MORE SECRETS by Nina Weinstein. $8.95, 1-878067-00-1. A beautifully written and sensitive novel for young adults as well as for survivors of sexual abuse of all ages, this coming-of-age story tells of sixteen-year-old Mandy's recovery from a childhood rape.

MOMMY AND DADDY ARE FIGHTING: *A Book for Children About Family Violence* by Susan Paris, illustrated by Gail Labinski. $8.95, 0-931188-33-4. Written from a child's perspective, this book tells about the confusing and sometimes frightening experience of living in a violent home. An invaluable resource for parents, teachers, counselors and day care workers, as well as a supportive and sensitive learning experience for children.

THE BLACK WOMEN'S HEALTH BOOK: *Speaking For Ourselves* edited by Evelyn C. White. $16.95, 1-878067-40-0. A pioneering anthology addressing the health issues facing today's black woman. Contributors include Faye Wattleton, Byllye Avery, Alice Walker, Audre Lorde, Angela Y. Davis and dozens more.

GETTING FREE: *You Can End Abuse and Take Back Your Life* by Ginny NiCarthy. $12.95, 0-931188-37-7. This important self-help book covers issues such as defining physically and emotionally abusive relationships; getting emergency help; deciding to leave or stay; the economics of single life; and how to be your own counselor. Also available on audiocassette, $10.95, 0-931188-84-9.

SEAL PRESS, founded in 1976 to provide a forum for women writers and feminist issues, has many other titles in stock: fiction, self-help books, anthologies and international literature. Any of the books above may be ordered from us at 3131 Western Avenue, Suite 410, Seattle, Washington, 98121 (please include 15% of total book order for shipping and handling). Write to us for a free catalog or if you would like to be on our mailing list.